Let's Go Into Business Together

8 Secrets to Successful Business Partnering

Revised Edition

By

Azriela Jaffe

DISCARDED
from the Nashville Public Library

Franklin Lakes, NJ

Copyright © 2001 by Azriela Jaffe

All rights reserved under the Pan-American and International Copyright Conventions. This book may not be reproduced, in whole or in part, in any form or by any means electronic or mechanical, including photocopying, recording, or by any information storage and retrieval system now known or hereafter invented, without written permission from the publisher, The Career Press.

LET'S GO INTO BUSINESS TOGETHER

Cover design by Barry Littmann
Edited by Karen Prager
Typesetting by Eileen Munson
Printed in the U.S.A. by Book-mart Press

To order this title, please call toll-free 1-800-CAREER-1 (NJ and Canada: 201-848-0310) to order using VISA or MasterCard, or for further information on books from Career Press.

The Career Press, Inc., 3 Tice Road, PO Box 687,
Franklin Lakes, NJ 07417
www.careerpress.com

Library of Congress Cataloging-in-Publication Data

Jaffe, Azriela.
Let's go into business together : 8 secrets to successful business partnering / by Azriela Jaffe.—Rev. ed.
p. cm.
Includes bibliographical references and index.
ISBN 1-56414-513-1 (paper)
1. Small business—Management. 2. New business enterprises—Management. 3. Partnership. 4. Success in business. I. Title.

HD62.7 .J34 2001
658'.042—dc21 00-057944

Dedication

This book is dedicated to my Mom and Dad,
Phil and Maude Ackerman,
who gave me life, guidance, and—always—love.

From my Dad, engineer and entrepreneur, I inherited my writing ability, attention to detail, and pride in a job well done.

From my Mom, a teacher and entrepreneur, I inherited a positive attitude, unyielding commitment to achieving my goals, and an appreciation for beauty and elegance.

I love you, Mom and Dad. Now the whole world knows.

P.S. You always said I could write.

✧

Acknowledgments

A special acknowledgment goes to my husband, Stephen Jaffe, my partner in life and in business. Without him by my side, encouraging my journey as an author, speaker, and coach, you would not be reading this book.

Lots of love to young children Sarah, Elana, and Elijah, who saw me less than they—or I—would have liked while I created this book.

Thank you to Dr. Tony Alessandra for his contribution of the Foreword and for his best-selling book, *The Platinum Rule.*

The following people lent their valuable assistance with editing, reviewing, and contributing to the manuscript in process: Stephen Jaffe; Lisa Roberts; Marti Childs; Jeff March; Scott Smith; John Nixon; Tom Wood; George Wood; Marc Levin; Jan Caldwell; and Tony Alessandra.

My mentor, Susan Page, author of three superb relationship books, continues to offer me love, guidance, and support.

Blessings to my spiritual guides, who remind me of the truth I already know and help me follow my path. I do believe that at times the words in this book came through me, not from me. My work as an author is always a co-creative process with whatever higher power is guiding me.

Although I have not listed their names here, many of the 125 entrepreneurial couples I interviewed for my first book, *Honey, I Want to Start My Own Business: A Planning Guide for Couples*, also informed my research for this book. *In Let's Go Into Business Together,* I choose to focus on business partnerships between friends, colleagues, and family members, leaving *Honey, I Want to Start My Own Business* to address the joys and challenges of intimate couples in business partnership. Much of the wisdom I learned in my research of entrepreneurial couples was applied to this book as well.

The following people generously offered me their time and expertise during interviews for this book. Some are currently in partnerships that work brilliantly. Others are struggling in partnerships that challenge them daily. And many others are not currently in partnerships but had a significant past partnership experience to talk about. They shared their joy, pain, sorrow, and wisdom, in candid detail, so that you could learn from their experience. In exchange for their candor, I have disguised and combined their stories to protect their privacy.

Bennett Abrams
Jay Ackerman
Maude Ackerman
Philip Ackerman
Tony Alessandra, Ph.D.
Kathleen Allen, Ph.D.
Sharron Alpert
Venus Andrecht
Michael Angier
Haim Ariav
Jamie Atkins
Michael Baley
Bonnie Barnard
Joel Baron
Paul Berenson
Valerie Bern

Melissa Blair
Anthony Blake
Ramsey Bowen
Roz Bowen
Ken Braly
Vikki Brock
Jan Caldwell
Deb Campbell
Marti Childs
Patricia Cobe
Philip Cohen
Patti Connell
Jim Corrigan
Georgann Crosby, Ph.D.
Cynthia Loy Darst
Dick Darveau
Jeff Davidson
Kathy Dawson
Carol Deckert
Chris-Anthony Delellis
Diana Edwards, Ph.D.
Dick Elliot
Melanie Erickson
Susan Ethier
Victoria Felton-Collins
Bill Fioretti
Lee Frankel
Andy Gerofksy
Sue Grigsby
Jan Groft
Gary Hanick
Gary Hasson
Steve Hinkle
Tiffany Holmes
Martha Hopkins
Chuck Huckaby
Michael Hutchinson
Carolynn Ishman
Linda Jacobs
Myron Jaffe
Greg Jenkins
Larry Kesslin
Joyce Kilmartin
Jeff Klunk
John Knowlton
Eric Kohner
Leon Krajian
Steven Krauser
Michael J. Lafave
Dr. Peter Littlehale
Randall Lockridge
Linda Locke
Carol Loshnowsky
Bill Lupinacci
Jeff March
Michael Mastros
Linda Matthie-Jacobs
Bruce L. McManis, Ph.D.
George Morrisey
Mark Mullins
Judi Neal, Ph.D.
Tom Neighbors
Beverly Nelson, Ph.D.
David Newton, Ph.D.

John Nixon
Bradford S. Oberwager
Washburn S. Oberwager
John Paino
Ellen Parlapiano
Fred Racey
Robert Rex
Audrey Riffenburgh
Martha Rogers, Ph.D.
Mitch Rosefelt
Shari Rosefelt
Howard Rothman
Lisa Roberts
Martin Rutte
Stephen Santiago
Byron Schiers
Ed Shea
Mark Smith
Scott Smith
Jane Smurawa
Steve Sotkin
Scott Stanley, Ph.D.
Jim Stevens
Erich Strebe
Robert Sullivan, Ph.D.
Mark Weaver
Joe Weber
Jerry D. Whitlock
Carroll Whitney
Joyce Wikcoff
Christian Winter
Tom Wood
George Wood
Ira Zapin
Bettye Zoller

Contents

Foreword

By Tony Alessandra, Ph.D.

Author of *The Platinum Rule* (Warner Books, 1996) and *Charisma* (Warner Books, 1998)

I am known in my profession as a partnering kind of guy. Most of the products and services I've created have been accomplished in collaboration. When I'm on the platform giving a presentation, I may be on my own, but when I am off the platform, behind the scenes, I am almost always working in partnership. I love the whole experience of synergy—two minds creating far more than one. My greatest pleasures in life, along with my marriage and my children, have come from mutually respectful, enterprising, powerful partnerships that stimulate my imagination and maximize my effectiveness. Most of my lifetime's "moments of magic" have resulted from being in partnership.

Some people form a business alliance as a one-time endeavor to get a particular product to market or to finance a startup venture. For me, partnering is an attitude, a way of life that integrates everything I do. Whether I'm teaching "collaborative selling"—partnering with customers to gain a competitive advantage in sales—reminding my audiences of The Platinum Rule, "Do unto others as they'd like done unto them," or evaluating a business proposition that a colleague invites me to consider, at the forefront of my mind is the belief that partnership and relationship are the keys to thriving in today's business environment. There is only one of me, and only so many hours in a day I am able to devote to work. Combining my strengths and resources with my colleagues' has opened doors and exponentially accelerated my professional growth. I would not be where I am today as a professional speaker, author, and consultant without the business opportunities I have created in partnership.

The partnerships I have created, whether they are a short-term collaboration on a book or audiotape series, or business alliances that span over several years, have one central theme: They are complex relationships that require the same kind of commitment and energy that I give to my marriage and closest friendships.

I was impressed when Azriela Jaffe contacted me for an interview as an expert on communication skills. Finally, someone was recognizing the critical role that relationships play in creating successful business partnerships. Partners, like spouses, often have common goals, but different approaches to achieving them. Though I have experienced many positive business partnerships, I've had my share of "for-better-or-worse days," when my partner and I had to work through emotionally charged objections in order to keep the partnership working. I've agonized over conflicts when a partner has responded to a client in a different manner than I would have, or when we've disagreed about the creative direction of a project.

Applying the Platinum Rule to my business partnerships—communicating with my partner the way he wishes to be communicated with, rather than always having it my way—takes great self-discipline and ongoing commitment to the greater good of our partnership. Just like a good marriage, business partnership sometimes requires giving up control, and yet I return to collaboration over and over again as my preferred style of doing business. I revel in the enormous satisfaction of brainstorming a new idea with a colleague and celebrating a signed contract we secured through our mutual efforts. Being an entrepreneur and professional speaker, on the road more than 120 days a year, can be lonely and isolating at times. My business associations bring me such joy and fulfillment that the question for me isn't whether or not to partner, but rather with whom to partner, and how to create the most beneficial and satisfying working relationship possible.

Let's Go Into Business Together is an invaluable resource for anyone considering a small business partnership or navigating a path through the relationship concerns that inevitably arise in all business partnerships. Although I have engaged in dozens of business alliances during the past 25 years, I still have much to learn about mastering the intricacies of partnering in business. *Let's Go Into Business Together* is an important contribution to any small business library and should be required reading for any individual considering or navigating the challenging and rewarding road of business partnership.

Introduction

"I wasn't trained to be a team member. I was socialized to be John Wayne, with lots of control. I was a poster boy for the old paradigm. But we can't do it that way anymore."

—Steve Hinkle

Welcome to *Let's Go Into Business Together.* I'm glad our paths have crossed. This book is for you if you are looking for some guidance in one of the situations listed here:

1. You are an entrepreneur or small business owner debating whether to expand your business by merging with a partner.
2. You are in conversation with a friend, colleague, or family member about the possibility of starting a business together.
3. You are currently working in partnership with at least one other person. You are concerned about maximizing your profits and strengthening your partner relationship(s).
4. You are struggling in your current partner relationship and are looking for guidance for how to remedy your troubles. You may even be looking for guidance that will help you decide whether to dissolve your current partnership.

5. You are a distributor in an MLM (multilevel marketing or network marketing) organization. You are seeking guidance about how to partner with your first-level downline in a way that will grow your business faster and more effectively.

   (Throughout this book, MLM and network marketing are used as interchangeable terms to reflect businesses, such as Amway, Mary Kay Cosmetics, and Cell-Tech, that sell their products through a network of distributors. Business owners in an MLM business earn profits from direct sales and royalties earned on sales made by their network of distributors—referred to in the business as their "downline.")

6. You are a family member or spouse of an entrepreneur working in partnership. The business partnership is affecting the quality of your life. You may have an ongoing relationship with your loved one's partner, even if you are not actively working the business. You seek guidance for yourself and also for the business owner you are connected to.

7. You guide and teach business owners and entrepreneurial students. You may be employed with an outplacement firm, a small business administration office, a women's career center, or a direct selling association. You are picking up this book as a resource to use in your workshops, presentations, and individual counseling sessions.

8. You are an associate in a partnership firm practicing law, medicine, architecture, engineering, accounting, advertising, or another profession.

9. You've been downsized, laid off, fired, or for some reason are in between jobs and searching for a new way to earn a living. You are considering partnering with

an established business owner as a good use of your talents or as a good investment of the severance pay you received or the savings you have accumulated.

10. You are in a corporate job you despise, and you dream of breaking free. You know you don't have the courage, the entrepreneurial skills, and/or the cash to do it alone, so you are looking at partnership as an alternative to corporate employment or going solo. You may not have a clue what you want to do or who you want to do it with—only of what you don't want to do anymore.

I am often asked if this book applies to people who are working in partnership but have not formed a legal partnership. The answer is a resounding yes! Only a small percentage of those who are actually working with someone else toward common business goals will form a legal partnership. They may incorporate, form a limited liability company, or only partner on projects, keeping their sole proprietorships.

Here are three definitions of partnership that would apply to the audience for this book:

1. "An association of two or more persons in a business enterprise." —*Webster's Dictionary*
2. "Two or more entities coming together for the purpose of developing synergistic solutions to their challenges." —Edwin Rigsbee, *The Art of Partnering*
3. "A relationship which occurs when two or more people voluntarily commit to help each other as part of achieving what each wants to achieve, independently." —Roger B. Tompkinds

The traditional model of partnership is changing radically as technology has spawned virtual partnerships we wouldn't have imagined 10 years ago. I interviewed several partners who are working in separate geographic locations as one company. In some cases, they met on the Internet and they've never even met in person. They rely entirely on modern technology to connect them toward achieving their goals. Whereas in the past most partnerships formed in mid-adulthood, entrepreneurs are now partnering right out of high school or college, throughout adulthood, and into retirement years.

In the past, with the exception of family businesses, most partners were in the same age group—basically homogeneous peers. Now partners may be 50 years apart in age and come from backgrounds as diverse as the United Nations. They may work with just one other individual or several, with or without employees, out of a home-based business or a large manufacturing plant. Partners may call themselves partners whether they have a traditional 50/50 equity arrangement or a 90/10 split of responsibilities and profit.

It is no longer unusual for a man and a woman who are not married to each other to be working as equal partners in a business. That notion was practically unthinkable 30 years ago. Now, the woman may leave her husband and children at home for days at a time while she travels with her male and female counterparts all over the world. The evolution of male/female partnerships reflects our changing societal norms for marriage, work, and raising a family.

Many entrepreneurs talk of a paradigm shift happening on the planet and in business. Traditional methods that value gaining control are giving way to collaboration and sharing control in an effort to succeed in the new global marketplace. The Internet encourages connections all over the world. Partnering opportunities are always available for those who are open and seeking such a vehicle for personal and professional growth. Working in a joint venture, partnering alliance, or partnership is fast becoming the norm, rather than the exception, for many small business owners. Besides enhancing profitability, it can also be fun.

Families are also returning to the working model prevalent at the beginning of the 20th century: joining together to support themselves in a family business. Husband-and-wife partnerships are becoming so popular that I've devoted an entire book to entrepreneurial couples' issues. It's called *Honey, I Want to Start My Own Business: A Planning Guide for Couples.* I've chosen to write *Let's Go Into Business Together* for business partners who are not married to each other. If you are an entrepreneurial couple, you'll certainly be able to receive assistance from this book, but be sure to pick up *Honey, I Want to Start My Own Business* for an in-depth exploration of how to successfully merge business and marriage.

Part of my job as the author of this book is to give you enough illustrations of successful business partnerships that you feel encouraged on your journey. Yes, there are thousands of partner disaster stories to be heard. As with any intimate relationship, staying on course requires patience, sacrifice, compromises, and a bit of good luck. Not everyone has what it takes or selects the appropriate partner to go the long haul with. Still, hopeful, optimistic stories about partnership abound. Here is one example, out of hundreds I've heard, that offers a positive perspective on partnership:

> My partner, Gail, and I have grown a direct-mail ad agency to $30 million in sales over a 25-year period. It is unheard of to have such a successful partnership in advertising, because most people in this industry have such big egos. We grew the business together, struggling from the very beginning. At one point it was so bad we had to share one car—Gail's old, beat-up Volkswagen, which we called the company car.
>
> The key to our success is mutual respect, admiration, and loyalty. We have similar values about the way customers and employees should be treated. We have integrity, and we hold up our end of the bargain. Over the years we've each considered getting out of the business; the long hours have taken a

toll on our families. In the end, we both keep sticking it out because our partnership, and what we've built together, is just too valuable to give up.

—✧—

The other part of my job is to better equip you for some of the difficulties of partnership. Imagine you and your partner(s) are standing at the foot of Mount Everest—or perhaps a mountain that's a little less challenging, if you want to be optimistic. This book won't get you up to the top by itself. You'll have to do the hard work, train to get into superb physical condition, and fight your inner demons when you feel like quitting. *Let's Go Into Business Together* is like a close friend who comes along on the expedition with you, giving you solid advice that will make your excursion less risky and more enjoyable.

Working in partnership requires different strengths, skills, and training than being successfully employed by a corporation or prosperously self-employed as a sole proprietor. Using the mountaineering analogy, suppose you were a long-distance runner and then you switched to mountain climbing as your sport of choice. Your physical and mental conditioning from long-distance running would give you a good head start. But your achievements as a long-distance runner would only go so far toward preparing you for mountain climbing. You'd have some new skills to learn, and it might take a while before your competence as a mountain climber was as well developed as your dexterity as a marathon runner.

If you are new to business partnering, respect the learning curve. Know that it may take you several years to master the art of partnering well. If you are a seasoned veteran of partnerships, you know from experience that the learning never ends when you are in partnership. Successful partnership centers around working in relationship with your partner, clients, employees, and vendors, and requires endless personal growth and dedication to improvement. With every new partner, you'll need to change some personal habits, tolerate differences in work style, accept criticism, and give up some control. What worked with one partner might not work at all with your next. Partnering is a lifelong course you never graduate from if you choose to do it well. Partnering favorably is, however, a learnable skill that you can dedicate yourself to achieving.

Ideally, you and your current or prospective partner will each read this book and complete some of the recommended exercises. If that isn't a viable alternative, you can still have enormous impact on the success of your partnership by doing this work alone. Refer back to this book at several stages during your partnership, from the initial selection process to the dissolution. Even if you are currently in partnership, you can still gain valuable knowledge from reading Chapter 1 through Chapter 5, which are dedicated to solidifying the beginning stages of partnership. Even if you and your partner scarcely argue about anything, you will find useful communication tools in Chapters 6 and 7, to help you converse more effectively. Even if neither you nor your partner is married, Chapter 8 will give you clues about the kinds of issues that could arise if either of you ever married. If you are just starting your partnership and termination is the last thing on your mind, you'll still prepare yourself best for your legal agreements if you read Chapter 9. No matter where you are in your partnership process, or where your partner exploration will lead you, every chapter in this book has something to offer.

The most powerful teachings of this book are revealed in the partner stories, gathered from interviews that took place for a full year with 120 individuals who are currently, or have been, in a business partnership. It is a blessing that we can learn from their experience and 20/20 hindsight. Imagine you had the opportunity to sit with 120 entrepreneurs for a couple of hours each, and you could ask each one: "What do you wish now you could have known then?" or "What are the greatest rewards you have received from being in partnership?" Their answers are in this book. You'll find these vignettes disguised and formed into composites to protect the privacy of those who shared their stories. All stories, however, are based on my research. In many cases, they are word for word what was said to me, with only the identities changed. Remember that when you read a story that seems too incredible to believe. Yes, all of these stories, no matter how fabulous or horrific they sound, happened to real folk like you and me!

Welcome to the base of the mountain. Got your gear ready? Mentally psyched? Physically prepared? Okay, let's begin the climb.

CHAPTER 1

Like a Marriage

"A business partnership is like a marriage—you get out of it what you put into it."

—Jerry Whitlock

The parallels between marriage and business partnership are evident in every step of the partnering process. Fatal mistakes, such as rushing into a marriage without knowing your mate well enough or failing to resolve conflicts, illustrate how business partnerships can fail as well. On the other hand, satisfying, thriving marriages are inspirational lessons for creating a successful business partnership. The best sources for tips on how to prosper in a business partnership can be found in expert guides for succeeding in marriage.

Many people have a cynical view of business partnership after hearing horror stories or participating in a dysfunctional partnership themselves. Though the divorce rate in this country is now over 50 percent, most of us still choose to get married because we have a dream of what a positive marriage is like and we want the rewards that only marriage can provide. We assume that we have made the right choice and that we'll beat the odds. Though fears and concerns about business partnership abound, millions still venture into this form of business every year because it remains the only, or the best, way for many small business owners to achieve their business goals.

The key is to understand and to accept that *a business partnership is an intimate relationship,* perhaps as complex, rewarding, and challenging as any marriage. If you don't treat your business partnership as you would a marriage, you are much more likely to be involved in one of the stories that proves how "impossible" it is to successfully grow a business in partnership. In this chapter, we will look at four developmental stages that almost every marriage and business partnership go through. We'll examine how they are similar and how you can apply the lessons of creating a stable marriage to building a solid business partnership.

Stages of Marriage and Partnership

Stage One: We're in Love!

Kelly and BJ met at a Parents Without Partners social event. According to both of them, it was love at first sight. "We're perfect for each other," raves Kelly. "He was worth waiting for. I was worried I would never find anyone else as good to me as my first husband was, but this guy is super! He's the strongest, smartest, sexiest man I've met since my husband died."

Kelly's feelings are echoed by BJ, who went through a nasty divorce five years ago and had despaired of ever finding another mate. "My kids adore Kelly," declares BJ, "and I love her kids too. We've decided to move in together—if the Brady Bunch can do it, so can we!"

David and Carol met by accident at the annual fly-fishing convention in their hometown of Atlanta, Georgia. "We only met because I hooked him by mistake, instead of a fish," laughs Carol. "He wasn't mad though—he is the most laid-back person I've ever met. We started talking and discovered that we both have a hard time finding good lures. He suggested we should start producing and selling our own, and I said, "Sure—why don't we give it a try?" Before you know it, we were getting together after our day jobs and working up a business plan. Both of us thought it would be cool if we could eventually quit our jobs.

David says, "Meeting Carol was real serendipity. I was looking for someone to help motivate me to get my fly-fishing idea off the ground. Carol and I work together perfectly because we are such opposites. I'm easygoing and she's always buzzing around, trying to get things done. She's focused mostly on how to get the business launched, and I'm the dreamer—I'm thinking of where we'll be in five years or so. I think we're the perfect match for business partners."

Parallels between failing in love and starting a business partnership

1. You may be looking for each other, or you may not be looking at all. You may meet by coincidence, and sudden attraction spawns the idea to partner together.

2. Romantic fantasy is the theme of your interaction. You are so excited about connecting with a kindred spirit that you see only positive qualities in the other person. If any negative characteristics emerge, you either ignore them or rationalize to yourself that it's no big deal, or that it could really be positive for you in the long run. *You refuse to pay attention to any details that would throw a wet blanket on your positive fantasies.*

3. Tunnel vision narrows your world to your new partner as you get charged up over your dreams of what you can create together. Your potential new partnership becomes the center of your universe and the object of your mental obsessions. It's hard to think of anything else.

4. You think in absolutes: "He is so smart," "She is so creative." You magnify the traits you are attracted to: "He is the smartest businessman I've ever met!" You even manufacture characteristics in the other that you believe are important for your well-being together.

5. The biological or financial clock is ticking. Now that you have found the perfect mate, you are overcome with the desire to rush forward into partnership. Urgency and "being in love" push out of your mind any logical constraint to slow down and get to know this person better before taking the plunge.

Safeguards for a business partnership in the "romantic" stage

1. Force yourself to slow down long enough to read through this book, do some of the exploratory exercises, hang out with your partner long enough to know him or her fairly well, and confirm to yourself that this individual is an ideal business partner for you.
2. If you aren't going to do any of that, at least prepare a partnership agreement that protects you in case this person ends up not being what you imagined.

   It's a good thing I insisted on forming a legal partnership with my ex-partner. She was against it because we were close friends and she didn't think it was necessary. Everything was fine between us until she married a guy who ended up being a real loser. She got totally caught up in the mess that he created in her life and stopped contributing to our business the way she was supposed to. I would have been in trouble without a written agreement. Since we had a buyout agreement, it was easier for us to dissolve the partnership when she became incapable of fulfilling her responsibilities. In all our years of friendship, I would never have predicted that she would fall apart like that. I guess that's why you need a written agreement—for those problems you can't predict.

   ✧

3. Beware of "always" and "never" talk, and remember that your partner is a fallible human being. Avoid creating fantasies that might be impossible for your partner to live up to: "My partner is always able to close a sale" or, "My partner would never walk out on this business, no matter how difficult it becomes."

I saw my partner speaking at a convention and I was mesmerized. It was the most powerful and moving speech I had ever heard. I approached him after the talk and told him I was involved in the same kind of work and would like to talk sometime. Several conversations later, we ended up merging our speaking and writing businesses. I felt like a million bucks being associated with this guy. Then one day, I guess he was having an off day, and I saw him give a mediocre speech. In a flash, he came off his pedestal. I realized that he was a fallible human being, just like me, and not every speech of his was going to be earth-shattering. At first it was a letdown, but then, it was okay really; it helped me feel less intimidated and more like an equal partner.

4. Fantasies about perfection are dangerous when entering a business partnership. You must be willing to examine, and feel comfortable with, the weaknesses of your prospective partner, as well as his or her strengths.

I hired an illustrator to co-author a book with me. During our preliminary conversations, he joked about being the "procrastinator type" and needing a tight deadline in order to keep himself on track. I didn't want to consider any possibility that this aspect of his personality could be problematic for our project, since I was entirely sold on his artistic talent. So, I ignored his offhand comments and hoped they wouldn't apply to our project. What a surprise: He was consistently late on all the deadlines associated with our project! Now I feel stupid for ignoring the warning signs.

5. "Live together" before getting married in a legal partnership. Work together on a few projects; test-drive each other in some manner before forming a legal partnership.

I got into conversation with the president of a company that served the same market I do. We brainstormed all kinds of ways that we could merge our services and serve our clients better, and bring in more revenue for both of us. This guy was a stranger to me, but he seemed sincere and trustworthy and I was impressed by his company. We started working together on a project, with bigger plans to partner more comprehensively within the year. Am I glad I had that opportunity to see how this guy operated! He consistently failed to return my phone calls or e-mail, to follow up on all the promises he made, and to complete his responsibilities on the project. I quickly determined that he wasn't the kind of guy I would want to partner with on a more permanent basis.

✧

6. Introduce others in your life to your intended business partner. Don't rely solely on your judgment, which may be influenced by your fervent desire for this partner to be "the one."

I have a good friend and mentor who has been working in my industry for over 30 years. When I was considering bringing on a silent partner, I asked him to interview everyone I was considering. I value his judgment and neutrality. He raised concerns about a few of the people I was considering that I never picked up on. When he finally did bless the guy I was most excited about, it gave me extra confidence to move forward with my decision.

✧

Stage Two: We're Getting Married!

The big experiment was working pretty well. Kelly and BJ lived together for six months before choosing a simple ceremony to tie the knot. They were content together, and the kids were getting along fairly well. Kelly had some concerns that BJ was stricter with her kids than with his own. BJ criticized Kelly for wasting too much time on the phone chatting with her friends, but for the most part they were very much in love and committed to raising their new family together.

After six months of hard work, David and Carol had several new types of fishing lures ready for the market, and some interested buyers. After they made their first substantial sale, word traveled fast in the fly-fishing community and orders started pouring in. Soon, they both realized that they would need to work the business full-time to keep up with the orders. They selected a lawyer and an accountant to draft a legal agreement for their partnership. They signed the agreement and quit their jobs on the same day.

Parallels between getting married and forming a legal partnership

1. You'll resist any discussion or legal paperwork that feels like a "prenuptial agreement" and suggests a lack of trust in the other, or an incomplete commitment to the partnership. You will be tempted to skip any discussion that would introduce "negativity" into the relationship.
2. It costs money to do this stage. You've got to hire the right professionals and put some time into planning the "ceremony." You may choose to create an entirely unique legal agreement—the equivalent of writing your own wedding vows—or to follow standard guidelines already established and used by millions of entrepreneurs before you. Even if you choose a standard partnership agreement, you are likely to add your own unique twist.
3. You feel mostly excitement, with a twinge of fear, at this stage. You are aware that getting out of this partnership will be harder from this point forward than when you were living together. Since you are mostly enamored of your partner, that doesn't concern you much—but you know that making this commitment is a big deal and could change your life forever.
4. You are going public with your partnership. Friends, family, your customers, and the public will form a new identity about you in their minds—you are now a "we" or a "them."

Safeguards for a Business Partnership in the "Getting Married" Stage

1. To reinforce the significance of your new venture, you might consider throwing a party and communicating to the public your solidified commitment. If you and your partners are geographically dispersed, or if your clients are all over the country, send out written announcements and go public with your new relationship on your Web site or other cyberspace communities you are connected with.

   When my partner and I merged our consulting practices, we invited more than 300 present and past clients to a big bash in honor of our new partnership. It gave us both an informal way to meet each other's clients, and it communicated to our clients how excited we were about our new partnership. It also gave us a feeling of celebration, which was a nice way to get started in our new business arrangement.

2. This book will provide you with many ways to articulate your commitments and expectations to your business partner, just as people getting married recite wedding vows. Don't underestimate the power of writing down your pledges to one another.

   My partners and I believe in the power of the written word to keep you on track and help you achieve your dreams. When we got together to create our legal agreements, we made sure that the written document was more than a legalistic contract. It also included job descriptions that we all pledged to fulfill and a mission statement that we created together.

3. You and your fiancé can't get married by yourselves. You need witnesses, and at least one professional to conduct the ceremony. At some point in your partnership, you'll want to bring in outside advisers who can help you get, and stay, on track toward growing your company and achieving your goals.

We pulled in a small business attorney, a CPA, and a business coach we selected mutually from a pool of resources each of us knew from working in the community. We called these three our "Board of Directors," even though we didn't officially incorporate.

4. Count your blessings. You are about to head into the stage where you may stop appreciating all the qualities of your business partner to the same degree you did when you "fell in love." Remind yourself of how rare it is to meet and partner with a compatible, like-minded soul, whether in business or in marriage. Serendipity, luck, and some hard work on your part have already led you from the dating stage to signing the agreement. Congratulations! Don't take this achievement for granted.

   A few years after my two partners and I started our company, we weren't getting along. An alliance formed between the other two, against me. I was jealous and angry. Most of our meetings were hostile and a waste of time, as we argued over our positions and refused to compromise. We had started out as good friends with respect for each other and great passion for our business. We called in a business coach and mediator in the nick of time. I think we would have split up without her assistance. She helped us get back to appreciating what we liked about each other in the first place. The day-to-day pressures of running a business had caused us to lose touch with our original vision and our faith in each other. She helped remind us of what we had forgotten.

Stage Three: Why Can't You Do Things My Way?

The honeymoon stage never lasts forever—in marriage or in a business partnership. Power struggles and disenchantment are painful but necessary processes that all intimate relationships pass through. You know you are in this stage when frustration, disappointment, anger, and resentment toward your partner start playing a more major role, and admiration and respect slip into the background.

In this stage, your partner can start driving you crazy. You discover, or finally admit to yourself, that your ideal partner lacks some qualities you wish he or she had. You notice that your partner possesses certain traits you wish he or she *didn't* have. Whereas romantic love is characterized by overlooking details, this stage is the opposite—now you scrutinize your partner and notice every fault, no matter how small. You may blame your partner for a host of business or relationship troubles, picking on his or her faults as the source of the problem.

You may transform differences that once pleased or fascinated you into sources of disdain and contempt during this stage. You and your partner(s) may rehash the same issues over and over again, not arriving at a solution, because your communication may become too distorted. Contrary to the romantic stage, you are now magnifying the negative, rather than the positive, in each other.

⟡

Kelly continued to keep quiet about BJ's coming down harder on her kids than on his as her resentment started to build. She finally snapped one night when her youngest son spilled his grape juice on the rug and BJ shouted obscenities at him and sent him to his room. Kelly confronted BJ: "You always punish my kids harder than your kids. If your daughter spilled something, you would calmly wipe it up. You treat my kids like little monsters."

"They are monsters," BJ shouted back. "You can't control them, especially since you spend most of your time on the phone yapping with all your friends, while your kids do whatever they want to. If you paid more attention to what goes on around here, I wouldn't be stuck cleaning up all the mess."

Kelly and BJ weren't accustomed to yelling at each other, and it shook them up. Did this mean that their marriage was starting to fall apart?

The fly-fishing business was exploding beyond David's and Carol's control. It kept them busy for long hours every day. One day, when Carol was racing around, she was irritated to find David sitting quietly at his desk playing solitaire on the computer. The laid-back quality she had once found so attractive in David was now the part she hated most.

"David," she yelled, "how can you just sit there? The new lure shipment is late, and you haven't called that new sporting goods store yet to set up their order! What do you think this is, a paid vacation?"

"Carol, relax," David protested. "I can't keep up the same pace you do. Every once in a while, I've just got to chill." But Carol couldn't relax. She spent her time fuming at David. "You don't take this job seriously," she accused. "I need a partner who wants this business to succeed, not someone who can waste hours playing solitaire when we're up to our eyeballs in orders!"

Carol and David were coming to terms with the differences in their personalities—and having trouble accepting each other's styles. Even though their differences had intrigued them in the beginning, they were now perceived as problems.

The parallels between marriage and a business partnership are especially noticeable once you've begun to feel disenchanted in the relationship.

1. You consider ending your partnership during this stage, at least every now and then. If that's not a viable option for you, you despair over how you will manage to stay happily partnered with such a difficult person.
2. You are tempted to focus most of your energy on trying to get your partner to change. You are less likely to be looking at your own behavior and owning responsibility for your part in the problem.

3. You may need to bring in outside professional help to mediate your conflict-resolution discussions/arguments. When you try to work out your differences on your own, the conversation often escalates out of control.
4. You are grieving for the ideal partnership you thought you had, and then lost. You are coming to terms with reality and learning how to accept who your partner really is and what your partnership can realistically be, instead of what you fantasized your relationship would be like.
5. It requires a great deal of commitment to the long-term future of your partnership to stick it out during the power struggle stage. Working through this stage of your partnership will ultimately strengthen your relationship and solidify your commitment to each other and the business.

Safeguards for managing the power struggle stage of a business partnership

1. Refer to Chapters 6 and 7 for different strategies to resolve conflict and handle your differences in communication style.

   My partner has a habit of avoiding conflict at all costs. I, on the other hand, want to process everything as soon as it's irritating me. That used to drive my partner nuts. In fact, she started avoiding me, and coming to the office less because she was afraid that I would take her hostage and start complaining as soon as she walked in the door. We solved the problem by setting up scheduled partner meetings twice a week. My partner is learning how to raise and listen to concerns in the meetings, even though it makes her uncomfortable. I'm learning how to postpone my complaints until a scheduled meeting. Often, by the time the meeting has rolled around, I've calmed down and we can have a much more productive conversation.

✧

2. Remind yourself, "This too shall pass." Every partnership moves through predictable stages, so if you find yourself in a difficult phase, know that it won't last forever.

It was a big relief for me to find out that every partnership goes through rough times, no matter how they start out. It took me by surprise, because my partners and I got along so well in the beginning. When we started fighting with each other, at first I thought that meant that our partnership was doomed. My parents are divorced, and once the fighting began, it never stopped until they split up. Luckily, we were able to work out our differences without having to end the partnership. I would reassure any partners going through hard times that, given enough time and hard work, most problems can be resolved. You don't always believe that at the time, though!

✧

3. Hire a relationship/business coach or professional mediator to help you get unstuck if you need it. Don't wait until you are on the verge of ending your relationship.

We call our coach "Mother Teresa." Really—she's a saint. When she came on the scene, my partner and I could barely stand being in the same room with each other. She was recommended to us by a colleague, and we figured we'd give it one last try before we dissolved the partnership. We should have asked for help before it went so far. It took us many months of counseling with Teresa before we were back to a productive partnership again. So much hostility had built up, it was like a volcano had to be released before we could have any calm conversation. I don't know how Teresa could even stand to be in the room with us in the beginning! Now we're grateful that we worked it through. We've got a great partnership now, and our company grossed over a million dollars in revenue last year.

4. Look in the mirror. Put the focus back on yourself and assess what you can do to enhance your relationship, rather than worrying about how to change your partner.

My partner accused me of being a nag. I defended myself—the only reason I had to nag him was because he never did what he was supposed to when he said he'd do it. If he would keep up his end of the bargain, I wouldn't have to nag. My arguments never changed my partner's behavior, although my logic made perfect sense to me. Then I learned about the vicious cycle that a lot of women create with male partners: I nag, then he rebels, then I nag some more, etc. So I stopped nagging. I put the focus back on myself and what I could do to contribute to our company's success. Lo and behold, when I stopped hassling my partner, he started contributing more!

5. Refer to Chapter 4. Revisit those exercises that reinforce your commitment to the partnership and to a joint vision. Like repeating your marriage vows, you may need to step back from the conflict and remind yourself of your original dream.

   I joined my network marketing company because I believed so strongly in its vision of creating world peace and an end to hunger. I was much more driven by the company's mission than the business opportunity. Then I got swept up in greed and started doing some unethical and ill-advised sales gimmicks with my partner in order to bring in more distributors. I lost myself and what initially grounded and anchored me. My body revolted and I became quite ill for several months. Being bedridden gave me an opportunity to reevaluate what I was doing and why I was doing the business in the first place. When I recovered from my illness, I approached our business in a much softer, kinder way. And of course the material rewards have come to me tenfold.

Stage Four: A Mature Relationship or Divorce

Entrepreneurs who are thriving in partnership struggle through the turmoil stage to solidify a stronger relationship.

It's not as if this stage happens only once in a partnership—you will manage conflict in your partnership at many different times in your work together. Each incident makes you more skilled at working through the conflict in a satisfactory way.

10 Characteristics of Mature, Satisfying Partnerships

Partnerships and marriages that have moved through romantic infatuation and intense conflict into committed devotion and respect exhibit the following characteristics:

1. They use the serenity prayer ("God grant me the serenity to accept the things I cannot change, the courage to change the things I can, and the wisdom to know the difference") in their partnerships. They keep the focus on what they can do to make their partnerships or businesses work better, rather than on how they can change their partners.
2. They see and accept their partners for who they are, warts and all. Though they may dislike some aspects of their partners' personalities, they keep things in perspective and maintain a sense of humor. They develop tolerance for their partners' imperfections and their own.
3. They risk being known by their partners, sharing about issues that matter deeply to them as individuals. They open themselves to the intimacy of the relationship and allow themselves to be seen and to be vulnerable. The partnership becomes a safe haven where they can let their guards down. The partners come to trust each other in the kind of way that can develop only with time and positive experience.
4. They demonstrate a strong commitment to the partnership. The relationship doesn't come up for question every time a significant disagreement erupts.

5. Each individual in the partnership believes his or her needs are being met. Responsibilities and contributions might not be exactly equal on any given day, but over time, each feels fairly treated.
6. Each partner experiences meaning or pleasure from helping the other partner fulfill his or her needs. They take genuine satisfaction in the accomplishments of their partners and will go out of their comfort zones to support their partners.
7. Individuals in the partnership have made their values and expectations clear to each other, and they honor the boundaries and requests of the other.
8. A thriving partnership is flexible and resilient enough to respond to unexpected life and business circumstances.
9. There is permission to express a full range of emotions, including fear, sadness, remorse, anger, embarrassment, and resentment. The partners have learned how to express such emotions in a way that won't cause their partners to react defensively or judgmentally.
10. The partnership has become a "we." They have created a shared identity, and at the same time, each partner gives the other the freedom to explore separate interests and to be unique within the partnership.

It takes time to make the transition to a mature productive relationship—often several years. Many partnerships fall apart before reaching this point, the partners unable to work through the disillusionment stage and electing to end the partnership instead. Because a partnership is different from a marriage, where a vow to lifelong commitment gives married couples the incentive to work out their conflicts, many entrepreneurs believe that if a partnership isn't working it's best to get out quickly and cut their losses before any further damage is done.

This may be true—some partnerships are a mistake from the beginning, best remedied by exiting as quickly as possible. Some partners turn out to be a serious liability, and the only solution is to end the partnership, learn from your mistakes, and move on. Equally true, however, is this fact: As in marriage, partners who are willing to do the hard work required to resolve their personal conflict will enjoy the benefits of a meaningful, rewarding partnership. Those who are not willing to do so risk losing a significant opportunity for prosperity and business success.

With the help of a counselor, Kelly and BJ were able to work through their disagreements around discipline. Kelly realized she was afraid that BJ wouldn't accept and love her children, and that this would put her in the impossible situation of having to choose between her husband and them. BJ realized he was jealous of the close relationship Kelly had with her kids, which he didn't share with his own. He admitted that he was trying to get his kids to love him more by being easier on them. Once Kelly and BJ understood why they were fighting so much, it was easier for them to resolve the disagreement.

Despite the financial success of their company, David and Carol started fighting so often they were on the verge of ending their partnership. They hired a mediator to help them talk through their differences and resolve whether or not to sell the company. After several weeks of mediation, they came to appreciate what they had been able to create together and agreed that neither one of them wanted to lose the business. Since the stress of trying to run such a sizable enterprise was making them crazy, they chose to hire a few employees to lighten their workload, rather than continue the way it was. They realized that the more they could relax, the more easily they could handle their differences. After coming to accept each other's work style differences, they concentrated on growing the company as a team.

Because you picked up this book, I will assume that you hope to create a seasoned, respectful partnership and that you are capable of working through the inevitable conflicts that arise in any intimate, long-term, committed relationship. Throughout *Let's Go Into Business Together* you will learn from experts about marriage and relationships because they are excellent resources to guide us through the analogous journey of business partnership.

Approach your business partnership with the same appreciation for the commitment and dedication that you bring to a marriage and you will greatly increase your chances of succeeding. A healthy, generous, pleasing relationship between you and your partner is the cornerstone of your business success. Everything else flows from that.

CHAPTER 2

UNDERSTANDING WHO YOU ARE

"I needed someone at the same level as me, worrying about the same things as I do. An employee doesn't share the same perspective—they aren't in the same boat."

—Jan Groft

BUSINESS MOTIVATIONS FOR PARTNERSHIP

When you are looking for a partner, or joining with a friend or family member to go into business together, the first step is to understand why partnering appeals to you as a business option. Reasons for partnering vary widely. Most often when we think of partnering, we imagine it is to find skills or cash we don't have on our own in order to launch an enterprise. Those are strong motivators, but reasons for partnering go far beyond these two criteria. I asked everyone I interviewed why they partnered, and often the desire to partner came first from the relationship already formed and second from a business drive. This kind of scenario is becoming more common all the time:

My partner and I were in the Marine Corps together. Fighting in the Gulf War as reservists, we became as close as any two people can get. When we were released from duty, both of us had trouble returning to the "real world." We could have just gone back to our lives and the jobs we left, but everything was upside down for us. Night after night, while we were in combat, we talked late into the night about our dreams for ourselves and our families—what we wanted to do with our lives when we returned. Fighting in a war has a tendency to put everything in perspective for you. Both of us wanted to do something more meaningful with our lives. When we got off the plane and returned to American soil, we reunited with our families, and then within days we started looking for something we could do together. We didn't know what kind of business we wanted to do, but we knew we wanted to do it as partners. We figured, what better training for business partnership than fighting a war together?

The quiz below summarizes 48 reasons for partnering I discovered in my interviews. When I began the research process, I was aware of basic reasons for partnering, like the need for capital or to create a stronger complementary team. I had no idea how many different motivations for partnership there are until I met several entrepreneurs who joined in partnerships for none of the reasons I was familiar with. The following list isn't exhaustive, it is just illustrative of the range of responses you may hear when asking, "Why did you decide to partner in your business?"

Use this self-assessment quiz to help articulate to yourself, and a prospective partner, your primary reasons for desiring a partnership.

Self-assessment Quiz

On a scale of 1 to 5, using the following criteria, enter a number on the line next to each statement below.

1: This motivation isn't meaningful to me at all.
2: This motivation has only slight meaning to me.
3: I wouldn't partner solely for this reason, but it would be a nice side benefit of partnering.
4: This motivation is a strong force for me in my search process.
5: This motivation is one of the primary reasons I am considering a partner at this time.

1. __ I enjoy being around my friend (colleague, sister, etc.) and would like to find a way to work together.

My younger sister and I have shared a bedroom since we were born. We chose the same college and have even dated brothers. We are inseparable and we can't imagine not being together in our work as well.

2. __ I believe in the whole idea of synergy: "The whole is greater than the sum of its parts."

I love the feeling that you get when you are part of a team that accomplishes a goal by working together. For me, that is much more satisfying than reaching a goal on my own.

3. __ I need someone around to stimulate my creativity.

It's part of my personality—I think while I'm talking. I need to be with people to be energized and creative, to get juiced up. I get excited talking with someone else, and I can't seem to access that part of myself if I'm working alone.

4. __ It's lonely and boring to work alone. Partnering with someone would be fun.

Working from home is too isolating for me. I need more stimulation and interaction than just me, myself, and I, and my computer. I either need to go back to the workplace, or find someone to partner with on a regular basis.

5. __ I'm burned out; I need a partner to breathe new life into my struggling operation.

I had operated my business for a year and I was tired. I wasn't even sure I was going to continue on. I only managed to break even after a year, and it was a lot of work. I met this really optimistic and enthusiastic guy at a small business seminar. We met for lunch at a pizza parlor, and he starts telling me: "You need to do this, and you need to do that..." I told him, "I don't have the time to do all those things," and he responded, "What you really need is a partner." A month later he joined me as my partner.

6. __ Going into business is like going to war. I want a buddy and a partner in the trenches with me.

I'm so grateful that my partner was with me when we went through the tragic loss of our business through an accidental electrical fire. It took us a year to recover financially and to be back on our feet again. There were many days when I couldn't bear to face it. My obligations to my partner made me hang in there when it would have been easier to quit.

7. __ My friend and I (family member and I) can't find a job.

My buddy Brad and I were best friends through high school and college. We had been biking together since we were 16 years old. We graduated college at a time when it was near impossible to find employment. Most of our friends were returning back home to live with their parents, and working in some retail store. We decided to open a bicycle rental and repair shop together. Sure beats looking for a job!

8. __ A partner would allow me to concentrate on the jobs I'm best at.

I'm spending way too much time on things that I'm no good at. If I worked with someone who excelled in bookkeeping and administration, I could spend my time with clients, which is where I belong.

9. __ I need a partner with financial and operational skills because I'm a creative person without much business experience.

When I joined Elizabeth's computer animation business it was a mess. Elizabeth had no business sense and her office was a jumble of bills to be paid, accounts receivables, and jobs to be finished. She had no idea how much money was in her bank account. What she lacked in business sense she made up for in computer animation genius. Elizabeth brought me in as a partner to give her control over her business. We are the perfect team. I had her business organized in two months and now she can not only write a check without worrying about bouncing it, but we actually are clearing greater profits, since she's much more organized and cash flow is improved.

10. __ I want a partner to share the risk with.

If I put in all of my life savings, then I'm screwed if it doesn't work. But if I keep some money in reserves and find a partner to help capitalize the business, it makes the risk more tolerable.

11. __ I don't have enough capital to buy, run, or expand my business.

This guy approached me when he read about my business in the local newspaper. He told me that he could help me grow my business a lot faster and he'd like to invest in the company. It's tempting to take him up on his offer, as I don't have any more money to invest and I know the demand is there for my business if I could purchase more equipment.

12. __ I need access to more cash or credit than I can get on my own.

I made some mistakes in the past and my credit rating isn't the best. I partnered up with a guy who hasn't paid a bill late ever, in his whole life. When we need to apply for another credit card, guess whose name it goes under!

13. __ I need a partner to save the company from going bankrupt.

In 1988, the prime rate went up to 20 percent. On a $1.3 million loan, I was paying $260,000 a year on bank interest! Banks were calling loans and wiping out companies left and right. It looked like I was coming to the end of the road. Just before the whole shebang went under, I found two silent partners who invested enough money so that I could refinance.

14. __ A partner will help me find new services, products, or avenues of distribution.

My forte is reaching the baby boomer market, but my products could easily be sold to senior citizens as well. I'm searching for a partner who knows that market and how to reach them.

15. __ It would enhance my business image and increase product sales to partner with someone well-known and respected in my field.

I'm only 22 years old. It's hard to be taken seriously by some of my clients. I want to partner with a gray-haired guy who looks like my father, for those clients who prefer to deal with a peer, instead of someone who reminds them of their sons.

16. __ With a partner, we'd be able to better serve our customers.

My partner and I own a computer repair company. We're open from 7 a.m. until 9 p.m. to better service our customers. We divide the hours between us so that the office is always covered. Our customers love the fact that when they call, or drop by, they always get one of us, instead of an employee who may not be as knowledgeable.

17. __ A partner will expand my networking contacts.

Networking is everything in business, but it takes *forever* to start from scratch and build a network. I just moved to a new geographic location when my husband accepted a job transfer. It will take me quite awhile to get to know the community. I'm searching for a partner who is already established in this town who can help open doors for me.

18. __ I would rather partner with someone and work for equity than work for anyone as an employee again.

I'm hoping to hit the big time by offering my skills and services in exchange for founding equity in a startup company. It's risky, but it could also make me a millionaire before I turn 40.

19. __ I need someone to take over the business when I retire.

For 25 years I've run my ophthalmology practice alone. I am looking forward to retiring within the next few years and spending more time with my wife and grandchildren. I brought Doug in as my associate partner right out of school. It's a win/win for both of us. He's learning how to run the business, and when I retire, he'll continue the practice.

20. __ I want a partner to help me grow my company into a major corporation.

I need the skills of someone who has played the corporate game. I could hire him or her, but many of them now want to work for equity and a stake in the company.

21. __ In my kind of business, it's detrimental to be viewed as a small solo proprietorship. A partner would help me compete with larger firms and be taken more seriously.

Most of my clients are accustomed to working with agencies with 20 or more employees/partners. I can compete on price, but I'm not always seen as a serious player in the industry. Frankly, I'd like to recruit a "name" in my industry to leave his or her big firm and come partner with me instead. That would be the best of both worlds, for both of us.

22. __ I'd like to gain entry into another field or industry.

I started my landscaping business right out of high school. It was a small affair and I did all the mowing and lawn care myself. A friend of mine, Jack, owned a tree-trimming service. He approached me and suggested becoming partners. Expanding my business in a whole new direction appealed to me. There are only so many customers you can get when all you offer is basic lawn care. I agreed to the plan and was pleased to see my personal income rise 25 percent the following year.

23. __ I need some assistance getting and staying organized. I'm not a very good office manager, and I can't afford to hire one.

One look at my office—especially the piles on the floor—and you'll see that administration is not my forte. If I could find a partner who could keep me organized, it would be worth giving away half of the equity in the company!

24. __ If I offer employees equity in my company, they will work harder and stay longer.

Our retention rate improved by 30 percent when we installed an employee stock ownership program. Employees think twice about jumping ship when they have several thousands of dollars in company stock that isn't vested yet!

25. __ I need marketing and sales assistance.

I discovered these fabulous waterproof watches while I was traveling in Japan. I thought I could make a killing by selling them to U.S. sporting goods stores. I imported $20,000 worth of product. The only problem was, I was terrified to make a sales presentation. The product was great but it sat in boxes around my warehouse while I procrastinated making the phone calls I needed to make. Tim was the answer to my problem—he was a superstar salesperson who sold me my last car. He was so slick, I suggested he join me in my company. He started working for me part-time, and soon I was so dependent on him I didn't want to lose him. I knew he could sell anything to anyone, and another sweet deal might come around. I gave him 40 percent equity in the company just to keep him on board.

26. __ I want to concentrate more time on marketing and sales. I'm too busy running the business and putting out personnel fires.

How did I become an employer of 60 people? I wanted to be a visionary entrepreneur, not an employer! Personnel issues are dragging me down. I'm starting to hate going to work. I want to give these headaches to someone else to handle and get back to doing what I love to do.

27. __ I want to become wealthy. I believe a partner will help me do that.

You can only grow so fast when it's just you.

28. __ (*Relevant for network marketers only*) I am motivated by the potential rewards of residual income that comes from partnering with my downline.

The secret to my phenomenal success in the multilevel marketing industry is that I partnered with six distributors in my first level who were most dedicated to growing their businesses. Rather than trying to bring huge numbers of new people into my organization, I concentrated my time and efforts on these six people, and partnered with them to help them grow their businesses. This strategy has rewarded me with a business that generates over $20,000 a month in residual income.

29. __ I need help but I can't afford to hire anyone. I'm looking for a partner who will work for equity.

I met this wealthy woman who wanted to work in a startup so that she could make a big difference in the world. She was driven by passion for the work she did. She didn't need the money. I offered her all kinds of stock incentives to join me, which she took, but I think she would have done the work for nothing.

30. __ I need someone, other than my spouse, to talk about the business with.

It's true—it's lonely at the top. I can't talk candidly to my employees about business troubles. I want a peer I can vent to and problem solve with.

31. __ I (or someone in my family) have (has) a medical condition that has prompted me to explore partnership as a business option.

My mother was paralyzed in a car accident while I was away at college. She lost the use of her legs and was unable to continue her job. She was on paid long-term disability but she was stuck at home, bored and lonely. I was really worried about her. I dropped out of college to give her the help she needed. My mother had always been a talented quilter and I urged her to start sewing again. We turned my mom's misfortune into a profitable business for both of us. Now Mom has something productive to do, and I display her work at craft shows and take orders for her custom-made quilts.

32. __ I want to partner with other people who have a strong desire to make a difference in the world.

I'm not doing this for the money. It's about social action for me. It would be a lot more fun to work in a team environment.

33. __ I want access to a partner's knowledge and patents/ copyrights.

I've got new technology and marketing whiz, but he's got the patent. Together, we'll be an awesome team! Why be competitors when we can work together?

34. __ I want to create a business opportunity for a family member.

I struggled for a year, bootstrapping my business with no capital to invest in decent equipment. My friend, Miriam, was losing her husband to cancer. Miriam's husband, Peter, wanted to be sure that Miriam had something to devote herself to after he died; a career to give her structure, purpose, and a reason to get up in the morning. While Peter was still alive, we planned for her to take the life insurance benefit and invest it in my company, and to join me as a partner. It gave Peter peace of mind before he died.

35. __ I'd like to merge with a partner who provides a service to his clients that would be a good fit for my clients as well.

I'm a chiropractor and I have partnered up with a massage therapist. We refer clients to each other all the time and share the cost of renting space.

36. __ Having a partner will allow me more time off.

I'm in the restaurant business. We never close. I desperately need some time off. It's hard to hire good help. Since I'm getting closer to retirement age, I've brought in a young kid who wants to buy the restaurant from me in five years.

37. __ There's just too much work to do. I need someone to share it with.

I was overwhelmed by a technical writing project and asked a friend who had recently lost her job to help me out for a few months. She stayed ten years. It evolved over time into a partnership, though we never planned on that initially. I gave her 10 percent of the business over time, in 2 percent increments at Christmas time. Even though I remained 90 percent owner, I thought of my friend as a partner, and introduced her that way to my associates and clients.

38. __ My partner and I can share secretarial support and overhead expenses, or, I would like to find a partner who will give me use of an office and equipment in exchange for equity in my company.

I started on a shoestring budget. My friend Joe let me use a piece of his office suite and his secretarial help in exchange for 10 percent of the company.

39. __ I'm just coming out of the corporate world. I know very little about being self-employed. I'd like to partner with someone who knows the ropes.

I wanted to open my own photography studio but I don't know the first thing about running a business. I'm searching for an established photographer who is slowing down, or who might want to sell me his business in a few years.

40. __ I want to join forces with a partner who is currently a competitor, so we can stop using our resources to battle each other and use them to make a profit instead.

My profit margins are disappearing because I'm always putting my merchandise on sale in order to beat the prices of my competitor down the street. I wish he and I could come to terms and merge in some way, so that we could stop spending most of our money and energy trying to fight one another.

41. __ I don't need another employee; I need a partner on my own level.

I franchised my real estate business and it grew faster than I planned. We were only four years into the expansion and I already had seven locations. Then I lost my top salesperson. I had to service her accounts in addition to handling my own workload. At that time, my current partner, Terry, was an employee at the company where I had worked before starting the business. I was complaining to him about how overworked I was and how I needed to replace my salesperson. He suggested bringing him in as a partner instead—he was looking for a change from his corporate job. I realized that I needed a partner more than I needed another salesperson. We hooked up and became partners. It was the best decision I ever made for my business.

42. __ I have a great idea for a new product but I don't have a clue how to bring the product to market, and I have no money. What choice do I have but to partner?

I invented a new baby product but the baby product industry is almost impossible to break into. I'm looking for partnership possibilities that would be win/win for both of us.

43. __ I've got employees working for me who depend on me for their livelihood. If I need to take on a partner for the good of the company, even if I don't want to do it for me, I'll do so for their sake.

It made me ill to do it, but when we were on the verge of bankruptcy, I agreed to a silent partner, a guy I don't even like, just to make payroll.

44. __ I want something to do during retirement.

My mom divorced my dad after 40 years of marriage. Dad was retired and spent his days and nights moping around the house. My husband and I were running a small coffeehouse at the time. I was six months pregnant and couldn't keep up with the hours anymore. We invited Dad to join us in the business as a partner. It was the perfect option for both of us. And, as an extra benefit of the arrangement, he fell in love with a regular customer and is getting married again next year!

45. __ The enthusiasm of a partner sharing the same goals motivates me. Without a partner depending on me, I would probably quit when it gets rough.

When my partner is up, I may be down. When I'm up, he may be down. We keep each other going and it's rare that both of us are down at the same time!

46. __ I'd like to partner with a mentor, or someone more experienced than I am, so that I can learn from him/her.

I opened a dance studio with a woman who had been teaching dance for 30 years in another city. She knew exactly what to do, and kept me from making thousands of dollars in mistakes, I'm sure!

47. __ I'd like to give back to a colleague or mentor who gave something important to me in the past.

I started a management consulting company, leaving a corporate job to do so. I had a really good friend, Fred, whom I met through a professional organization. Fred helped me through a difficult time in my personal life, and he was really supportive of my starting my business. He lined me up with the corporation he was working for as my first major client just when I was having trouble paying the mortgage. A few years later, Fred was fired—we both believed it was age discrimination. It gave me great pleasure to offer him a partnership in my company as an alternative to looking for another corporate job.

48. __ I want to give back to my family.

I dream of making my dad wealthy in his retirement. I have the greatest respect and appreciation for him. It would give me no greater pleasure than to partner with him in the company, show him what I'm made of, and then generate profits that will make him and my mom comfortable in their later years. It's the least I can do after everything they've done for me.

✧

As you can see, the range of motivations for partnership is surprisingly vast. Review the motivations you gave your highest scores to—the fours and fives—and keep these in mind as you move into Chapter 3, where you will be assessing the match between you and a potential partner. You needn't have identical motivations for your partnership to work. But it is helpful for you and your partner(s) to understand—up front—what is motivating you to desire working in partnership. Knowing what motivates you will be one of the most important tools you have for selecting the right partnership opportunity.

Motivations for Partnership That May Get You in Trouble

"I've learned that I would rather have the stress of overwork than the stress of a bad partnership."

—Patti Connell

A woman, age 39, with her biological clock ticking loudly, rushes into marriage, pressured by the urgent need to have a baby—and then divorces a few years later because she wasn't really compatible with her husband. She's a lot like entrepreneurs who rush into partnership for a variety of understandable, yet dysfunctional, reasons. Some of those partnerships work out; many do not.

My interviews included many sadder but wiser entrepreneurs who acknowledged that unhealthy impulses for partnership led them to unrewarding or difficult partnership experiences. Any of the following life events or circumstances can make you vulnerable to choosing a partner, or being approached for partnership, for misplaced reasons. It could work out fine, but proceed carefully if any of these 11 red flags are present in your life or your prospective partner's.

A note about these cautions: They are designated as cautions, not entirely unreasonable motivations for partnership. I am not suggesting that a partnership motivated by these criteria can't work, or that it is automatically on a shaky foundation. For example, one of the cautions speaks to partnering with someone who can't sell a product and is approaching you to bring your sales expertise to the table. Reaching out to a partner who has skills you don't have is a natural and healthy reason for partnering. Getting help when you are a technician and not a natural salesperson may be a very appropriate and healthy response to business troubles. The reason it is listed as a caution is because it has the potential to create trouble. For example, resentment can build in the partner who is bringing in all of the new business but giving up half of the profits. The inventor's inability to speak about the company's product or service with others could harm the company's reputation or puzzle customers. This is one of those motivations for partnership that could be entirely healthy and productive or could lead to trouble.

If you recognize any of these motivations as hitting close to home, do an honest inventory and ask yourself the following questions: Could this motivation create any unhealthy or potentially harmful dynamics in my partnership? Is it leading me to feel a sense of urgency or panic, based primarily in fear? Is it distorting my thinking and making me more vulnerable to making a poor or rushed partner decision? If so, you may still choose to proceed with your partnership plans, knowing that your motivations aren't entirely healthy. Recognizing that, you can protect yourself with the safeguards that follow each caution.

1. Death or disability of a business partner leads to a search for an immediate replacement.

   In October of 1994, I gave birth to my first child. Two months later, my mother—and business partner—died suddenly of a blood clot that lodged in her heart. Six months after Mom died, when my daughter was only eight months old, I found out I was pregnant again. So, here I was. Mother of two babies and president of a growing company, without my mother's assistance as my partner, best friend, and mother. I didn't feel I was strong enough to do it alone, so I went through a string of three different business partners, trying to replace my mom. I lost thousands of dollars and ended up firing all three partners over a three-year period of time. The partner I was searching for all along, I didn't really need. It was really about growing up and letting go of my dependence on my mom.

Safeguard: If your business partner suddenly becomes disabled or dies, you'll feel as if the rug has been pulled out from under you. Though you might have addressed this possibility in your partnership agreement, and in the back of your minds you always knew this scenario was a possibility, you didn't believe that it would happen to you. Suddenly, you are faced with running an organization that has always depended on your partner's input and skills. That's why you partnered in the first place!

The key is to separate the need for temporary stopgap assistance from the desire to return as quickly as possible to partnership as a structure for managing your company. Just as rebounding from a divorce into another marriage too quickly can spell trouble, rebounding into a new partnership just to fill a sudden void can also create problems. Rather than looking for a clone of your previous partner, use this time to evaluate what you really need. You are likely to be disappointed if you seek someone to fill your previous partner's shoes exactly. It may be in your best interests to hire an employee or contract worker who can perform some of the critical functions that your partner did, while you sort out what is best for you and the company in the long term.

2. Your self-esteem and self-confidence are too low to run a business alone.

> I've tried to figure out the lesson in my miserable experience with my ex-partner, Steve. Looking back, I think it had something to do with believing that I needed a guy to take care of me. I was initially attracted to a really controlling, overbearing partner who was just like my dad. I gave away my power to him and nearly lost the company, and my mind, in the process.

✧

Safeguard: It is helpful prior to partnering in business to have done some introspective work, either in therapy or on your own, to know what family and self-esteem issues you are still working out in your adult life. Harville Hendrix, Ph.D., a relationship guru, posits in his imago theory that we all have a tendency to marry someone similar to the parent with whom we have unfinished business. This way we can work out those differences with our spouse and heal those old wounds in the safe haven that marriage can provide. We may do the same in our partnerships, unconsciously choosing a business partner with whom we can reenact unresolved family conflicts. Some of these issues run so deep you may need counseling to work through them. Look for why you feel so comfortable in an old, familiar way with a prospective business partner. If he or she reminds you of someone you have a troubled relationship with, beware.

The adage about marriage that two halves don't make a whole also applies to business partnerships. It's fine to seek out a partner who will expand your skills and make the business better than it can be with you alone. It's dangerous to seek a partner because you don't believe in yourself or your business enough to make it on your own.

3. I just sold my business (got downsized, fired, or inherited a bunch of money), and I need something to do with my time and my extra cash.

   When I sold my company for $3 million, I was a sucker for poor investments; I was 43 years old and I had all this free time and no plans. I became a silent partner in four different companies, and none of them worked out. I was too anxious to do something fast, and I rushed into partnerships without getting to know the players well enough.

Safeguard: We define our identities in the world by what we do for a living. Especially for men, but increasingly for both sexes, when we are jousted out of paid work, we are especially vulnerable to jumping into something inappropriate or harmful just to be able to tell ourselves and others what we do for a living and to feel useful and productive again. William Bridges, in his insightful book, *Transitions*, speaks about how agitating it can be to be in the "wilderness," like the biblical Israelites who started reminiscing about how good Egypt was once they had been released from slavery. When we've left our version of Egypt but we don't know where we are headed, feeling ungrounded and up in the air instills a strong drive to go running back to the familiar—or to find a new destination as quickly as possible.

In my coaching practice I have counseled entrepreneurs, or aspiring entrepreneurs, who are checking out a business opportunity and want to talk through their options with me. I always encourage them to examine what is driving them in this direction. Is it the positive attributes of the business opportunity or fear of and impatience with their present circumstances?

Receiving a lump sum severance check or a significant inheritance can spur sudden business partnering decisions. A good rule of thumb is, the larger the paycheck, the more time you should take to evaluate your options. Don't let a high-pressured salesperson take advantage of your newfound or unaccustomed wealth unless you have thoroughly checked out the opportunity and you believe it is exactly what you have been wishing for. Then, of course, the lump sum deposit can be the venture capital that permits you to get started.

4. My husband (or any significant family member) recently died or became disabled.

   I went into business with a friend only one month after my husband died. I was numb, acting like a robot, and barely functioning. In hindsight, I should have waited at least a year, but my husband didn't leave much of a life insurance policy and I was worried about supporting my kids.

Safeguard: In the ideal world, you wouldn't be left a widow or widower with an urgent need to support your family. You would have enough of a life insurance settlement to cover you for a period of time while you recover from the shock and grief. In the real world, work becomes a salve for grief, a place to focus your attention and a reason to pick yourself up and keep moving. Also, few people have enough life insurance to protect their families for long. So, the death or disability of a family member may be a reasonable motivator for partnership.

However, consider getting a job or doing some joint venture projects before actually forming a legal partnership with someone so soon after a family tragedy. Whenever possible, make your partnership decisions with a sound mind and stable heart—after you've had some time to heal from unexpected tragedy.

That said, I've heard stories of successful businesses launched from tragedy. That's often where the need for a particular product or service is first identified. The key is to be able to discern whether you are emotionally and mentally capable of handling the demands of a business.

5. I'm lonely. I find the isolation of self-employment to be really problematic.

   I've learned that I can seek a brainstorming opportunity without having to partner with someone. I used to form a partnership every time I wanted to launch a new idea, because I'm one of those people who doesn't work well alone. But none of those partnerships worked out. Now, I use a co-mentoring group for brainstorming; we meet once a week, and it fulfills the need I have to connect with other professionals without losing control of my business.

✧

Safeguard: Working from home or running a business can be a lonely endeavor—especially if you are accustomed to working within a corporate culture. Though many of us yearn for the freedom and flexibility of self-employment, we are often unprepared for how isolating it can feel. Joining with a partner may be a completely valid solution to such distress. The key is to first see whether there are other alternatives to partnership that would meet that need. For example, sharing an office suite with other entrepreneurs, joining community organizations, connecting online, or attending professional trainings. Second, assess whether you are well suited for all the other aspects of business partnership that arise when you seek a partner for companionship. Bringing on a business partner may just trade one stress—loneliness—for other stressors—sharing control, clashing work styles, reducing your income, and so on.

6. I have big dreams but no capital, so I'm looking for an investor who wants to get rich by financing my company.

   Avoid getting into a partnership where one person is putting up all the capital and the other is working the business. I financed a stranger's company because it sounded like a cool idea and I had some money to invest. This guy was dead broke, so I put up all the capital. He was supporting a family, so I paid him a salary as well. After a year, he left the partnership and took a higher paying job. He had much less to lose than I did—all he lost was a year of his time, but I lost $150,000.

Safeguard: It is not uncommon for the inventor of a product to seek investors. Inventors might have little or no cash of their own to invest. This scenario can work just fine, but beware of potential hazards. When someone has no money at stake, only time, he or she might have less incentive to stick it out against serious setbacks, or to work with the same fervent passion as someone who has a significant amount of money on the line. It's a good idea for each party to put in some investment, even if the amounts aren't identical. You might want to consider each partner's investing a similar percentage of available assets, so that each person is feeling the same financial motivation for making the business work.

7. I am a magnet for desperate entrepreneurs in big trouble. I like being a hero.

   The truth is, my ego really gets off on rescuing entrepreneurs who need my money to make their businesses work. For years, I didn't look carefully enough at why a business wasn't working. I took what the entrepreneur said at face value. Then, inevitably, I'd find out down the road that part of the reason the business wasn't working was him or her. At first I thought maybe I was just one of the most unlucky investors you'd ever meet, because all my partners ended up being idiots, thieves, or bums. I was becoming very cynical. I finally listened to my wife, who accused me all along of being drawn to dysfunctional people who would worship me. Now I consult with her before I consider investing in anyone's company.

✧

Safeguard: This gentleman had a wife who was able to point out to him his troublesome motivations—he couldn't see them himself. Initially, he thought he was just "unlucky." You may or may not be fortunate enough to have a watchdog like that in your immediate circle. The first step is to take responsibility for your own outcomes. If you have a pattern of partnering with losers, it is unlikely that you are just a victim of unlucky circumstances. What are you doing to contribute to your misfortune? Earlier, I mentioned the tendency to choose partnerships and marriages based on a need to heal childhood wounds. Many entrepreneurs go into business with a drive to satisfy their egos and a need to be the helper or rescuer. This impetus can produce fabulous results and worthwhile companies. Many of us search for ways to make a difference and to be needed. Where it becomes problematic is if this drive so overwhelms your reasoning power that you fail to pick up the signals of a dysfunctional and incompetent partner. Then you may spend most of your time and money applying CPR to a dying company.

8. I'm not very well connected. I need to partner in order to expand my network, because I haven't developed one of my own.

   My partner was like a leech. Every time I went to a business meeting, chamber of commerce happening, networking event of any kind, he'd be right there at my arm, butting in on the conversation. He wasn't able to initiate any new relationships for our firm; he was only feeding off the ones I generated. When I first met him, I thought it was a bit odd that he didn't have any friends or colleagues. He's such a genius, I thought he was just too busy inventing products to take the time to socialize. When I joined his firm, we understood that I was bringing in far more contacts than he had—that was his original motivation for partnering with me. That was okay with me, but I didn't realize that he was so socially inept. I didn't want to be partnered with someone who embarrasses me in front of my colleagues.

✧

Safeguard: Some entrepreneurs are more naturally extroverted than others. It is an excellent idea for someone who is introverted and shy to partner with someone who is more comfortable with the people-oriented aspects of the business. Many successful partners respect each other's strengths and spend their time doing what they do best. That's different from partnering with someone who has social skills that actually damage the company, or impair your ability to grow the company as you would like. Although an introverted person will be unlikely to bring into the business the same number of contacts as a more extroverted counterpart, you want to partner with someone who represents the company well, even if only to a small circle.

9. I can't sell. I need a partner to sell my product and services so that I can develop my business.

   If you can't sell yourself, or the product you feel so passionately about, how do you expect someone else to? That doesn't mean you can't partner with someone who enjoys sales more than you do—but be careful of partnering with anyone who is so terrified of selling that he or she is bringing you on board as a rescuer. You want your partner to at least be able to talk about the product or service with prospects and customers. If your partner is a lone ranger, and the sales process paralyzes him or her with fear, sooner or later you'll resent bringing in all the new business but giving up your partner's share of the profit.

Safeguard: It is rare that the person who executes day-to-day operations with precision and passion is also equally as skilled and excited about getting out into the community and selling the service or product. A reasonable solution to lacking sales skills is to bring in a partner with stronger selling skills than you have. Beware, however, of someone who is approaching you because he or she has little or no track record of being able to sell a product. Is it a sign that this product lacks a viable market? Is it a signal that the person is unwilling or unable to handle some of the rejection that is inevitable in any business pursuit? Does this person have the fortitude to manage the hardships of self-employment?

When one partner is bringing in all or most of the new business, but is taking home only half the profit, he or she might appreciate a partner's attention to running the business on day-to-day matters but begin to resent sharing of profits equally. When the partnership dissolves, the person doing all or most of the sales often expresses the feeling that he or she should be better compensated for bringing in the clients—even if the partnership agreement was a 50/50 arrangement.

10. I want to partner so that I can make more money and work only a few hours a week.

   In a multilevel marketing business, I discovered that many people want to partner with me (their sponsor) to get me to do all the work for them. They figure, since I'm going to be collecting residual income from their business, why shouldn't I do the work? This kind of partnership is easy for them to get out of, and the investment is low, so people's commitment wavers very easily. I've wasted a lot of time partnering with distributors who aren't worth my time, because I didn't screen them carefully enough. I was making it a numbers game, bringing in as many people as possible, instead of looking at the quality of the people involved.

Safeguard: This dilemma occurs frequently in the network marketing industry but applies to other industries as well. Often, new distributors look to their sponsors to pave the way for them to get wealthy. They want to ride their sponsors' coattails, doing as little as possible and benefiting from their sponsors' knowledge, efforts, and connections. This type of person will burn out sponsors in no time flat—unless the sponsors set boundaries. The sponsors need to gauge in their distributor-selection process who is willing and able to commit the time and money that warrant their individual attention and support. Then they can focus their limited time and resources on the people who are most likely to use that support to build a thriving business.

Beware of anyone who is looking to partner in order to significantly reduce workload and increase income—at the same time! It's valid to seek a partner in order to have more freedom to take time off from the business, or to receive assistance for having more work than you can handle on your own. It's also reasonable to partner in preparation for slowing down and retiring. The key is not to have unrealistic expectations that your partner will make it possible for you to quadruple your income while working at a quarter of the pace.

11. My dad expects me to go into the family business. I don't know how to tell him that it isn't what I want to do.

> From the time I was a little kid, my dad has been talking about my going into the family business. I worked there all through college and graduated with a degree in business, just like my dad insisted. I'm working full-time now running production, just like dad wants. Dad's getting older and his health isn't great. I'm afraid I'll give him a heart attack if I tell him that I'd rather be anywhere but in this business. I don't feel like I chose this partnership. I feel like I was railroaded into it.

Safeguard: Entire books and consulting firms have formed to serve the family business market—and for good reason. These businesses are often fueled by complicated emotional dynamics that interfere with sound business practices. The best advice I can offer here is to seek the counsel of a consultant trained in family business issues and to read the books and literature currently available on family businesses. If your motivations for entering or continuing in a family business are unhealthy and not addressed, you can be sure that this inner turmoil will disrupt the business in some manner.

If any of these scenarios ring even slightly true for you, consider them warning signs. Life is unpredictable; even the most toxic and desperate of reasons for partnership have led to successful companies and rewarding relationships over time. However, you'll have your work cut out for you, since you might have to overcome some roadblocks that will interfere with your peak performance.

Propensity for Sharing Control

I interviewed several individuals who entered partnerships with reasonable and trustworthy motivations, but they still reported a negative experience. (I'm not talking about a successful partnership with a difficult ending, but rather a rocky partnership all the way through.) Not everyone is cut out to work in partnership. Just as it takes a certain kind of personality to create a successful marriage or enterprise, a profile emerges of an individual who will have trouble partnering successfully, regardless of any sound business reasons they have for partnering. These people are better off creating brief joint ventures, hiring contract workers, or entering partnerships that are not considered equal partnerships, since they are typically unable, or unwilling, to give up the control necessary to work effectively in an equal partnership. (Some partnerships, structured 70/30, or 80/20, work just fine with a partner who has difficulty sharing control—but only if the other partner[s] accept this individual as their leader.)

A gentleman I interviewed who has given up on partnering as an option after a series of tumultuous experiences, exhibits a profile of a poor candidate for successful partnering:

> I'm a road map to disaster when it comes to partnership. I'm so driven to be successful, I'll do anything to make a buck. My ex-partners have accused me of being unethical. I think I'm just a smart businessman. I work really hard and burn out my partners. I only need four hours' sleep a night. I'm up until 3 a.m. working, and I start expecting my partners to keep pace with me. If a partner wants to discuss business, I'll talk with him

for 20 minutes. I'm not going to sit with him for three or four hours—it's a waste of time. And I don't have the patience for all that relationship processing crap when I'm running a business. If my partner is a whiner or complainer, I'm outta there.

I think I'm easy to get along with. But according to my wife, I'm into control and directing things I care about. I guess it's true. All of my partners have quit in a short period of time. I guess I'm not what you'd call a partnering kind of guy. The only partner I'll have now in business is my wife. She knows how to handle me.

This gentleman might sound like your worst nightmare when it comes to partnership. His language is a bit harsh, and may not be your style, but does any part of his attitude ring true for you? Can you acknowledge the part of yourself that is resistant to letting go of control, or tolerating the work style differences in your partner, or spending time working out relationship concerns instead of focusing strictly on business tasks? Entrepreneurs are by their nature strongly attached to having freedom and control in their work life, so resistance to partnership is natural; how much control you need determines whether you are well suited for partnership.

Need to Control: A Self-discovery Exercise

Answer the following questions honestly, not as you would like to appear but, rather, as you know deep in your heart you are naturally inclined to behave. There is no correct or incorrect answer. The world needs both leaders and followers, autocrats and democrats. Your honest self-assessment will help you choose the right kind of partnering option for you.

Score the following 10 questions according to this scale:

1: That doesn't resemble me at all.
2: That sounds a bit like me, depending on the circumstances.
3: That's like me most of the time.
4: That's like me almost all of the time.

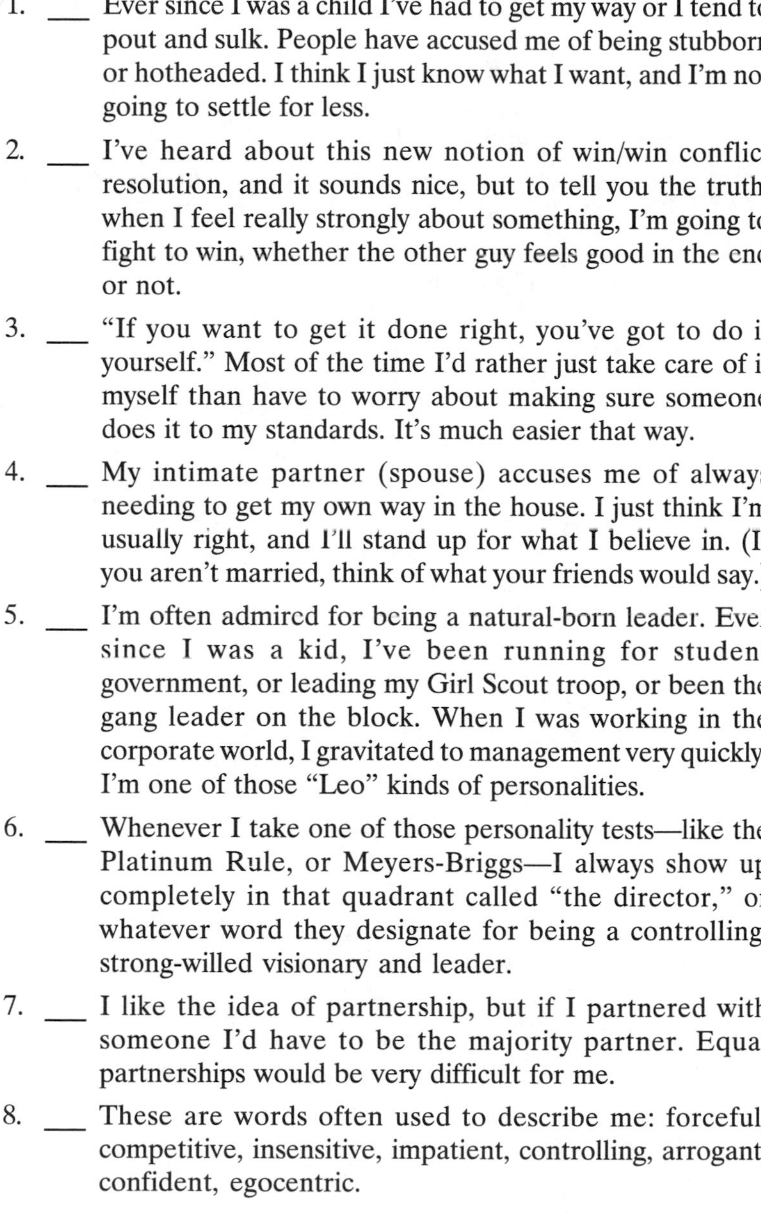

1. ___ Ever since I was a child I've had to get my way or I tend to pout and sulk. People have accused me of being stubborn or hotheaded. I think I just know what I want, and I'm not going to settle for less.
2. ___ I've heard about this new notion of win/win conflict resolution, and it sounds nice, but to tell you the truth, when I feel really strongly about something, I'm going to fight to win, whether the other guy feels good in the end or not.
3. ___ "If you want to get it done right, you've got to do it yourself." Most of the time I'd rather just take care of it myself than have to worry about making sure someone does it to my standards. It's much easier that way.
4. ___ My intimate partner (spouse) accuses me of always needing to get my own way in the house. I just think I'm usually right, and I'll stand up for what I believe in. (If you aren't married, think of what your friends would say.)
5. ___ I'm often admired for being a natural-born leader. Ever since I was a kid, I've been running for student government, or leading my Girl Scout troop, or been the gang leader on the block. When I was working in the corporate world, I gravitated to management very quickly. I'm one of those "Leo" kinds of personalities.
6. ___ Whenever I take one of those personality tests—like the Platinum Rule, or Meyers-Briggs—I always show up completely in that quadrant called "the director," or whatever word they designate for being a controlling, strong-willed visionary and leader.
7. ___ I like the idea of partnership, but if I partnered with someone I'd have to be the majority partner. Equal partnerships would be very difficult for me.
8. ___ These are words often used to describe me: forceful, competitive, insensitive, impatient, controlling, arrogant, confident, egocentric.

9. ___ When I'm strongly motivated toward a goal, it's difficult for me to tolerate anything—or anyone—that slows me down or gets in my way. I can work long hours, and I get frustrated with any outside distractions that are taking me away from my work.

10. ___ I'm not likely to demonstrate emotion—like crying, anger, or fear—in public. That would make me appear vulnerable and out of control. I pride myself in maintaining my composure at all times.

How did you score?

30 or greater: You will be most successful if you choose a partnership option that allows you to run the company and maintain authority in most business responsibilities to give you autonomy and leadership within your area of expertise. At times you'll insist on getting your way, and at other times you'll give in to your partner. You'll pick your battles and be open to compromise.

15 or less: Since your need to dominate or lead is fairly low, you are well suited for partnerships that include even entrepreneurs with a high need for control. You would be open to a minority stakeholder position. You could be in an equal partnership where you aren't responsible for management, and be quite satisfied, since your need to lead or direct is low. If you are in an equal partnership with individuals with an equally low need for control, your decision-making process will likely be consensus.

✧

Now you have a sense of what business need motivates your search for a partner and whether your need for control makes you a good candidate for partnership. Understand that you will not be completely giving up autonomy and control when you partner. Usually, each of you will be responsible for certain functional areas. However, you will be unable to be the captain of the ship in all instances.

The last important step we'll look at in Chapter 2 is exploring your personal values. Knowing your core values will be important in Chapters 3 and 4, when you are evaluating your partner choice and creating a joint vision for your partnership.

Defining Your Personal Values

Personal values are the wind behind your sails—they empower you. According to the dictionary, a value is "a principle, standard, or quality you consider worthwhile or desirable." You will want your business partnership to reflect your deepest core values and your partner to honor your values. Therefore, before you can select a partner wisely, you need to understand your personal values.

Think of the driving forces in your life that have motivated and encouraged you to take certain paths or make major life decisions. Consider what determines your nature, why you chose your mate, the way you raise your family, and the kind of company and partnership relationship you seek. If you've been an employee, supervisor, or business manager, think of those values that influenced your thinking about how to treat customers, employees, vendors, your boss, and others.

Personal Values Assessment Quiz

Individually, scan the following list of 100 values. Rate each of the words below according to the following scale:

8 to 10:	Absolute motivator; essential for making my life and this partnership work.
5 to 7:	Strong preference; having this in my life and our partnership would be ideal.
1 to 4:	Not a big deal to me. If it's there, great; if not, I can live without it.

__ acceptance
__ accomplishing goals
__ accuracy
__ achievement
__ admiration
__ advancement
__ ambition
__ analysis
__ appreciation
__ approval
__ beauty
__ calmness
__ caution
__ challenge
__ clarity
__ commitment
__ communicating
__ community affiliation
__ community contribution
__ companionship
__ compassion
__ completion
__ contribution
__ cooperation
__ creativity
__ culture
__ decisiveness
__ directness
__ discretion
__ education
__ effectiveness
__ efficiency
__ encouragement
__ environmental stewardship
__ excellence
__ family
__ fidelity
__ financial return
__ financial security
__ flexibility
__ follow-through
__ frankness
__ freedom
__ friendship
__ frugality
__ fun
__ gratitude
__ harmony
__ health
__ honesty
__ humor
__ independence
__ influence
__ ingenuity
__ intimacy
__ joy
__ kindness
__ leadership
__ learning
__ logic
__ love
__ loyalty
__ luxury
__ making a difference
__ marriage
__ mastery
__ neatness
__ openness
__ optimism
__ order
__ originality
__ organization
__ persistence
__ personal growth
__ personal legacy
__ philanthropy
__ planning
__ political freedom
__ political power
__ professional growth
__ prosperity
__ protection
__ punctuality
__ quality
__ raising children
__ recognition by peers
__ recreation
__ reliability
__ resourcefulness
__ respect
__ risk taking
__ safety
__ service
__ spirituality
__ stimulation
__ synergy
__ systemization
__ trustworthiness
__ uniqueness
__ volunteerism

Keep your "8 to 10" values in mind as you consider various partnering possibilities. You'll be asked to refer back to this list in Chapter 3, "Look Before You Leap."

✧

Conclusion: Who You Are Changes Over Time

Understand that discovering and defining who you are is a fluid process. Your needs and wants will change over time; partners, or partnership options, that appeal to you today might be unsuitable in a different phase of your business or your life. For example:

✧

> My partner and I worked well together for many years. We grew our business from a startup to a $10 million-a-year operation. I'd say our motivations were pretty much the same, and we shared control fairly easily. But when we hit our 50s, everything in our lives changed, and so did our business as a result. My partner got divorced, married a much younger lady, and started a family again. He didn't want to work such long hours anymore, and he and his new wife decided to move across the country. My wife and I were sending our kids off to college and looking forward to spending some relaxing time together. My partner and I decided to sell the company and we parted amicably.

✧

This is by no means a failed partnership. Rather, these two individuals partnered very successfully for that part of their lives when their business motivations and personal values were in harmony.

Know who you are at the moment and what you and your business need to be profitable, productive, and fulfilled. Know the basic themes of your life that are unlikely to significantly change, regardless of your age or business interests. (For example, your marriage, raising kids, living in your current location.) If you are clear about what you want before you set out on your search for the right partner, you will be much more likely to create a partnership that gives you satisfying results. If you get these steps backward, and focus first on evaluating your partner without knowing yourself, you'll have no mechanism for determining whether your partner is a good match for you. A prospective partner may be a good person, a sound businessman or businesswoman, a good candidate for partnering with someone. If you understand who you are, you'll know better whether that someone should be you.

Chapter 3

Look Before You Leap

"Don't be too quick to make a decision. An ineffective partner is much worse than no partner at all."

—Bob Sullivan

Evaluating a Partner or a Partnering Opportunity

I'm often asked whether any of my research findings surprised me. The answer is yes. I was astonished at how many partnerships form by accident or serendipity, with one or both individuals reporting: "I wasn't even looking, but it came around at just the right time." Or, "We never really talked about getting into a partnership. We just came together on this one project, and it evolved from there." Or, "This person came into my life, and we got along so well we decided to find a way to work together."

Some entrepreneurs do the business partnership equivalent of getting married after the first date; they rush forward without evaluating more than superficial impressions about their intended partners. Some impulsive business owners enter a partnership because it seems like a good idea at the moment, not giving a whole lot of thought to whether they are well suited for working in partnership. Some individuals team up with total strangers, and others partner with family or close friends. Cautious folks spend months evaluating their partnering decisions, involving a team of lawyers, accountants, and other professionals; others throw caution to the wind and move forward with little structure or formality.

Here are some examples from my interviews that illustrate the range of evaluation that people give their prospective partners before leaping into partnership:

⟡

I went on a gut instinct, though my partner was practically a stranger.

⟡

I was looking for a partner, so I put out a posting on the Internet in one of my news groups. I received 12 responses, narrowed it down to two, met each of them in person once, and selected my partner. I didn't have time to waste. Luckily, it turned out great.

⟡

I met my partner while doing volunteer service. I didn't know much about her, but we really hit it off and discovered we had some common interests. I figured: "If she'd spend her Sunday dishing out soup for the homeless, how bad could she be?"

⟡

I'm the kind of person who makes major decisions based on my gut feelings. I don't bother with all kinds of reference checking and research. I've been lucky so far—my instincts haven't let me down.

⟡

I didn't know my partners well, but others whom I trusted knew them.

⟡

I was playing golf with a buddy. I told him about my latest idea and asked him if he knew of anyone who might be interested as an investor. He hooked me up with Bill, another member of the club. Bill had just received an inheritance and was looking for investment opportunities. We had lunch several times and got to know each other.

⟡

I met with a trusted psychic a few times a year. I asked her about my latest venture and the partner I was considering. She gave it a thumbs-up, and that was good enough for me.

Within my network marketing company, my sponsor has a reputation for being a really effective and generous person. I don't know her personally, but when I heard such great things about her from some friends, and then saw her speak at a conference, I decided to sign up as a distributor under her line.

My partner was referred to me by a friend I have known for 10 years. If she says that this guy has strong character and is a trustworthy person, that holds a lot of weight with me.

I knew my prospective partner well before joining together in business.

My partner and I used to work together as employees in the same firm. I left to start my own company. I had tremendous respect for Carol when I worked with her, so when I was in need of assistance a few years later, I recruited her to join me as a partner.

I partner in everything I do. First I find someone I really like and respect. Then we figure out some kind of business to do together. It's easier to hire skills than to find a person with whom you are compatible.

Of course I know my partner—she's my sister. We've grown up together all our lives and still live in the same town. I feel like I know her as well as I know myself.

I was a customer of my current partner for many years, so I knew how he operated in business; I liked what I saw. When he approached me with the idea of going into business together, I jumped at the chance to learn from such a successful businessman.

My partner and I were friends first, business partners second. We raised our kids together and were neighbors for many years. We did discover new aspects about each other we didn't know once we started working together, but the basics remained the same.

The Choice of Due Diligence

I originally entitled this section "The Importance of Due Diligence." I wanted to make an impression about how essential to success it is to "look before you leap" into a partnership. I wanted to scare you with some of the horrendous partnership stories I've heard that could have been avoided by a background check and attention to details in the beginning of the association. But here's a controversial truth I've come to know from my research and my own life experience: Lots of partnerships work out fine without intense up-front evaluation.

Many business owners create successful, prosperous partnerships with only superficial knowledge of the person they are joining with. Some people will do everything mentioned in this chapter—dot their i's and cross their t's—and their partner still ends up being a jerk. Evaluation is a subjective, and only partially effective, process. You won't always know the whole truth about who your partner is—and even if you could know that, people can change. It would be irresponsible for me to suggest that if you do everything in this chapter, you won't run into trouble down the line—or that if you don't follow the suggestions in this chapter you are doomed.

Does that mean I would endorse skipping this chapter, or giving it less importance and going straight to Chapter 4? No. It means I respect your choices about how much due diligence you want to give the evaluation process and how much risk you choose to take. It depends on how you and your partner approach making major life decisions. It depends on how much money you have at stake, how well you know your prospective partner (or think you do), and how much of a rush you are in. It depends on how much you need this partnership to work out. If I preached to you about the importance of doing everything in this chapter, you might think I just don't understand your current circumstances. "Looking before you leap" means different things to different people—and that's okay. This chapter will give you a glimpse into choices available for evaluation that you can do regarding your prospective partner. You'll choose what feels essential for you.

A chapter called "Look Before You Leap" would be incomplete without at least a few scary stories—the best inspiration I can give you to do some of the work of this chapter. Here's an example from my interviews:

> Two guys approached me to put up the money to buy a luncheonette. I knew nothing about restaurants—it was just an investment. A year later I discovered they weren't paying payroll and sales taxes. The day I found out I marched them down to the lawyers and sold them my share for a dollar, because I was criminally liable. I didn't know these guys and they ended up being losers. I didn't check them out because they were referred to me by a friend. They left the state, and the IRS came after me for the back taxes because I was a partner during the period they failed to file those taxes.

Seven Characteristics to Evaluate in a Prospective Partner—And How to Do It

1. Suitability for Entrepreneurship

Your prospective partner might have a brilliant idea, be flush with cash, or be just the sales superstar you need. Perhaps he or she is passionately interested in your venture because he or she hates a boss and is looking for something new to replace a job he or she is miserable in. The person could be a best friend, or a family member, and someone you feel confident about working with.

No matter how perfectly someone measures up to any other criteria, it's a good idea to evaluate someone on this question first: "Is my prospective partner well suited for being self-employed?"

This question might be an easy one for you to answer if both of you have been self-employed before. But if one or both of you have never been self-employed, you must be aware of the risks and challenges of self-employment as a lifestyle, and decide whether each of you is well suited. For example, can your prospective partner handle:

- ✦ The financial risks.
- ✦ The self-discipline required.
- ✦ Likely long hours.
- ✦ A certain amount of rejection and criticism every small business owner receives.
- ✦ The staying power required when times get tough.
- ✦ The emotional roller coaster of being a business owner.
- ✦ The impact on his or her spouse and family of being self-employed.
- ✦ Potential loss of staff support, irregular paychecks, a change in benefits, and loss of other perks of corporate employment.
- ✦ The challenges of working from home, if working from home is being considered.

Even if you find someone who seems like a perfect match, if that person isn't well suited to the entrepreneurial lifestyle, you can run into a situation similar to what happened for this woman:

> I pressured a friend of mine, Sheila, to quit her corporate job to join me in my network marketing business that was growing so fast I could barely keep up with it. She was always griping about her job anyway, and she loved my products, so why not? It was a mistake to push her. She needed the structure of corporate life and the steady paycheck. She missed socializing with her co-workers. After three months of constant complaints to me about our business, she went looking for another job. I didn't realize that someone could be so attached to a way of life that I couldn't stand and would never return to.

Just because someone is unhappy in a job, and griping to you about it, doesn't mean he or she is well suited for partnering with you or anyone in business. Ask first: Is this person cut out for business ownership? If the answer is yes, you can then determine if the person is well suited for working with you.

2. Compatible Business Goals and Values

In Chapter 2, you assessed your business motivations for partnering and the core values that drive your business decisions. Ideally your prospective partner will complete the same assessment tools, so that you can compare your responses. You don't need identical answers on these assessments to be compatible enough to proceed as partners. In fact, it would be highly unusual for you to share the same profile.

If your motivations for partnership are entirely different than a prospective or current partner, your partnership may still work beautifully.

> Peter joined Rebecca's printing business after he retired from his insurance sales job. He had not been looking forward to a retirement of watching football games and playing an occasional round of golf. Rebecca asked for his help with the

sales and marketing end of her business, and he jumped at the chance to go back to work. He wasn't concerned with making a lot of money—he just wanted to be useful in his retirement.

In Chapter 4, you'll learn how to merge diverse business goals and values into a unified mission statement, values commitment, and vision statement.

The key at this stage is to determine if there are any conflicts around your business goals and values that would prohibit or jeopardize your ability to successfully partner together. For example, if you yearn to run a multimillion-dollar corporation and your friend desires a small home-based business, you would be unlikely to partner well. If you want to create a secure economic future for yourself and your family and a prospective partner is single and open to taking large risks in order to increase potential return, your values may be in conflict. If you are pursuing self-employment so you can spend more time with your family and your partner expects 60-hour workweeks, you may not partner well—unless you agree at the start that you will work less hours than your counterpoint.

Putting together a business plan, or at least starting to sketch out the process, is the best exercise for determining whether your business goals are in harmony. You might, like the woman in the following story, elect not to proceed with your partnership if the business planning process reveals significant differences in your long-term goals and approach.

It wasn't until my partner and I sat down and started trying to flesh out a business plan that we realized how fundamentally different we are in our approach to business. Talking in generalities didn't illuminate that point. The conflicts were only revealed when we had to get specific about how much money we were going to spend, and on what. We realized that we'd probably be arguing over every point in our business and it wasn't worth the aggravation to either of us. We dropped the whole idea of partnering together.

Discovering differences in your business planning process doesn't have to mean the dissolution of the partnership. On the contrary—such a complementary approach will strengthen your business decisions if you are able to consider all points of view and arrive at a solution that draws upon your experiences.

Although different demographic and socioeconomic backgrounds and values may negatively affect your partnership, they can also open your eyes to another's way of viewing business and the world. The key at this juncture is to recognize whether you hold an absolute value that your partner must share in order for this partnership to work.

Refer back to Chapter 2, the quiz for identifying your values. There, you'll find a list of value words you were asked to rate according to their level of importance. Look at all of the "8 to 10" words on your list and your partner's list and discuss whether any of your core values are in conflict. Would you have a hard time supporting any of the values that you notice are highly rated by the other person? (Hint: Distinguish between essential and desirable values. For example, you may desire that your partner share your love of Jesus, but believe it at least essential that a non-Christian partner have some spiritual foundation that guides his or her work. Depending on the kind of business you are in, it may be essential for you to find someone with the same religious orientation. When I was the human resource director for Lutheran Social Services of New England, I was the only observant Jewish person on the corporate staff. They appreciated my dedication to my spiritual life, even if I wasn't a Lutheran. However, when we recruited for the vice president of development position, that individual had to be a devout Lutheran.)

If you partner with someone who doesn't respect your values, your relationship will be filled with strife and dissatisfaction. These individuals shared with me their feelings about finding a partner with compatible values:

Philanthropy is a strong value for me, as is my spirituality. I would have difficulty partnering with anyone who was an atheist or who refused to tithe any of our profits.

I'm a recovering alcoholic. I would find it impossible to partner with someone who didn't have his or her drinking under control.

Fidelity is a strong value for me. I ended a partnership with a partner who started having an affair while we were working together. I know it's none of my business, but I lost all respect for him when he did that.

I started my own business because I wanted to use my creativity and have fun. If I can't have fun, I won't do it. I'm single and I don't have to worry about anyone but me, so I'm willing to take some risks. My partner, Jim, was laid off from his job when he was in his fifties. He has three adolescent children to send through college—he worries all the time about money. He came into business with me because he was looking for a way to create a livelihood that no one could take away from him because of his age. Jim's looking for security, and I'm looking for a good time. The two don't always mix.

If you partner with someone who does share your core values, your relationship will be much more harmonious and rewarding.

I met my partner in a spiritual studies class. We had both been studying with the same spiritual master for a number of years and continued to study with him after we partnered together. We use these spiritual teachings to resolve conflict in our partnership, which has been immensely helpful to our relationship.

✧

Both my partner and I are work-at-home moms. We respect each other's values for raising our children in a healthy, loving way. We won't allow the business to interfere with our primary commitment to be good mothers.

✧

3. Complementary Business Skills and Business Competence

What are each of you bringing to the partnership in terms of skills, knowledge, work experience, and strengths? Most people do not want to partner with a clone of themselves, even if that might make for easier conflict resolution. The key is to identify the gaps in your skills and abilities and to find a partner who is able to fill some of them. This is usually the stage of your relationship where you welcome differences and applaud a different way of thinking and skill sets you have not acquired.

You will also want to be sure that your partners are competent at doing what they say they do on their resumes. If you haven't had the experience of working with them before and don't have firsthand knowledge, you'll have to rely on personal and professional references—and perhaps on a demonstration of their work and abilities.

Apprentice your partner for a while before you offer him or her partner status. Work together on a joint venture before you form a legal agreement. Look for evidence of prospective partners' ability to perform in the past—check out their products, speak to their clients and vendors—anyone they've done business with. Find out if they belong to any trade associations or community organizations, and talk to members of those organizations about their experiences with your partners.

Review their promotional materials. If appropriate, visit their current enterprises and talk with their employees. Observe them at work.

—◇—

> I am a professional speaker. I was approached by a gentleman who speaks on the same subject matter I do. His brochures and promotional material were impressive. He was a nice guy, and we began a series of conversations about merging our speaking businesses into one partnership. A few months later, I heard him speak for the first time. It was immediately clear to me that he and I weren't at the same skill level. He reminded me of where I was a few years ago. I should have seen him speak before engaging in any serious conversation about partnership.

—◇—

Check out your gut feeling about partners' work—don't let impressive brochures or references be your sole sources for evaluation. For example, for my next book, I was seeking a humorous business cartoonist. I received a portfolio from a gentleman with a long list of awe-inspiring credentials. He had been published in most of the well-respected entrepreneurial magazines and national newspapers, including *The Wall Street Journal, Barron's*, and so forth. I should have felt lucky to attract his interest in my project. The problem: His cartoons didn't make me laugh. I didn't hire him for the project. I kept searching until I found a cartoonist with equally strong credentials and a style that was more personally appealing to me and to others I showed his work to. The cartoonist I selected for the project had no brochures, no business card, and even sent me his correspondence on a handwritten note, since he doesn't own a computer. Yet, his cartoons were funny, his list of magazine placements impressive, and his personality delightful.

Depending on the kind of company you each have, and what you are considering doing together, you may ask for a balance sheet with assets and outstanding liabilities. (Once you become a person's partner, you may become liable for his or her debts.) You might hire an accountant or an attorney to look at financial statements to be sure there aren't any areas of concern.

If your prospective partner has been in business for a while, contact the Better Business Bureau in the area where your prospective partner does business. There are nearly 175 Better Business Bureaus, with more than 11 million consumer contacts each year. They will give you a 900 number to call (at the time of this writing, you are charged approximately $3.80 for the call). The BBB will give you the background on any company in its files. If there have been complaints, you'll find out what they were and whether they were resolved. If you join the BBB in your area, you and your partner(s) can take advantage of the free dispute resolution service available to BBB members. You'll pay little or nothing for the service beyond your BBB membership.

Check out your partner's company on the Internet. Ask news groups and relevant cyberspace communities what they know about this person and his or her company. I'm on the active e-mail mailing list of other authors and publishers. Every day someone posts a message that reads something like: "I'm considering X (person/company) for Y responsibility. Has anyone had any experience with them?" Even if your partner's company isn't publicly held, the Internet provides a mechanism for checking out a company's performance.

The most reliable predictor of what your partner will provide for your company in the future is what he or she has done in the past. People can change, and past accomplishments aren't a hundred percent accurate when forecasting the future. But when you are evaluating someone you scarcely know, past records of achievement are the best clues you have available to you.

4. Solid Credit History and No Trouble with the Law

If prospective partners present themselves as being trustworthy and competent, but you find out that their credit histories are shaky, that they filed for personal bankruptcy during the last seven years, or that they are carrying fifty grand in credit card debt, do you think that would be relevant to your partnering decision? How about if they are being sued, or if they are delinquent on custody payments for their kids? Such knowledge would be critical for some partnerships. Depending on how much money is at stake in your partnership, how well you know your prospective partners, and what kinds of financial responsibilities they will have, credit and criminal checks may be appropriate. If a prospective partner becomes immediately offended and hostile about your suggestion that such checks be done, it could be a warning sign that there's trouble behind the scenes. (Of course, you must be willing to provide the same for your prospective partners as you are asking of them.)

Because any financial pressure your partners are experiencing will directly affect their business motivations and behavior, it is fair to ask about their level of personal debt. Since you will be placing your livelihood in their hands, it's appropriate to ask for evidence that they can handle their own financial affairs. You are gambling with your reputation by aligning yourself with one or more individuals. Therefore, you want to be sure they aren't in any kind of legal trouble that might have a negative impact on your enterprise.

Perhaps you didn't realize you had access to this kind of information. You do, if you have a permissible reason for requesting it. Joining with someone in a business partnership is considered a permissible reason according to the Fair Credit Reporting Act, the national law that governs the credit industry.

Here's a simple way you can check your partner's credit—or your own. According to Kelley Lutz, vice president of the

Credit Bureau of Lancaster, Pennsylvania, there are credit bureaus in virtually every city in the country. Without being a member, you can complete a form and get a rundown of your credit record, right on the spot, when you drop by the office. The cost is minimal, just a bit over $8, and it's free if you have had an inquiry within the past 60 days. ("An inquiry" means that someone has checked your credit report—for example, a credit card company, bank, appliance store, or even your new partner.)

You can become a member of your local credit bureau if you want the ability to check out potential business partners' credit histories. On the application, you must state that this is your intent, since your desire must be for a permissible reason. For example, you can't get a credit history on someone you've started dating just to be sure he or she is good "marriage material"! The law imposes civil penalties and significant fines for abusing your access to credit information. The cost for membership in Lancaster is $63 a year. It takes only a few weeks to receive approval, and then you can ask for a report on any prospective partner.

You can also directly approach the three largest national credit reporting agencies—Equifax, TransUnion, and Experian. Credit bureaus receive their information from these agencies and act as go-betweens.

The simplest and most expedient way to approach credit histories is for all partners involved to agree to acquire their own credit reports and to share them with each other. You risk angering potential partners if you don't tell them you are investigating their backgrounds until you find something troublesome on a report. Your name will appear on their credit reports as a recent inquiry, so you can't keep the search hidden from them.

Kelley pointed out that the courthouse offers a wealth of information on the background of potential business partners as well. As a matter of public record, you can, in just one visit to the county or municipal courthouse where your potential partners live, ascertain if they have any liens against their homes, back taxes owed, restraining orders, delinquent child support, or litigation pending. You can find out if they have been sued or are suing anyone. You can even determine if they have criminal records. You have access to anything that is public record just by asking for it.

These steps are overlooked or avoided in most partnerships, seen as an unnecessarily cautious step that will slow down the process and introduce hostility into the relationship. Consider insisting on a credit check or visiting the courthouse if your potential partner is a stranger to you, if you pick up some vibes in your initial conversations that raise some concerns, and/or if you are risking a good deal of money or your reputations by affiliating with that person.

5. Compatible Money Goals and Values

Money is an emotionally charged, sensitive topic for almost everyone. You are risking this precious resource in the hands of a practical stranger—even if you feel you know your prospective partner fairly well. (Consider the number of marriages that end in divorce due to money clashes.) Money conflicts tear apart families, partnerships, and marriages like a late summer hurricane. I mentioned earlier that I am often asked what surprised me in conversations with the people I interviewed. I don't know if this surprises or just saddens me, but conflict over money is just as prevalent in successful businesses as in unsuccessful ones. When you are penniless, you and your partners are worried about having enough money to keep the company alive and to pay your family bills. When you start to make money, you are each worried about getting your fair share.

When you are rolling in dough, you may still fight about who is contributing more time and effort than the other. When you eventually end your partnership, you'll need to negotiate fair financial terms for each of you. Money negotiation will be present at every stage of your partnership. So, partner with someone who shares your goals and values about money.

As with sex in a marriage, you may avoid discussing this potentially awkward and embarrassing subject in the early stages of your partner selection process. It can feel as if you are getting too intimate, crossing an invisible boundary of social etiquette. And yet, it's important to determine early on whether you and your partners view money and risk in basically the same way.

Here are 12 questions you can discuss to help evaluate whether you and your partners share similar values and expectations about money.

1. What kind of income do you need to make in order to support yourself and your family?
2. What level of income were you accustomed to earning in previous employment?
3. How long can you go without income, if that's what the business requires?
4. What are your three-to-five-year financial goals? What is your long-term financial vision? What would you like to be doing 10 years from now?
5. How much do you think your time is worth per hour? How many hours are you willing to work in this business to reach your financial goals?
6. How much money, or what percentage of revenue, do you believe should be reinvested in the company once the business is profitable? Do you envision forgoing a significant portion of salary and profits in order to expand the business?
7. Do you have any dreams of growing the business to become a publicly held company?

8. When do you want to retire? What would your financial situation need to look like before you would feel comfortable retiring?
9. What percentage of your financial assets are you investing in this business? (For example, are you risking everything you have, or will this business require only a small portion of your available assets?)
10. When it comes to money, would you consider yourself risk averse, risk inclined, or somewhere in between? What kind of financial risks have you taken in the past? If you've invested in the stock market, has your portfolio been high risk, balanced, or low risk?
11. How important is it to you to be debt free, in this company and in your personal life?
12. What are the family obligations you are concerned with meeting (mortgage, college education or private school for children, health care, retirement)?

6. Family Commitments

I think it helps that neither my partner nor I have any children. One of us is 34 and the other 38, so it could still happen. I think that would change everything between us. It would be harder for both of us to put in our 50 percent if we were divided in three ways—business, spouse, and family.

My partner and I had an immediate, good, gut feel about the other. I appreciated that both of us had wives at home full-time with our children, reflecting similar values, and the same pressure to make a living.

> It struck me how Sam talked about his wife—it was clear that he had a happy marriage. I took it as a good sign—at least I knew that he was capable of making an intimate, long-term partnership work.

⟡

Because your family relationships and obligations will directly impact your daily actions in your business, discuss these commitments before entering your partnership. Many of the partners I interviewed reported that one of the greatest rewards of their partnerships was the support their partners gave them to care for family matters. To the extent that you know as you enter a partnership what kind of flexibility you will need from your other partners, talk about it—up front! You don't want to find out after the partnership agreement is inked that your partner and your family have irreconcilable expectations of you.

One woman in a position that required frequent travel brought her newborn on the road for the first year of his life so that she could continue nursing. She got prior approval from her male partners to be sure they could handle it—she even asked how they felt about her nursing her baby in front of them. Another entrepreneur expressed gratitude for his partners because they accommodated his erratic schedule so he could be available for his handicapped son's physical therapy treatments. And still another business owner told me about her unusual working hours, blessed by her partners, so that she could manage a complex joint custody schedule for her children. All of these individuals counted on their partners to support their family commitments, and in return they gave their partners the same understanding and consideration.

If these kinds of issues are relevant for you, they must enter your preliminary discussions if you are to avoid serious misunderstandings in the future. Consider this woman's story:

⟡

I was a single parent raising five children when I decided to go into business with Jack. He was a parent of three himself—though married. I assumed he would understand how much flexibility I needed in order to care for my kids' needs. We made the mistake of not discussing it before we signed the partnership agreement. Then he started giving me grief for not always working eight-hour days and weekends, just because he did. I tried to explain to him that I didn't have a wife like he did and I needed more flexibility during the days than he seemed to need. We should have gotten it straight right from the beginning, because there was no way I could please him and also be there for my family too.

7. Compatibility of Cultural and Religious Differences

These individuals articulated why considering cultural and religious differences may be a necessary part of your evaluation process:

I'm black, and my new business partner is white. When we discussed going into business together, I looked for any prejudicial attitudes in his language or casual, off-guard behavior. Of course he would never admit to such a thing, but it can be unconscious or subtle. I spent several weeks just hanging out with him and his friends, until I felt reassured that this wasn't an issue.

I come from a large Italian family. We're very close and all of the adult children live within twenty miles of where I grew up. My partner needs to understand that my large extended family will be dropping by the business all the time. I wouldn't partner with anyone who wouldn't give my family royal treatment. My family comes before anything.

I am an Orthodox Jewish doctor. When I discussed merging my medical practice with two colleagues, I made it clear to them up front that I would not work from Friday sundown to Saturday sundown, nor on various holidays throughout the calendar, unless we had a life-threatening emergency. The "on-call" schedule would have to accommodate my religious commitments or the partnership was not going to work for me.

✧

I am a Jewish female. I partnered with an Egyptian man who seemed to be the perfect business match. We were an excellent partnership in terms of our complementary skills, but there was one major problem for me I hadn't predicted. In Egypt, Jewish women are treated like second-class citizens. Even though this gentleman had been in the States for twenty-five years, his negative stereotypes about women were deeply rooted in his psyche. No matter what the partnership agreement said, he couldn't see me as an equal partner.

✧

Now that you are aware of seven areas for contemplation or discussion with your potential partner, you are ready to move on to the last section of this chapter.

At some point in your evaluation process, you'll make a decision. You may put the brakes on and walk, or run, from this partnership opportunity, proceed cautiously, or go forward without reservation. One thing is certain: You can't stay in the evaluation stage forever.

Traffic Signals For Your Partnership—Red Light, Yellow Light, Green Light

I'd like a dollar for every person who has expressed to me something like:

> Looking back, I can see that all the warning signs were there that I was getting into partnership with the wrong person. I didn't want to see it then—I ignored the obvious—so I had to learn the hard way.

You don't have to learn your lessons only in hindsight. You can look squarely and honestly at your choice of partners, including their blemishes and weaknesses, and decide: Is this the person I want to risk my business with? Is this the person I trust enough to give my hard-earned money, time, and heart to? You may always have a bit of uneasiness going forward with such a major decision as a business partnership—most of us are a bit squeamish on our wedding days. However, there's a big difference between a cautious concern and a voice screaming at you: "Run! Get out of this before you get in too far!"

As you complete your evaluation process, you'll probably interpret the signs in one of three ways:

1. Red light—warning signs serious enough that you should put your partnership plans on hold, temporarily or permanently. This person, or this business opportunity, isn't stable or trustworthy enough for you to align with at this time without serious jeopardy to your business, your bank account, and/or your psyche.

2. Yellow light—you aren't looking at this partnership through rose-colored glasses. You know your partner isn't perfect, and neither are you. You proceed cautiously, taking extra precautions, like reference checking and formalizing your agreements, to protect any concerns you have. You tell yourself it doesn't have to be forever, but for now, this partnership could work.

3. Green light—this partner seems to be destined, a gift from heaven, exactly what the doctor ordered at this time, the business equivalent of a soulmate. You can hardly imagine a partnership that would be more ideal. It's "all systems go" as far as you're concerned!

Twenty Red Lights That Should Signal Stop or at Least Slow Down, Heading into a Prospective Partnership

Beware of partnering with any individual or individuals if any of the following red lights show up during your "getting to know each other" period:

1. He or she is currently being sued and isn't forthcoming with you about the circumstances. You find out in your own investigation. When you ask about it, you hear something like "Don't worry. It's nothing, really—just a frivolous lawsuit."

I was seeking a partner to lower the overhead of my psychotherapy practice. A friend of mine introduced me to another psychologist, Craig. Craig was relocating from across the country and would be reestablishing his practice in our town. Craig and I hit it off. While we were negotiating the agreement, my friend called me in a panic, telling me that he had just heard a rumor that Craig was being sued by a former patient for trying to molest her during a therapy session. No wonder he left town! Craig had told me he moved to be closer to his adult children. When I confronted Craig, he shrugged it off as "a disgruntled patient, and nothing more." I wasn't satisfied with his explanation, and I was angry that he had withheld such vital information from me. The deal was off.

2. There is no track record of success. They have no actual accomplishments to back up their claims of what they are bringing to the table—only lots of excuses for why they haven't made it yet and sky-high promises of what they will do for you in the future.
3. You witness them speaking abusively, or in a derogatory manner, to their employees, spouses, strangers, or to you. This could also include evidence of race, age, or gender prejudice.

My husband introduced me to a colleague, Ben, who was interested in buying into my retail store. We had some productive initial meetings; I was starting to seriously consider his offer. Then my husband and I went out to dinner with Ben and his wife, Gloria. Ben was so nasty to Gloria—bossing her around, making fun of her, and calling her a pig for ordering dessert—we could barely get through dinner without choking on our food. If that's the way he treats his wife, imagine how he would treat me.

4. They rage to you about how they are suing the SOBs who screwed them in their last partnership. Or they complain incessantly about what a horrible partnership they had and how it was all their partner's fault.
5. You do a credit check and discover that your prospective partners' credit ratings are abysmal. They filed for personal bankruptcy a few years ago and/or have a chronic habit of not paying their credit card bills on time.
6. They refuse to put any of your verbal agreements in writing. They either "don't have the time" or insist that such formality would be too constraining.
7. You catch them in a blatant lie about their backgrounds, abilities, or the products they represent.

Gary worked for me for three years, and I was considering making him a junior partner in my law firm. My wife and I socialized with Gary and his wife several times and they looked content. So imagine my shock when I was entertaining a client in a nearby town and I saw Gary holding hands over dinner with another woman! The next day I casually asked him what he had done the night before. He said, "Nothing I was just home watching television with my wife." What Gary does with his personal time is none of my business, but I wondered how I could trust him when he could lie so easily to me—and his wife.

8. You do some reference checking, and people are either hesitant to talk openly with you or warn you to stay away.
9. They are committed to so many projects it's unlikely you will receive the attention your business needs and deserves. They appear rushed, burned out, and exhausted every time you see them. They assure you "It won't be that way once we start working together."
10. They are in the middle of a divorce or other serious life crisis and their personal lives are in a shambles. They are too distracted, broke, enraged, and/or stressed out to be dependable, solid partners. (They may be just fine after their personal crisis passes.)

Martha and I started our partnership just as she was on the verge of adopting a baby girl from Russia. She had to fly to Russia a few times to finalize the details. Then, when she finally brought her new daughter to the States, the baby had all kinds of problems adjusting. Martha took several leaves of absence to take care of her. It took almost a year before Martha's attention was back to our partnership. Though I had done most of the work launching the business, Martha and I still split our profits, as outlined in our partnership agreement. I felt like I was being ripped off.

11. They've been fired from their jobs—for incompetence, letting personal problems interfere with their work, or other reasons. Their story to you is that they are being framed. You ask some of the other people involved and learn there's another side to the story that troubles you.
12. They are charged with a crime, and legal action is pending.

Since I was a little kid, I always wanted to own my own roller rink. A roller rink in town went up for sale. I had recently been laid off from my job and my wife encouraged me to follow my dream. We were short on capital, so I approached this old buddy of mine, Jim, who offered to put up the $50 thousand we needed. Jim had been fired from his job when he was arrested for molesting a woman in the parking lot after hours at his office. Jim insisted he was innocent and I believed him. I really didn't think he was capable of such a thing. I jumped at the opportunity he was offering me, and we bought the rink. Four months after our business opened, Jim was convicted of his crime and sent to jail. To make matters worse, I found out he had been hitting on the teenage girls coming to the rink as well. Word spread so fast in our small town, it put me out of business in three months.

13. The partner you are considering acts in a way that you find exceedingly distasteful, heartless, or rude. Your immediate instinct is "I don't like this person."

I blew my cork after an experience that had nothing really to do with the business. I had just seen a widow drop dead from a heart attack at her husband's wake, and it really shook me up. I was telling my prospective partner about it over the phone, and she suddenly started talking about going to the ballet. She had no response, and I thought, What kind of person is this? Am I talking to a banana peel? This is not the kind of person I want to be in partnership with.

14. You discover that your prospective partner is a complete pessimist who always has a bad word to say about something or someone (and nothing is ever his or her fault).

I needed a partner for my growing computer business. Judy had a lot of contacts and was referred to me by a customer. I agreed to meet her for lunch. We had only been there for five minutes when she started complaining. She hated the table where we were seated and the service was too slow. Then, of course, her meal was undercooked. She griped about her husband, her clients, her kids, and virtually everything in her life. It appeared that she was interested in joining my business because she hated everything about her own. I couldn't imagine partnering with such a negative person.

15. Your antennae should go up immediately if a prospective partner is offended if you want to check references and says something like "If you don't trust me, and you feel you need to get references, I don't think we can work together."
16. Be careful of partnering with a heavy drinker (or recreational drug user) who tells you that he or she indulges only on off hours and you needn't worry about it interfering with work.

I knew Nathan, my fraternity brother, was a bit of a party animal. I didn't think he would let it interfere with his work. We started a video production company together right out of college. For the first few months of our partnership I never saw him drunk on the job. Then I started to smell alcohol on his breath when he came to the office in the morning. I didn't mention it, hoping he would get it under control. Now it's progressed to the point that he frequently shows up late on Monday mornings and cuts loose by 3 p.m. on Fridays. I don't know how to confront him without ruining our friendship.

17. You have worked with this person in another work setting and you've seen him or her act unethically, irresponsibly, or incompetently.

Scott was the top salesman where we both used to work. I had seen Scott fabricate all kinds of promises just to make a sale. When he asked me if he could join my sales force, once I had started my own company, I hired him with some reservations. I warned him not to pull the same tricks with my customers. But he didn't listen. He made such exaggerated sales pitches about the software's ability that I got stuck giving refunds to hundreds of angry customers. I should have known that Scott wouldn't change his true colors. I fired him after three months.

⟡

18. When discussing roles and responsibilities in the company, this individual emphatically refuses to do any of the routine work required in a lean startup. This person is accustomed to having secretaries and staffs, and is a prima donna. (You might choose to work with such individuals if what they have to offer is so valuable that you are willing to do most of the work or if you don't plan an equal partnership.)
19. They focus most of their conversation on what they are going to get from your partnership rather than what they are going to give.

⟡

I interviewed Sharon as a prospective partner for my growing interior decorating company. When I met with her, I was immediately turned off by her approach. She was only concerned about what my company could give her. Her first questions were about how much she would get paid, when she would get a company car, and how much vacation she would receive. Then she had the nerve to tell me that she expected me to change the company's name and logo to reflect her being part of the firm. I was waiting for her to tell me that I needed to get new office furniture!

⟡

20. The prospective partner is asking you to invest a great deal of money and pressures you to grab this opportunity right now, before someone else does. If it sounds too good to be true, it is.

Twelve Yellow Lights That Should Signal Slow Down, Proceed Carefully

The following scenarios are the kinds where, if the business goes well, you tell yourself, "Good thing I didn't let it stop me."

If the partnership becomes problematic, you say to yourself, "Why didn't I pay closer attention to those warning signs! How could I be so naive?"

In other words, it could go either way. Don't rule out the possibility of partnering based solely on these concerns. Slow down, and candidly discuss your apprehension with your prospective partner, trusted professionals (lawyer, accountant, family adviser), friends, and your spouse. Follow your intuition; it usually doesn't lie, unless you practice self-deception.

1. Your prospective partner wants you to save his or her failing company. These people are candid about their troubles. If everything were going smoothly, they wouldn't need you. They have made some mistakes, and they are acknowledging their weaknesses. They want to strengthen their management of the company and/or they are looking for money. This may be a golden opportunity for you—if the product is viable and the entrepreneur has strengths that complement yours. The key is to investigate thoroughly enough to determine the true source of the trouble—and whether you hold the key to fixing it.

When Linda first started her office furnishings company, she ran the office and gave the sales presentations by herself She barely made enough money each year to pay the bills. After two years of trying to run the company alone, she decided to take on a partner. Linda asked Michele, a satisfied customer, if she would consider quitting her job to join Linda in the business. Michele was hesitant to join a struggling business, especially since she'd have to give up her steady paycheck. But after seeing Linda's products, she was convinced that the business could be profitable, so she decided to take the risk. Michele brought to the business the sales skills that Linda was lacking, and within the year the business was out of the red.

---

2. Your prospective partner has just emerged from a problematic partnership or has failed in more than one. Why did the previous partnerships fail? What role or responsibility belongs with your prospective partner? Has he or she learned from the experience? Everyone is entitled to a mistake. You want to be careful, though, not to be the next one.
3. You notice that your prospective partner interrupts you, dominates the conversation, talks about himself or herself, rarely asks you questions, and appears to be highly competitive in his or her work and personal life.
4. The individual you are considering has never been married and/or never been in a successful business partnership. He or she has been a lone eagle—a sole proprietor—for a long time. What habits has he developed? Is she too set in her ways to adapt to a partnership now? What motivates him to make the change?
5. Your prospective partner offers an appealing service or product but acknowledges that sales are poor. Why? Is it the company's marketing or sales strategy, the product, the demographics of the market, the competition? Until you know more about why sales are low, you won't know whether you will be able to help solve the company's problems.

I joined Ned's sporting goods business because he claimed to need some help in sales. He told me sales were low because he couldn't find a decent salesperson. He offered me equity in the company if I would join him. It wasn't long before I found out that the reason for low sales was a line of defective products, not ineffective salespeople. Customers were returning the equipment as fast as they bought it. Within a few months, the reputation of our merchandise killed any possibility of staying in business.

6. You notice that your prospective partner is consistently late for meetings with you or others. How much of an issue is this for you? Is this a reflection of the person's dependability in other ways? If you are a stickler for timeliness, this irritation could drive you nuts.
7. You are working on a project with someone you are considering as a partner. This person exhibits troublesome behavior. He or she misses deadlines, doesn't return phone calls or e-mail, makes promises and then doesn't deliver, and generally acts in an unreliable manner. The beauty of this project is that you get to test-drive your partner before merging your companies. Don't expect that these character defects will somehow change if you join forces. Can you live with your concerns? Is your partner open to modifying his or her behavior if confronted with it?

Sarah and I decided to co-write a cookbook. We were under a tight contract with our publisher and Sarah started missing deadlines. She was so disorganized, she drove me crazy. Even though the first book sold well, when the publisher asked us if we would be interested in writing a second book together, I declined.

8. Divergent financial needs: One partner has an urgent need to be profitable, and the other is cushioned financially and in no rush. This kind of financial inequality can work if all parties are aware of the difference and plan roles and responsibilities according to individual needs and motivations. Be careful about making the assumption that the person with no pressing financial needs will work at the same pace as the individual with urgent cash needs.
9. Your prospective partner exhibits some personality traits that concern you, given the kind of business you are in and the role that person would be playing in the business.

It could be personal insecurity, or shabby personal appearance, or stuttering, or a fear of flying on airplanes. How much of a concern this is depends, of course, on your circumstances.

I'm a professional speaker, giving seminars around the country. As my business started to grow, I decided to bring in an office manager who could help hold the fort down while I was on the road. Mary was interested in joining me only if I gave her some equity in the company. I was so impressed with her office management skills, I agreed. My only concern was, I had an image to uphold. Mary didn't dress as classy or professional as I would have liked. It was awkward for me to bring up the subject, but I told her that she would need to upgrade her wardrobe if she wanted to work with me. Not only was she open to the idea, but she asked me to go shopping with her!

10. At first you admire your prospective partner's other commitments to family, church, and community. Then you have to ask the question: Will this person have enough time for the business? What will he or she give up, or what evidence is there that the person can make room for more in his or her life? What kind of demands do you expect the business will require, and how will you divide the workload?

I own a sports uniform store that was interfering with my ability to manage as a single parent. I went looking for a partner. Allen told me when I approached him that he would need lots of afternoons off because he coaches high school sports year-round. I admired his commitment to coaching and thought his connections would help our business. We agreed that he would cover the store early in the morning, giving me the ability to get my kids off to school and get some household chores taken care of.

11. You have reason to believe that you don't share the same personal values to a great degree. To what extent are these differences relevant and important? Do you care if your partner is in favor of legalized abortion, goes hunting on weekends, or is politically right or left wing? Different political affiliations may be irrelevant to most partnerships, but what if your business relies on fund-raising from a particular political community? A clash in values can be a reason to avoid a partnership or just something to be cognizant of as you move forward.
12. When you invite your prospective partners to do some of the exercises in this book, or to discuss some of the issues the book raises, their responses are lukewarm to cold and they offer plenty of excuses for not doing it "right now." What is the basis of their resistance? Is it an indication that they will be less committed than you to working out relationship concerns once your partnership is launched and under way? You should seek assurance that their reluctance to discuss these issues is not a warning sign that they are unwilling to give your relationship the consideration it requires.

Green Light—Positive Signs to Move Forward in Partnership

Partnering is an art and a science—there's no way to eliminate all risk and unknowns. I have heard countless stories of partner shock and betrayal: teaming up with someone who seemed like an angel in the "dating" stage and turns devil incarnate after the "marriage" begins. Sometimes, hindsight provides some clues. Other times, it catches us entirely by surprise. Partnering is risky business. Even if your evaluation in this chapter turns on a green light for you, and you proceed forward with every confidence that you are in good hands, you can run into trouble later. That said, summarized in this section are positive signs of a good candidate for a partnership. If you see the following traits in your prospective partner, and in yourself, you are more inclined to have a positive partnering experience.

Looking for the Green Light

Consider the conversations you've had with your prospective partners, and what you know about them and their histories. Evaluate all your research of who you believe they are and have been in their precious working experiences. Ask yourself how they rate on the following 20 characteristics, using the following values.

1: I don't see this trait present in my prospective partners at all.

2: This trait seems to be developing in my prospective partners. I believe it will strengthen over time.

3: This characteristic describes my prospective partners most of the time.

4: This trait is one of my prospective partners' greatest strengths and assets.

1. ___ They are eager to make a contribution to our business, and have skills, knowledge, and resources to offer.
2. ___ They demonstrate an interest in working out conflicts and optimizing our partner relationship. They are open to doing relationship exercises or to seeking outside counsel if we need it.
3. ___ They appear to be capable of sharing decision making and control, and have done so in a working environment in the past.
4. ___ They seem genuinely interested in me as a person. They are good listeners.
5. ___ They are specialists in their area of expertise, but they are also versatile and will do whatever is needed. They aren't too full of themselves to fill the role of janitor if it's needed.
6. ___ I appreciate their balance between optimism and realism. They are aware that things can go wrong, and are

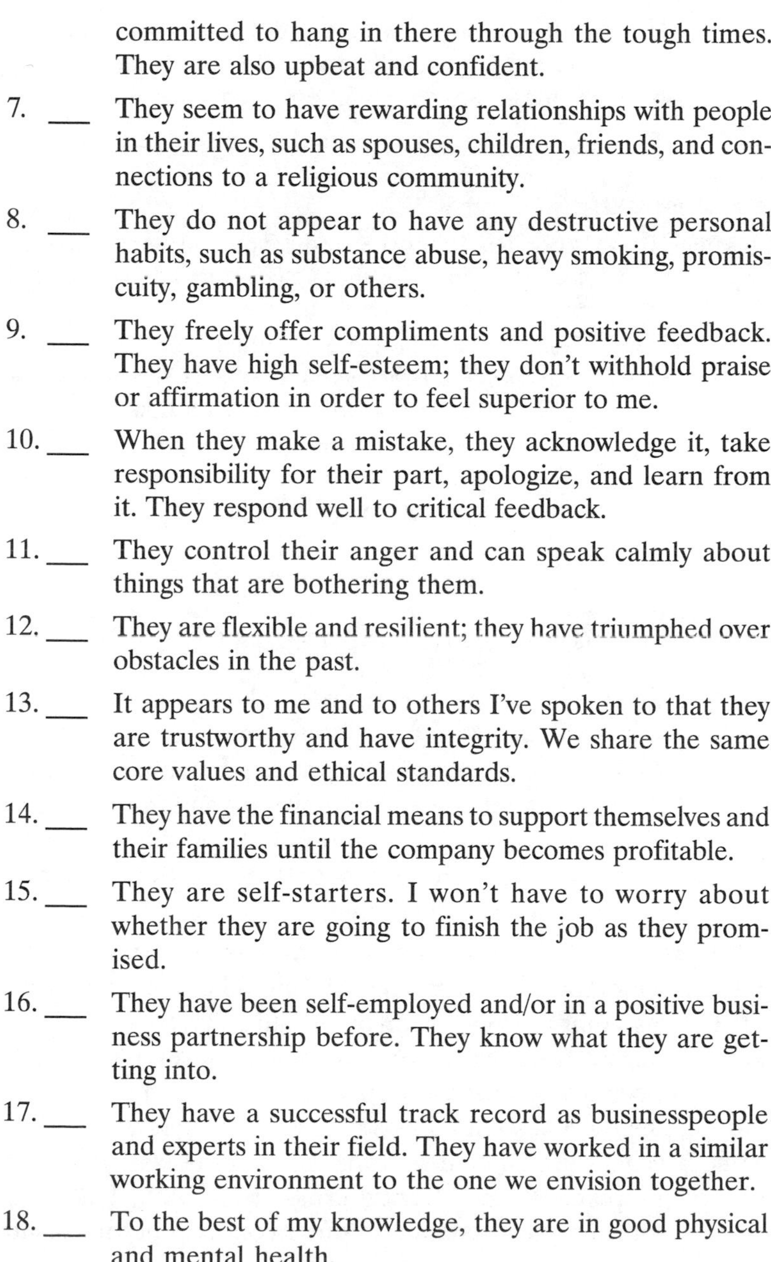

committed to hang in there through the tough times. They are also upbeat and confident.

7. ___ They seem to have rewarding relationships with people in their lives, such as spouses, children, friends, and connections to a religious community.

8. ___ They do not appear to have any destructive personal habits, such as substance abuse, heavy smoking, promiscuity, gambling, or others.

9. ___ They freely offer compliments and positive feedback. They have high self-esteem; they don't withhold praise or affirmation in order to feel superior to me.

10. ___ When they make a mistake, they acknowledge it, take responsibility for their part, apologize, and learn from it. They respond well to critical feedback.

11. ___ They control their anger and can speak calmly about things that are bothering them.

12. ___ They are flexible and resilient; they have triumphed over obstacles in the past.

13. ___ It appears to me and to others I've spoken to that they are trustworthy and have integrity. We share the same core values and ethical standards.

14. ___ They have the financial means to support themselves and their families until the company becomes profitable.

15. ___ They are self-starters. I won't have to worry about whether they are going to finish the job as they promised.

16. ___ They have been self-employed and/or in a positive business partnership before. They know what they are getting into.

17. ___ They have a successful track record as businesspeople and experts in their field. They have worked in a similar working environment to the one we envision together.

18. ___ To the best of my knowledge, they are in good physical and mental health.

19. ___ If they are married or with a significant other, that person is supportive of our venture. If they are single, they have no one to answer to except themselves.

20. ___ They appear to be happy, grounded, reasonable, and kind.

How did you score?

Less than 30: Your light just turned red. If your partner scores that low on so many of these characteristics, you should look for other options.

31 to 59: Your light is yellow. Your partner could shine in several of these categories but exhibit a few troublesome traits that make you proceed with caution.

60 or higher: It looks like a green light—if all of your other evaluations in this chapter checked out to your liking and your gut instinct says "Go for it!"

When The Traffic Signals Aren't Mutual

If you and your prospective partners take the previous quiz, you may not score each other in the same manner. One of you may put the brakes on, or slow the process down because of a concern, while the other is ready to move forward immediately. That's normal. One of you may be more cautious than the other. One of you may have a more serious obstacle to overcome than the other, or a lower risk threshold.

My husband, Stephen, says he knew from our very first date that he wanted to marry me. I thought he was a neat guy, but he was going through a divorce, had physical custody of two adolescent boys, was more religiously observant than I, and had been a vegetarian for 20 years. At the time, though I was looking for a husband, I was precisely trying to avoid marrying a "vegetarian Orthodox Jewish man with kids." It wasn't part of my plan. When Stephen crossed my path, I needed time to work out my resistance to these concerns before I said

"I do!" Luckily for me, my husband waited for me to catch up; we were engaged within a few months and married a year later. (We're still happily married after seven years—just because the traffic signals for partnership aren't mutual in the beginning doesn't mean your partnership can't evolve nicely once you are both on the same wavelength.)

You may need to be patient with a prospective partner who needs to work through his or her concerns before partnering with you. If you rush people into partnering prematurely, they will express their anxiety about unsettled issues when you are trying to focus on launching and running the business. On the other hand, don't allow a prospective partner to pressure you into partnering before you are ready. If you find yourself stalling for too long, it may be a sign that this partnership is not well suited for you.

When Your Light Has Turned Green, What's Next?

Moving on to Chapter 4 and beyond in this book assumes that you have selected a partner who meets your needs and passes your evaluation. You are now ready to merge your individual enterprises, dreams, and goals into one unit with a joint vision. You will find that doing so is far easier when you have worked through the first three chapters in this book:

- When you are both (or all) committed to your partnership with the level of dedication you would find in a marriage.
- When you know yourself and your business well enough to identify what you are looking for in a partner and whether you are well suited for partnership as a means of running your business.

- When you have evaluated a prospective partner for his or her compatibility with your personality and business goals.

If you have taken the time to read the first few chapters of this book, congratulations! You are several steps ahead of most partners who neglect to give their relationship this kind of attention in the initial planning stages. You are creating a solid foundation for your partnership to come.

Chapter 4

Creating a Joint Vision

"You've got a problem when no one has the sign on his desk 'The buck stops here!' Someone must be the final arbitrator."

—Bruce McManis, Ph.D.

Creating a Joint Mission and Vision Statement

As a business owner, you likely understand the need to create a mission statement for your enterprise. The importance of articulating your mission statement to your employees, customers, and yourself is clear. As a customer, you've seen the mission statements of other small business sites posted on their establishment walls. Your personal mission may very well be what drove you to pursue your entrepreneurial dreams in the first place. Your company vision is what keeps you on the path when you are, as a client of mine once said, "up to your neck in alligators." A deeply felt mission gives you the strength and courage to hang in there for the long haul. A well-articulated mission helps you regain focus and equilibrium when conflicting demands on your time take you away from your stated purpose.

And yet, I'm willing to bet that few of you reading this book have ever actually articulated your personal or company mission, in writing, to yourselves, to your customers, or to your partners. Why? Because such an activity is usually viewed as a luxury, something to do when you have some "spare time." Developing and articulating a mission statement falls much farther down the list than such urgent activities as raising capital, prospecting for clients, delivering product, or responding to a customer complaint. After all, one could argue, what good is a written mission statement if you don't have a profitable business or a useful product or service to deliver?

This rationalizing is understandable. I would insist, however, that for two or more individuals entering into a partnership, defining and articulating a mission statement is not a luxury but an essential step to creating a solid, effective partnership. Why? Because until you take a few hours to go through such a process, and actually create a written mission and vision statement that unites both of you, you and your partner are operating on assumptions.

Let's say you've clicked in your initial meetings—it seems like a perfect match. You and your partner are in high gear, celebrating the synergy that flows between you and feeling optimistic about the successful company you will create together. Maybe you've been working together for months with little conflict. You are anxious to get your product to market, to show the world what you have to offer, and to reap the financial rewards of your brilliance. You aren't interested in doing anything that will slow you down. You figure: "If my partner and I have a conflict about the direction we're headed in, we'll deal with it when it comes up. Why worry about it now?"

The planning process for a mission and vision statement does take a few hours, maybe even a full day or two of your time, but it will save many more hours in the long run. When you are evaluating distribution alternatives, considering an expansion of your product line, brainstorming how to expand your client base, or confronted with an employee relations problem, knowing where you and your partner stand and having a joint vision—in writing—give you a strong foundation from which to work and the criteria for evaluating your decisions.

Discussing your mission isn't enough. Writing it down is a ritual that helps to solidify your commitment and symbolically demonstrates your unity as a partnership. It isn't my mission, but our mission; it isn't my vision for the company, but ours. It isn't the written mission or vision statement itself that contributes so much to strengthening your partnership—it's the process you and your partner will undergo while creating that statement.

Buzzwords such as growth, profit, success, and quality product mean different things to different people. Though you may assume that you and your partner mean the same thing when you say "We want to bring a quality product to the market and make a lot of money," you could actually be operating in different universes. If you don't take the time to discuss your goals and personal desires, you may discover, after investing many hours and thousands of dollars, that you and your partner are traveling separate paths. Consider what happened to Mark and Jerry.

> I am committed to spending quality time with my family. I don't want to be consumed by business 16 hours a day—I just want to make a decent living. My ex-partner, Jerry, is divorced, with grown kids, and work was all he seemed to care about.
>
> Jerry and I worked great together for a year or so, until the business started becoming profitable. Then Jerry got a case of "more-itis." The more money we made, products we developed, customers we served, the larger he wanted to grow the business. He got greedy and lost sight of our original commitment to serving a loyal base of customers with a quality product.
>
> We should have discussed more thoroughly our dreams of where we wanted to be in one to three years. We assumed that each of us had the same vision for the company, but it turned out we had radically different long-term goals. After two years of fighting over how fast to grow the company, my partner bought me out and we went our own separate ways. Last I heard he had doubled the company's size in a little over two years. I wouldn't want to manage that kind of headache—I'm glad I got out when I did.

Jerry and Mark assumed that they shared virtually identical intentions and desires for growing the company and delivering a quality product. Since their partnership worked so well in the bootstrapping startup stage, they didn't see the need to clarify their long-term vision beyond the initial conversations that led them to partner in the first place. And yet, if they had spent just a few extra hours developing a company mission statement, they might have discovered they were driven by radically different personal and company missions.

We naturally assume that people we like share our personal passions or commitments. What if you are partnered with someone you feel you know intimately, and you are confident that you share a similar vision, both short-term and long-term, for the company? Is it a waste of time to create a written mission and vision statement? Perhaps, like Scott Smith and John Nixon, co-founders of EntrepreneurPR of Sacramento, California, you are best buddies of several years, know each other better than you know your wives or mothers, and feel confident that your partnership is the perfect match.

I asked Scott and John to participate in an experiment. When I interviewed them, they came across as an ideal partnership. They complement each other well, finish each other's sentences, and have a friendship as close as you can ask for and a shared passion for growing their successful company. EntrepreneurPR publishes a yearbook *Entrepreneur Illustrated* profiling several hundred small businesses throughout the country. Their in-demand company provides the media with easy access to unique and newsworthy stories and information existing, but perhaps hidden from public view, in the small business community. By matching up the media with small business icons, EntrepreneurPR also provides small business owners with PR opportunities that have resulted in substantial new business for hundreds of companies.

Like many business owners in partnerships that are going well, Scott and John hadn't taken the time to write down a mission or vision statement. They thought about it, even started it once or twice, but urgent business demands took precedence, and it fell farther down on the priority list. I invited them to work with me to create a mission and vision statement in exchange for sharing their experience with you. They immediately agreed. (The success of their partnership is no accident; they demonstrate one of the secrets of partnering success—embracing and encouraging outside support when it is available, and always being willing to grow to the next level.)

I asked them, "Scott and John: You have been in business together for about two years. Why haven't you gotten around to writing a mission and vision statement?"

> Urgent issues such as media interviews, book design and distribution, Web site development, client recruiting, and employee relations kept pushing back finalizing our mission statement. We met on several occasions to do it, but it remained an important, yet unfinished, project. Then, as more people got to know about us, we were being asked about our mission and it was time to address it.

Defining Your Mission

A mission statement is a road map for growing your business. It is the compass that points you in the right direction and redirects you when you are veering off the path. When you and your partner are arguing over a decision that must be made, it is the place you return to for help. According to Laurie Beth Jones, author of *The Path: Creating Your Mission Statement for Work and Your Life*, a mission statement has three simple elements: first, it is no more than a single sentence long; second, it can be easily understood by a 12-year-old, and third, it is recitable from memory at gunpoint. The following steps for creating a mission and vision statement are adapted from the process suggested in *The Path,* a highly readable and insightful book.

Some mission statements are longer than one sentence—up to a few paragraphs perhaps—but ideally you will be able to synthesize your mission statement into one sentence that you can say at a networking event when a prospective client or colleague asks, "So, what does your company do?" Try to avoid generic phrases such as "We are here to serve our customers," which is just rhetoric that doesn't inspire, clarify, or inform.

A useful mission statement always communicates action, not just philosophy. And it does so in specific enough terms to be meaningful to you and your partner. Therefore, every mission statement includes at least one action verb.

Instructions: This is where you and your partner start the mission statement development process. What action words turn you on? What motivates you, expresses the behaviors you wish to be engaging in while running your business? The word organize might be practically orgasmic to one partner, but it might be a turnoff to another, who prefers to spend his or her time in cluttered chaos. There are thousands of verbs you can choose from; it is normal to find that you and your partner are attracted to different verbal expressions. Your goal is to find those action words that energize, excite, and motivate both of you—or, at the very least, to create a mission statement that includes verbs that appeal to each of you.

Mission Statement Exercise, Part A—The Action

Separate from your partner, scan the following list of 172 verbs I've compiled from *The Path,* several other research sources, and the dictionary. Write down or circle your top 20 favorites, and then narrow them down again to the top 10.

✧

accomplish	alert	assemble	balance
acquire	alleviate	assist	bestow
advance	alter	attain	brighten
affect	amplify	attract	build
affirm	analyze	augment	calm

catalyze
cause
choose
claim
coach
collect
combine
create
command
communicate
compel
compete
complete
compose
conceive
confirm
connect
construct
contact
continue
counsel
defend
deliver
demonstrate
detect
devise
direct
discover
distribute
dominate
dream
drive
educate
elect
embrace
encourage
endow
energize
engage
engineer
enhance
enlighten
enlist
enliven
entertain
enthuse
evaluate
excite
explain
explore
express
extend
facilitate
finance
fix
follow
foster
franchise
gather
generate
give
grant
guard
guide
heal
help
hold
host
identify
illuminate
implement
improve
influence
inform
inspire
instruct
integrate
involve
launch
lead
locate
love
make
manifest
master
mediate
minister to
model
motivate
move
negotiate
nurture
open
organize
participate
perfect
perform
persuade
play
possess
prepare
present
prevail
produce
promote
provide
pursue
quest
reclaim
reduce
redefine
reflect
reform
regard
regulate
relate
release
renew
restore
return
revise
safeguard
satisfy
save
sell
serve
share
solve
spark
speak
stimulate
strengthen
summon
support
surrender
sustain
touch
trade
translate
travel
triumph
uncover
understand
use
utilize
validate
value
verbalize
volunteer
venture
write
yield

✧

Join your partner and compare your top 10 verbs lists. Do you share any verbs in common? Don't be surprised if they are entirely, or substantially, different. Now the goal is for the two (or more) of you to choose your top three to five favorite verbs, narrowed down from the 10 each you currently have on your lists.

When Scott and John did this exercise, Scott's top 10 verbs were:

build	entertain	satisfy
communicate	help	travel
create	organize	distribute
promote		

John's top 10 verbs were:

attract	help	stimulate
connect	motivate	strengthen
demonstrate	provide	explore
satisfy		

When Scott and John came together, they narrowed down their list to the following top three choices:

build	promote	provide

This is what they had to say about that process:

Being forced to narrow down our verb list to just three words helped us to focus on our true mission. Surprisingly, our combined list of 20 words shared only two words—help and satisfy—and neither of those ended up on our final list! Although we were worried at first about having so few words in common, the narrowing process took us only a few minutes.

Mission Statement Exercise, Part B—The Who

Now that you have chosen the most meaningful verbs, it's time to decide who are you here to serve, to help, to safeguard, or to inform. (Insert whatever verbs you chose in Part A, above.)

Be as specific as you can in your discussion about who you are serving. To create a one-sentence mission statement, you may articulate the "who" in fairly general terms, but it is still useful for you and your partner to first brainstorm the segments of your market. Be careful not to narrow your mission statement "who" to a one-product market or to a group of people who will buy from you for only a short period of time.

For example: The mission statement for my company, Anchored Dreams, is: "To provide practical assistance and emotional support to individuals, couples, and partners in business." In 1996, when HarperBusiness published my first book, *Honey, I Want to Start My Own Business: A Planning Guide for Couples*, my primary audience was entrepreneurial couples or small business owners concerned with issues related to marriage and family. When I wrote *Let's Go Into Business Together*, I added "partners" to my mission statement. I am now the author of eight books. My audience still fits under the umbrella I created in my mission statement. If the "who" of my market should change, I can always reevaluate and rewrite my mission statement.

Instructions: Separately from your partner, jot down on an index card three general categories of customers you currently serve, or hope to serve, and up to twenty subcategories of smaller market segments under those headings. Get together and compare notes. Ideally, especially if you've been working together for a period of time, these lists will be fairly compatible. However, you'll likely find a few differences that prompt discussion and clarification. Maybe one of you harbors a secret dream that your company will expand services to include a market your partner hasn't considered. Now is a great time to share your vision. Don't be alarmed if this part of the exercise also creates conflict, or if one or both of you express interest in serving a market that doesn't appeal to your partners.

My sister and I came together in business because we both adored our mom's mouthwatering spaghetti sauce. Whenever we made it for friends and family, everyone wanted the recipe. We decided to bottle it up and start selling it to our friends and neighbors. Initially, we had modest dreams for our little company—we were just looking for a part-time activity that would be fun, bring in a bit of discretionary income, and honor Mom. But then my sister came up with the idea of getting the ingredients donated by local supermarkets and serving the poor in our community by selling our sauce at rock-bottom prices.

My sister has always been the "Mother Teresa" in our family. I felt like a scrooge telling her that I wasn't on board—it sounded like a lot more work than I was prepared to do, for too little payback. She would have been satisfied with being the community "do-gooder," but it wouldn't have been enough incentive for me. Eventually, we compromised. We agreed to tithe 10 percent of our slim profits to organizations in our community serving the poor. That satisfied both of us, and we didn't have to radically shift our targeted customers.

Mission Statement Exercise, Part C—The Product/Service

The last element of the mission statement is the "what"—what is the service, product, or benefit you will be providing your target customers? Again, the "what" of your mission statement should be broad enough to extend beyond your current product and to articulate the greater vision that you and your partner share. If my mission statement for Anchored Dreams spoke only of books, it wouldn't capture my coaching or speaking business or my newsletters for entrepreneurial couples and small business owners, and my syndicated column. So I chose "practical assistance and emotional support" to communicate all of the various services and products my company provides.

Instructions: With your partner, list all of the products and services you currently offer or hope to offer. Be specific.

Now look for the similar themes. If relevant, group your products and services into similar categories. Seek ways to phrase your products and services in terms of the benefit you will provide your clients and customers. Does your company manufacture umbrellas or do you keep people dry in the rain?

For example: EntrepreneurPR offers the following products and services:

- Public relations.
- *Entrepreneur Illustrated.*
- Online version of *Entrepreneur Illustrated.*
- Web page design, consultation.
- Expert writing and editing services.
- Article reprints.
- Wall plaques of articles.

These can be grouped into one benefit statement, such as: "Affordable, effective, and convenient national media exposure."

Mission Statement Exercise, Part D—Putting It All Together

Now Scott and John were ready to create their mission statement. They had their three most attractive verbs chosen, customers defined, and the benefits of their services articulated. This is what they came up with:

> The mission of EntrepreneurPR is to help small businesses and entrepreneurs build their companies by providing them effective, convenient, and affordable national media promotions.

Articulating Your Vision

For the last two years, Scott and John have been waking up early in the morning and imagining what it will be like for each of them when their company reaches its goals. Late at night, when they are still at work, they motivate themselves by their fantasies of what it will be like a year from now, or two or three, when cash flow exceeds their wildest expectations. They have shared in general terms their visions of the future—each assuming that the other understands what he is saying. But their fantasies may in fact be quite different. Imagine this scenario:

> John says: "It's going to be so cool when we get the X account. We'll finally be bringing in some serious cash." *(He is visualizing buying his wife and kids the swimming pool they have been asking for.)*
>
> Scott says: "It's going to be so cool when we get the X account. We'll finally be bringing in some serious cash." *(He is visualizing giving out a Christmas/holiday bonus to the employees who work so hard to help service the account.)*

Visualizations are highly personal and individual, and yet, when two or more partners join together they must find a way to create a joint vision. A vision statement is an expression of what your life and work together will look, feel, sound, and be like when you are fulfilling your mission statement. Written in the present tense, as if it has already been accomplished, a vision statement is filled with descriptive details and is always positive.

Your vision statement can include a description of your ideal partnering relationship and hoped-for relationships with customers, clients, colleagues, employees, and vendors. A vision statement articulates in detail how you are making a difference in your clients' lives, how you are spending your time, what you are feeling about your accomplishments, how much money you are making, the lifestyle improvements that your business success has enabled, and so much more.

Consciously creating and expressing a vision statement will feel like the least urgent task in front of you as a partnership—and yet, it can be one of the most fun and rewarding activities you can engage in. You can rely on this vision statement to pull you along and to keep you motivated when you hit the "quitting days" you will inevitably encounter. A vision statement expresses your individual and collective dreams in a way that will unify and energize you.

Instructions: There are two ways you can create a vision statement. I recommend both if you are willing to spend the time. I gave Scott and John the option of doing one or the other, or both. First, create a visual image that expresses your success; it can be something simple. When my book *Honey, I Want to Start My Own Business* was released, I went to the bookstore and took a picture of the book sitting on the New Releases shelf. Then I took a picture of the *New York Times* best-seller shelf. When the pictures were developed, I cut out the picture of Honey and taped it over one of the books in my best-sellers picture. I also doctored a Business Best-Seller list from the newspaper. Both of these visual images sit on my desk and nurture my dreams.

A few years ago, I created a collage to help me positively visualize making the transition from corporate human resource director to self-employed author, coach, and speaker. I am someone with little artistic ability, but I can cut out pictures from a magazine. One night, I surrounded myself with piles of old magazines and began cutting out images and words that appealed to me. I glued them together into a large collage—and created a "vision statement" that I had framed and hung on my office wall.

With your partner, or separately, create a vision statement with magazine pictures, or any visual image that captures your hopes and dreams for the company you are growing together. When you have something that appeals to both of you, make sure it goes on the wall of your office or some place visible to both of you.

The second part of this process is to create a written vision statement. I recommend that you each write your own vision statement and then share it with each other. Look for the places in which your vision statements are synergistic, and places where they differ. Create a joint vision statement that articulates in one voice what you dream of together. Whereas the mission statement should be as brief as a sentence or short paragraph, the vision statement can be several pages long, depending on how much detail you get into. Take an evening out, over dinner or some brew if that appeals to you, and let your imagination soar. Growing a business is such hard work—allow yourself this simple pleasure! Here's what Scott and John wrote for their vision statement:

> To be the news media's best source for locating and reporting on innovative entrepreneurs and small business owners. To be the country's most affordable, effective, and convenient national public relations firm for entrepreneurs and small business owners. To be known as the founders of the country's first, and leading, public relations firm dedicated to helping the national news media, and entrepreneurs and small business owners, discover each other.

Scott and John went on to tell me:

> Our personal vision statement centered around providing for our families. Despite our relatively young ages, we are rather traditional in our agreement of males being the main providers for a family. This is true even though we both came from much different backgrounds. Scott, the eldest of four boys, was raised in the rural foothills of central California by a supportive and hardworking single mom, who, even without child support, quickly got off the welfare roll though she could have really used the extra help. John, by far the youngest of three boys and two girls, was raised in a very upper class neighborhood in the San Francisco Bay Area by dedicated and supportive parents who never divorced.

Here's what Scott and John came up with for their personal vision statement:

> To be involved with and supportive of the lives of our families. To provide our families with what they need to live comfortably and prosper. To continue to

build and maintain our many friendships. To travel and experience other parts of the world. And finally, to never forget to have fun along the way!

If you enjoy the activity of creating a mission and vision statement you can do it again. Ideally, you will revisit both for guidance, inspiration, or conflict resolution.

Committing To Your Values

In Chapter 2, we defined those personal values that were driving forces in our lives. In Chapter 3, we emphasized the importance of partnering with someone who shares your values and ethics. Repeatedly in my interviews, when partners described a partnership that worked, they would say, "We share the same values."

Gershom and Samuel, cofounders of a multimillion-dollar media company in New York City, crossed paths on Compuserve. Though they came together as strangers, they felt an immediate synergistic connection once they met, much like two people on a blind date who instinctively say, "This is the one." Gershom summarizes his feelings about their early meetings:

> We both had an immediate good gut feel about the other. We shared similar values, at work and at home. We both had wives at home with young children and shared the same commitment to support our families so that our wives could be home full-time with our children. In our previous companies, we each made business decisions according to what would make the customer happy; we didn't cut corners financially at the expense of customer service just to make our own pockets a little fatter. We instinctively trusted each other from the first meeting, and our partnership is working very well three years later.

Gershom and Samuel saw certain values in the other that were important to them, and made the decision to partner accordingly. Here, in Chapter 4, we look at values in a different way. Assuming that you have chosen a partner who holds the same basic values as you, how do you honor those values in your business and your partnership? Once again, assumptions can get you into trouble. Just because you both have stay-at-home wives doesn't necessarily mean that you both have the same understanding about balancing business and family, or how much money you want to earn. Being married to two stay-at-home wives is a starting place for shared needs and lifestyle approaches, but only that. The next step is to take the time to really get to know what your partner values, how your partner wishes to express his or her values in the workplace, and then to commit to honoring that.

Let's say that you both value "commitment." The word commitment can mean different things to each of you, such as:

- Keeping your word when you make a promise.
- Backing your partner decisions when employees complain to you about him.
- Working the hours it will take to make this business work.
- Not leaving the partnership, even if you go through hard times together.
- Remaining faithful to your wife or husband.
- Fulfilling your responsibilities as defined in the job description.

If you agree, for example, that commitment is a core value for both of you, how will you know if you are honoring this value in your partnership? You'll need to define for each other what commitment really means to each of you. Assuming that you went into business together because you found enough shared values to feel comfortable with one another, now is the time to commit to creating a partnership that honors those values.

Marti Childs and Jeff March are co-founders of a successful California marketing communications business venture, EditPros. They offer writing and editorial services to corporate and institutional clients across the country. Their partnership has been working fabulously ever since they started their company six years ago. During our interview, I was struck by how many shared values they expressed and their creative ways for honoring those values.

When we conceived the idea for our own business, Jeff and I were both runners and seriously into physical fitness. Realizing that our business would eat away at the time we used to have to exercise, we intentionally rented a post office box five miles away from the office. Every day we ride our bicycles, side by side, to the post office and back. That way, we get out of the office for an hour every day, keep each other informed, and as an added bonus, we stay in shape.

If Marti and Jeff didn't share a strong commitment to physical fitness, riding their bikes ten miles each day might have been too demanding for one of them. For this partnership, it's one of the secrets to their success. I asked Marti and Jeff if they would be willing to participate in the following exercise—to bring their implicit and shared value commitments into focus and to express them in a written commitment statement to each other. They readily agreed to participate and to share the results with you.

Partnership Commitment Statement

Instructions: When we get married, we recite wedding vows as a way to express our heartfelt intention to honor and support each other "in sickness and in health, till death do us part." Such a vow of commitment wouldn't make sense for a business partnership. And yet, expressing your pledge to uphold and support your partner's values can be a powerful means for affirming a partnership that satisfies each partner's deepest needs. If you feel out of alignment with your values, you will likely leave the partnership, even if you are prosperous, and you will suffer a great deal in the process.

Refer back to the exercise in Chapter 2 defining your personal values. You and your partner should individually complete the exercise again if some time has passed since you were considering partnership—otherwise, just use the results from the first time you did the exercise.

Write on a piece of paper all of the words that each of you rated an eight or higher, meaning "This value is an absolute motivator, essential for making my life and this partnership/company work."

Select the top six values you agree to support in your work together. They may be shared values, or you may choose three from each list. You may aim to have all values on the list that are eights or higher for both of you, or you may choose to incorporate the three highest values for each of you, regardless of whether they are shared. It doesn't matter, as long as you select a final list of six or more to work with that you both are willing to commit to. (The number six isn't set in stone. If you want to include more than six values, that's fine.)

Now complete the following sentence using each of the values on your list: We honor ____________ in our partnership, so we will ____________, and we won't ____________.

For example: We honor commitment to our families in our partnership, so we will keep work hours to a five-day work-week, and we won't expect either of us to work more than 45 hours per week.

Or: We honor philanthropy in our partnership, so we will tithe 10 percent of our profits to a charity we jointly select, and we won't let greed or fear interfere with that commitment, even if cash flow gets tight.

Here are the two lists of values rated eight or higher that Marti and Jeff came up with when they did this exercise.

Marti's top five:

family	independence	trustworthiness
financial security	personal and professional growth	

Jeff's top five:

communicating	kindness	trustworthiness
family	reliability	

The six words that they both agreed make up their "highest values for the partnership" are:

family	communicating	financial security
trustworthiness	independence	reliability

Marti had this to say about the process of selecting the six highest values for their partnership:

What I found most interesting is that my words "financial security, independence, and personal and professional growth" related to the fact that until we founded EditPros, I felt controlled and held back by my employers. I've always wanted to have control of my own future and be able to take care of myself and my family if I had to. I never really thought much about it until I compared my words to Jeff's.

We both agreed on the words we used from each of our lists to develop our partnership commitment statements. Looking at them now, I notice that although we both constructed the sentences, I wrote three of them and Jeff wrote three of them. That's pretty much how we work together on a daily basis.

Jeff had this to say:

I found the self-evaluation and comparison with Marti interesting and valuable because it reaffirmed that we are truly in synch with each other's values and motives.

Here are the six value commitment statements Marti and Jeff created for their partnership:

1. We honor family in our partnership, so we will balance our personal and professional needs as we see fit, and we won't allow others to control when and how we spend time with our families.
2. We honor trustworthiness in our partnership, so we will be certain to keep promises we make to each other and to our clients, and we won't agree to any promise that we can't fulfill.
3. We honor communication in our partnership, so we will discuss problems as they occur and work out solutions together, and we won't make important decisions without first discussing them with one another.
4. We honor independence in our partnership, so we will continue to diversify our client base and range of activities, and we won't allow ourselves to become reliant on any individual client.
5. We honor financial security in our partnership, so we will make business decisions with potential for long-term stability, and we won't let disorganized, noncommittal activity by business prospects distract us from our long-term goals.
6. We honor reliability in our partnership, so we will try to live up to each other's expectations, and we won't disappoint our clients or each other.

I encouraged Marti and Jeff to hang these on an office wall or place them in a file folder to refer back to at an opportune time.

Different from a mission statement, your values commitment statements are not designed for the public, but rather to support your partnership. You might choose to share them if someone asked, but you probably wouldn't print them on your business stationery.

Setting Business Goals

The process of expressing your values leads perfectly into the process of setting goals. Now, when you work together on your business plan or review your monthly or quarterly goals, you have a framework for discussion. Most of the partners I interviewed had no trouble being convinced of the importance of setting business goals in the startup phase. Often, though, these goals weren't written down, nor were they revisited when the business started heading in a different direction, or going at a different speed, than originally planned. A business plan is a living document whose usefulness diminishes substantially when it is viewed as a onetime activity just to get started.

When you are working in partnership, communicating about your business goals takes on added importance compared to being a solo proprietor. If you are working alone and you don't write down your goals, you might not be as focused as you could be, and the financial risks might be greater. If you are working in partnership and you don't communicate your goals, you run the risk of heading in separate directions and setting individual goals that conflict with your partner's. Here's an illustration of how important it is to be congruent:

> My partner and I brought in a consultant to help us reach our end goal—to sell the company. Having the sale of the company as our end goal influences every major decision we make. It would be very difficult if my partner and I didn't agree on this most basic intent. Our entire partnership is influenced by this goal. We are careful of accounting so that the books look good. We are developing products not only for today but for the future as well. It's like living in a house that you renovate in order to sell.

The most successful partners I interviewed regularly set, discussed, and revisited their business and partnership goals.

You must find the communication style most comfortable for you, given your personalities and the nature of your business. Marti and Jeff from EditPros like meeting every day. Some partnerships have weekly partner meetings. Others meet once a quarter in a marathon meeting that lasts two or three days. (This style is most common when partners are geographically separate from each other.) Your business plans may be elaborate documents or scribbled notes. The key is to meet the needs of each member of the partnership. If you prefer tight order and structure, and your partner operates with a looser style, you will both need to compromise.

Creating New Visions And Directions

> My partner and I have such different life goals, we are struggling with how to grow the company and stay in partnership. My fear when we first started out was that we were going to fail, but my partner Theresa's fear was that we were going to be wildly successful and she would lose her leisure time. My goal is to make enough money so that we can sell the company and play—I'd love to go back to school just to learn. I see our company as an international company, with several hundred employees, and my partner and I and an executive team running the company. My partner doesn't want a huge operation with hundreds of employees. She wants to take a month off when she feels like it. She's not motivated to grow the company if it's going to mean she'll lose her freedom.
>
> We love working together, so we are searching for a way to make it work. Right now we're considering making Theresa the manager of one subsidiary of the company, with only a few employees, and I'd run the rest of the company.

It is common in successful moneymaking partnerships for one or more partners to say "I want more in my life. This is nice, but now there are other things I want to do." Or one might say "This isn't enough for me" or "I'm tired of working all these hours." Lifestyle decision breakups are usually more amicable than those due to nonperformance. Ideally, your partnership is prepared for such a possibility in advance. One gentleman told me he entered his current partnership with such a plan:

> I've got a five-year plan. At the end of that five years, I'm going to be out. This is what I'm going to contribute for the next five years, and when I leave, this is what I'm taking with me. I have no intention of staying in this partnership for longer than five years, no matter how successful we are.

Partnerships and life evolve, taking detours and unexpected turns that often land each individual in a different place than was originally intended. When a partnership is working well, each individual will stretch to find a new way for the partnership to accommodate the other individual's changing desires or family needs. Sometimes the partnership will break up, but not always. Consider this highly successful partnership that has been working harmoniously for more than 15 years:

> Six years ago I decided to cut back to half-time to pursue my interest in writing by going to school for a master's in business. At that point I wasn't asking more of my partner. I was just managing to do the same amount of work more efficiently, and working more nights and weekends. The larger we grew, the more I started passing stuff along to him—"Will you take payroll? It needs someone who is here all the time." He naturally became more involved in managing the business because I wasn't always there.
>
> Then I unexpectedly got pregnant. There are 17 years between my kids. Now I'm only in the office one day a week. I've become more like a silent partner than an active partner. My partner has essentially taken over the day-to-day operations. A year ago we hired our first executive VP to begin a succession planning process.

The first thing my 3-year-old is going to write, when she can write, is a thank-you note to my partner.

I asked the partner left running the business whether he resented the disparity in hours worked, given that they are still compensated as equal partners. Remarkably, he is at peace with the situation:

My partner suggested selling the business to me, but I don't have that kind of money. Besides, I don't want the burden of running this business by myself. I would rather have my partner part-time than not at all. I'm happy for her and her new family, and I like what I'm doing. It still works for us, even though it's different than the way it started out. I don't forget that she's the one who started this company. I'm grateful she's given me the opportunity to benefit from all the risks she took in the beginning. We're still a team, regardless of how many hours each of us works.

Defining Roles and Responsibilities

Two years of research for *Honey, I Want to Start My Own Business* revealed a secret of success for entrepreneurial couples running a business together: Define your roles and responsibilities, and make sure that each of you has a separate area of authority. This applies just as well to partnerships between individuals who aren't married. Your business may be small or new enough that a clear division of labor seems inefficient or inappropriate. You may have more of a "go with the flow" approach, everyone pitching in to get the job done.

There is certainly value in each partner's being willing and able to do everything. But the likelihood of conflict is greatly reduced by clarifying the boundaries of authority and decision making. Often partners rush into a business opportunity without discussing "who is going to do what, when." For partners already past the startup stage, roles and responsibilities change and need to be reevaluated. The secret to success is giving each partner an area of responsibility aligned with his or her strengths and a chance for his or her ego to shine in some particular area. When each has the ability to make decisions without checking with the other, you diminish the resistance most entrepreneurs have to losing autonomy and control.

Decision Making and Role Responsibilities

Imagine that you and your partner are co-captains of a ship and a hurricane is on its way. One of you wants to batten down the hatches and weather the storm; the other wants to return to shore. If you have a crew, they will need to know which captain to follow. While you and your co-captain are arguing about what to do, the turbulence is about to capsize the boat. Within your partnership someone has to be in charge, either of the entire company or of a particular area of responsibility. Though many partnerships start out hoping for a democratic process, where no decision is made without full consensus of all partners, most find that this fantasy is difficult to fulfill.

Chances are that one of the primary reasons you partnered in the first place was to bring together complementary skills; it only makes sense, then, to divide responsibilities for decision making and day-to-day operations according to skill and expertise. You and your partners must decide where the lines of authority are to be drawn and what kinds of decisions can be made unilaterally or must have partner involvement and approval.

The best approach seems to be a compromise in which major business policy decisions are made with full involvement of all partners and other decisions are made according to the responsibility assigned to a particular partner: "My partner makes operational decisions, and I make the marketing decisions," or "My partner goes out into the field and makes the promises, and I'm the lady who makes sure we deliver."

Many of the business experts I interviewed cautioned against the 50/50 partnership approach, especially if clear lines of authority were not defined. Dr. Kathleen Allen, professor of entrepreneurship at the University of Southern California, warns: "One person has to take the lead, even in a partnership." Otherwise, you can end up hopelessly deadlocked and decisions can take too long to make.

Few small business owners take the time to create job descriptions in the customary manner of larger corporations. But doing so is a wise move. You may believe that you have a clear understanding of each individual's roles and responsibilities, but when a disagreement surfaces, you will wish you had your mutual understanding in writing. Objectively evaluating a partner's contribution is impossible without written objective criteria for performance. If a job description includes concrete goals and a time line for achieving them, partners have a more impartial way to hold each partner accountable.

Conclusion: Goal Setting Is A Fluid Activity

Life is unpredictable; individual, family, and partnership needs change over a period of years. It is the norm, not the exception, that a partnership will need to reevaluate goals, reshape to accommodate life changes, and adjust its mission and its vision in relation to unexpected growth or disappointment in reaching business projections. If you get too attached to the status quo in your partnership, you will experience great stress when goals need to be adjusted or reconsidered. If you accept from the beginning that you and your partners are developing a living organism that cannot be entirely controlled or predicted, you will relax more into the process. Think of goal setting, and mission and vision statement creating, as a lifetime activity, not a one-shot deal.

CHAPTER 5

Formalize Your Agreements

"One of the biggest tasks of any partnership is to decide up front how it's going to dissolve."

—Jan Caldwell, attorney

Use this chapter as a resource that outlines the questions to ask, and the issues to consider, when formalizing your partnership. You will discover what every partnership agreement should cover and the consequences of not committing your agreements to writing. You will learn about various compensation arrangements and the experiences of others that have led to success or disaster.

In the Recommended Resources section, you will find several excellent resources for learning more about the different legal structures of business ownership and the advantages and disadvantages of each. I strongly recommend you pick up Nolo Press's *The Partnership Book*, and if appropriate, consult with an attorney and accountant before entering a formal legal agreement.

When you work through money, trust, and control issues in the beginning, you are more likely to identify significant problems ahead of time.

Virginia and I were both therapists in private practice. We had worked well together on many collaborative projects. We decided to launch a counseling program in Israel. After six months of planning we consulted a lawyer to help us create a nonprofit corporation and a partnership agreement.

> Virginia started making very unreasonable demands. We couldn't reach an agreement, and the partnership dissolved before we could get the program up and running. I wish we had discussed these issues earlier; it would have saved a lot of wasted time and money.

First, let's draw a distinction between a joint venture, a strategic alliance, and a legal partnership. Individuals involved in a joint venture share work activities on a specific project. When that project is over, their enterprise concludes, unless they choose to work together on other projects. In a joint venture, you and your partner typically present yourselves to the public as individual businesses, merging for a brief period of time to create a specific product. You might have no intention of forming a long-term legal partnership, or you might use the joint venture as a testing ground for a future official partnership.

For example, if an author teams up with a cartoonist for one book it might be considered a joint venture. If that same author and cartoonist team up to write a series of books, offer seminars as a team on the subject, give their endeavor a distinctive name, and create a syndicated column together, they will probably form a legal partnership. (As a joint venture, the parties should still commit their agreements to writing—even if they do not enter an official partnership.)

In a strategic alliance, two or more companies come together to gain a competitive edge by sharing products, information, and customers. For example: McDonald's and Burger King enter into strategic alliances with the makers of children's toys to please children with their kids' meals.

According to the Uniform Partnership Act, a regulatory code that's been adopted by every state except Louisiana, if you willingly and openly work with another person and share ownership of a business, whether or not you use the term partnership or have a partnership agreement, you can still be subject to the conditions specified under the Uniform Partnership Act. Even if you elect not to write down or formalize your partnership arrangement, the UPA governs your actions anyway. Wouldn't you rather set down the understandings that will govern your partnership? Writing down your agreements can help you check your assumptions, clarify your goals, and articulate your visions.

Begin With the End in Mind

Do you imagine you will still be working with your current partners when you are 90 years of age? Unlikely—unless you are married to your business partner. The end of your partnership is inevitable; "till death do us part" is not a sound partnership approach.

"Begin with the end in mind" articulates an approach to partnering that obliges partners to plan for various eventualities and possibilities. When we marry, divorce is generally the last thing on our minds, unless we've already gotten divorced and we are marrying for a second time. Partnership is like that, too. When we enter a first-time partnership, we resist thinking it will end. We worry that if we demand a contract, like a prenuptial agreement, it means there will be trouble. Unfortunately, only when a first partnership has ended poorly does the business owner readily agree to formalize the next partnership—if he or she is willing to partner again at all.

A partnership agreement isn't created for the sole purpose of addressing the end of the partnership. Its more important function is to express how you want your business, and your relationship with your partners, to operate. It could be used as the operating agreement for the business, like a business plan. The process of forming the agreement compels the discussions that partners should have and provides a document to refer to when disagreement emerges or significant change in direction appears necessary after launching the business. Most entrepreneurs don't prepare for the fact that their partner relationships will change over time. A partnership agreement acknowledges this reality.

Why Most Businessowners Skip the Formality

Professor Bruce L. McManis, Ph.D, head of the department of economics and finance at Nicholls State University, estimates that 80 percent of partnerships skip the formalization stage or rush through it with an inexperienced lawyer because money is short and they don't want to consider the possibility that something bad will happen. "They see a business opportunity and they want to be a millionaire by next Friday," McManis observes.

Here are the most common reasons offered by the business partners I interviewed for avoiding the formalization process:

> Lawyers are too expensive and they take too much time. We'd rather put our time and money into making the business work than worry about what might happen if the business does or doesn't make it.

> We're such good friends and we've known each other so long; we can talk to each other about anything, no matter what happens.

> We're a mother and son partnership; putting these kinds of agreements on paper is awkward. How do you codify the trust between family?

> We've been operating on a handshake for nine years. The first contract my partner gave me to sign was too one-sided and I wouldn't sign it. We never came up with another contract.

> In the back of my mind, I know what we should do, but we're so caught up in the day-to-day running of the business, we just don't take the time.

> We went to a lawyer and discussed the buy/sell agreement if one person wants out. We were in the glow of "we're in this together," and we didn't want to hurt each other's feelings. So we didn't finish putting the agreement together.

✧

We're focused on launching the business. We don't want to distract our attention from where it needs to be, or get our partnership off on the wrong foot, by fighting over money we haven't even made yet.

✧

We did have a partnership agreement, but we never got around to signing it.

✧

Levels of Formalizing Your Agreements

An official partnership structure is not essential to business partnership success. Plenty of partnerships operate well on a handshake. That said, to protect yourself and your business, you should at least discuss and then write down your understandings of such basics as compensation, work responsibilities, and contribution (covered in detail in the section called "50 Questions to Answer in a Partnership Agreement").

Consider the following criteria for determining where you and your partner choose to be on the spectrum from scribbled notes on a piece of loose-leaf paper to a formal document prepared by an attorney and your accountant:

- How long you've known your partner, and in what circumstances.
- The trust in your relationship.
- How much and what is at stake if the partnership doesn't work out.
- Amount of money invested, and where it is coming from.
- Expected financial return from the business.
- Comfort level with legal agreements.
- Likelihood that the business will be launched.

- Length of time you expect the business to last.
- Family considerations—protecting family assets.
- Tax consequences—choosing a structure that minimizes tax impact.
- Your risk tolerance.
- Your desire for spontaneity versus structure.
- How much time and money you have to invest in the formalization process.
- How much of a rush you are in.
- Clarity around business goals, work responsibilities, and compensation agreements.
- Availability of an attorney you trust and can afford.
- Your age, health, and other personal considerations.
- Whether your liability is already protected because you are a corporation or a limited liability company.

A colleague was preparing a partnership agreement for a new venture. She asked me, "What type of partnership arrangement would work best for us, keeping in mind we want the simplest type, with the least amount of paperwork, as we don't even know if the business will take off or not? Do we really need a lawyer when the trust factor is so strong between us?"

There are some circumstances where forming a legal partnership may not make sense. In the case above, where the business is just in the idea stage and might never get off the ground, a written partnership agreement could suffice. These partners can wait to form a legal partnership until they are sure their ideas will take root. They are in the formative stages, concerned about clarifying their agreements, protecting themselves from potential harm, and solidifying their partnership. They should consider how much money each partner will invest to launch the business and how committed each of them is to putting energy and resources into creating this business. If they are just in the dating stage, and not sure if they wish to be married for a length of time, an informal written partnership agreement that still covers the essentials may suffice until the venture becomes more tangible.

Legal partnerships make it more complicated to exit the partnership. Depending on the actual agreement, one partner can become obliged for the other partner's business debt. Formalizing your relationship can also take a great deal of valuable time and scarce money. These deterrents keep some people from forming legal partnerships—and for good reason.

I interviewed a gentleman who joined with four other men in a virtual high-tech company. He had a strong need for structure and formality, but his colleagues were in favor of the "just do it" approach.

> The window for this opportunity was narrow, and we didn't have time for due diligence. I said to my partners, "We're going to run into a bunch of problems down the road we could avoid by writing down our agreements and consulting with an attorney ahead of time. As long as everyone is willing to take responsibility for the fact that we're taking this risk, I'll go along with it."

A psychologist in a three-person partnership recalls:

> We spent so much time hashing out our investor agreement, instead of focusing on getting the product to market, we almost didn't have a product at all. Who cares if you get 20 or 30 percent of the profits if there's no product?

Given the valid concerns raised above, why write your agreements down, or structure a formal partnership? Here are a few reasons to consider.

Reasons to Formalize Your Agreements

1. Partnership agreements and exiting agreements are like buying life insurance. You hope you'll never need it, you know you will eventually, and by the time you do, it's too late to buy it. The time to put the words and agreements on paper is before any money is involved, when the partner relationship is upbeat and relaxed. Just as a business plan is a road map for business development, a partnership agreement is a road map for the people doing the business.

   Sam and Jeff were college buddies who had to have their arms twisted by their parents to properly formalize their soccer accessories Internet business. Because their parents were their major investors, they had little choice. It's a good thing they were pushed to do so. The young friendship didn't stand the test of entrepreneurial pressure and it wasn't long before the best friends were barely speaking to each other. When they decided to close the business after just a year, it was much easier to do so, as they had properly prepared themselves for the possibility of its ending.

2. A partnership agreement formally acknowledges the bond between you and your partners. It adds professionalism to your endeavor. A well-done written agreement will lessen the uncertainty and fear you have about partnering.

   It was strangely reassuring to me to pay a lawyer and draw up a bunch of paperwork that was filled with legal mumbo jumbo I didn't even understand. It was like making a statement to the world: "We're to be taken seriously. We're a *real* business!"

3. Preparing a partnership agreement is a fabulous way to learn whether you and your prospective partners are in full agreement and have what it takes to create a successful business. It is another opportunity for you to check assumptions, clarify goals, and articulate your vision.

Matt, Ryan, and Chris started a surveying company. Chris put up most of the initial investment required for equipment because Matt and Ryan already owned the building where the company would be headquartered. They assumed they would all be equal partners but never actually discussed the details. The cash started to roll in before the partners had a chance to solidify their agreements. Chris demanded a higher share of the profits because he had invested most of the money. Matt and Ryan argued that they should get equal shares because their share of the investment had been the building. They ended up hiring a mediator to help them work out their differences and a professional appraiser to assess the value of the building.

4. If you are uncomfortable discussing money, decision making, and working responsibilities at the beginning of your partnership, it doesn't bode well for working together. A partner who is incapable, or unwilling, to commit in writing is flying a red flag you need to heed.

   When Susan and I started our antiques store, we had no trouble verbalizing a partnership agreement for our business. But because I didn't know Susan too well, I asked her to set aside time to visit a lawyer so we could have the agreement formalized. Susan readily agreed, but whenever I made an appointment, she had one excuse or another for why she couldn't make it. For six months I pressured her to at least write down what she thought our agreement was. When we needed to make a decision on a five-year lease, I gave her an ultimatum—a signed legal agreement or no lease. She stormed out of the store and I haven't seen her since. I signed the lease by myself and became a sole proprietor.

5. A binding agreement protects your friendship and your partnership by providing objective guidelines to follow when conflict arises. A subjective process that relies on good will and trust has more potential to endanger your friendship than handling the issues required to prepare a useful partnership agreement.

Francine and Missy had only been friends for a couple of years. They knew that they hadn't really come up against any major adversity together, so they were leery about how they would handle business troubles, should they develop. Would they scream at each other, or would one of them quit, or worse yet, would one of them be a crybaby and have a meltdown anytime there was a problem to discuss? Concerned for how working together might affect their friendship, and vice versa, they met for a couple of sessions with a therapist to discuss their personal styles for handling conflict. It was useful for Francine to acknowledge to Missy that she had a tendency to fly off the handle with a hot temper. Missy admitted that she tended to head for the door as soon as a voice was raised. Knowing this in advance helped them map out a strategy for handling heated moments.

6. Life circumstances will intervene and affect your partnership in unforeseen ways. Death, disability, illness, geographic relocation, and other major life changes can and will happen. Don't take the chances this business owner did:

I started an architectural firm with a colleague. We had a thriving business and a great relationship, so we put off formalizing our agreements. Tragically, my partner was killed in a car wreck. According to his will, his stake in the business was left to his wife. Overnight, I was in business with my partner's wife, a lady with no architectural training and a nasty personality—which worsened when she became a grieving widow. I didn't have the cash to buy her out, so I was stuck. We should have had key man insurance [which protects the remaining partners should a partner who is key to the business become disabled or die] and a buy/sell agreement at the very least.

This partner in a rapidly growing Internet company shares his wisdom:

When my partner was diagnosed with cancer, she had to scale back her involvement in the company. She sold back most of her shares. With our legal agreement in place, it was a piece of cake working out the details, and much easier to bring in new investors. When my partner was going through chemotherapy, devastated by depression and illness, it would have been the worst time to start negotiating how to handle this. I would have given away the store because I felt so bad for her and her family. She was in no shape to focus on anything but getting better. We were both devastated by the potential loss of our partnership. We needed a straightforward, fair system to guide us.

✧

7. There are significant tax advantages and financial issues to consider when forming a partnership. The form of partnership you choose will determine the amount of money you take home from the business and the level of risk you incur.

When we decided to form a partnership of eight practicing physicians and healthcare providers, we consulted with an accountant who specializes in setting up these kinds of practices, so that we were creating an arrangement that would be most beneficial to all concerned.

8. You will not be able to seek venture capital and outside investors without a written partnership agreement.

I was filled with dread at the thought of writing a business plan, but it wasn't even an option to skip this step. We couldn't move forward without a serious infusion of cash, and no one except maybe my mother was going to lend us money if we didn't have a strong business plan to back up our claims. Then, because we were going to be working in partnership, the VCs wanted to know exactly how our partnership would work, and who would do what. It forced us to answer those questions for ourselves before discussing the business with other people.

Equity Arrangements for Rewarding Contribution

Before you create a written partnership agreement, one of the primary matters you need to settle is how each partner will be compensated for his or her contribution to the company. There are as many different ways to structure compensation as there are partnerships. Develop a plan that rewards partners for both contributions and performance. One common error is a compensation structure that assumes each partner will deliver what he or she promised, with no method for measuring performance or adjusting compensation if the partner doesn't work up to expectations.

You will need to revise the compensation plan as your company grows. Like a business plan, it is a living document that needs regular revision to reflect current circumstances and changing goals. Your partnership agreement should address how you will settle disagreements related to compensation, and it should define periodic review sessions to evaluate whether your working relationship needs to be adjusted.

Some partnerships organize around the classic 50/50 partnership arrangement, in which all investments and profits are split equally (or 33/33/33, for three partners). You can be creative in your compensation agreements. Here are 16 different equity arrangements I discovered in the partnerships I researched for this book. They are useful as starting points for your partner discussions, but you need not limit yourselves to these arrangements:

Our partnership is 50/50. Jerome works more hours because I kept my day job, but I invested more money to compensate for less time in. We brought together 20 practitioners and structured it as a partnership. Everyone was considered an equal partner, with an equal vote. Some of us put in more money in the beginning, but we were all compensated equally in salary. Those of us who invested larger amounts looked at it as a long-term investment, expecting to profit substantially in five to 10 years, when we sold the practice.

I have a 50/50 retail operation with my partner, Gloria. I've also opened up a separate store that has nothing to do with Gloria. Since the new store will take my time away from the original company, I gave Gloria 10 percent of the profits from my new store. That way she won't resent my inability to put in the same kind of hours she puts into our business.

We decided to compensate each of us with an equal salary, regardless of how many clients we brought into the business. There was a whole year when my partner brought in twice the business I did, and we considered whether to revise our salaries. We both agreed that I was prospecting some bigger clients with longer lead times, so it wasn't fair to penalize me.

In a two-person partnership, I recommend structuring a partnership 49/49/2. The third person can be an attorney or someone both partners agree is neutral. This structure helps facilitate conflict resolution and decision making.

—Bob Sullivan, Ph.D.,
author of *The Small Business Start-Up Guide*

Originally our compensation system assigned a salary to each partner based on goals. One of the four partners, Miriam, was hitting only 50 percent of her goals, but she was being compensated as if she had achieved them. This went on for about three years and created a lot of resentment in the other partners. Finally we revamped the compensation system to pay only for goals actually achieved. Miriam wasn't able to make a living with the new system, so she left the partnership.

My partner has 51 percent of the company because he came up with the idea, but we both view it as an equal partnership.

A former colleague began an advertising firm two years before I joined. I didn't invest any money into the partnership. We agreed that I would work for two years with no salary and then I would become a 40 percent owner.

I've been working with two other guys. The majority owner, who came up with the product and does all sales and development, has 60 percent ownership. The other two of us have 20 percent each. Even though I'm only a 20 percent owner, I'm the CEO of the company because I'm much better at running the company than the inventor of the product is.

We divided up the company stock, but each of us only has a right to our target percentage of stock if we stay for three years; we don't vest any interest in the company until that time. Also, vesting is contingent on satisfactory performance as measured by the goals we've set and agreed to accomplish.

I opened up a satellite office for an existing company. I put in 50 percent of the financial resources required to open that office, and the three existing partners put in the other 50 percent. My partners get a 50 percent cut of any revenue I generated.

Originally we each took a salary plus a percentage of the business we brought into the firm. When we received the same salary, but one of us wasn't performing up to the standards of the others, that created resentment. So we switched our compensation plan to "You eat what you kill." Now we each take a much smaller salary, and our compensation is based primarily on the amount of business we bring in.

When I formed a partnership with a friend, we each put up equal amounts of cash to get the business started. When it came time for the second round of refinancing, my partner didn't have it. We rewrote our original 50/50 agreement to 60/40 to reflect my larger investment.

My original partner and I put up capital in a 60/40 ratio. Ownership shares were based on our initial investment. When we took on a third partner who contributed an additional 10 percent, we adjusted the ratio accordingly. The new partner wasn't willing to quit his job and join us unless there was an equity situation, so we brought him in as a minority partner.

I'm a physician right out of school. I joined an established physician's practice as an associate. I invested several thousand dollars, and gave him a percentage of my billings. We plan on my taking over his practice when he retires. I'll buy him out according to a five-year schedule we've agreed to.

I sponsored my partner into our network marketing company. We each receive different residual income based on the performance of our organization, but we pool all overhead and marketing expenses and split them equally.

Clarifying Expectations

"When a working relationship seems good, we often take it for granted that we understand each other. We assume that someone already knows what we need, want, expect, and value. There's a tendency to leave portions of our verbal and written communications unstated, relying on assumptions or on what we imagine someone wants rather than asking about it directly. Sometimes our expectations and feelings remain below the surface because we think people already know them or because we simply don't have time to go into the necessary detail to explain our views in depth. As a result, only half of our message gets communicated clearly, leaving the other half vague or missing altogether."

—Paul and Sarah Edwards, *Teaming Up*

You bring to your partnership a host of expectations about yourself and your partner. Most of these expectations are implicit, never vocalized until you or your partner fail to live up to them. Then anger erupts, and the expectation becomes evident when a conversation begins with "Why didn't you...?" or "How could you have...?" Let's say you were shown a field with land mines throughout and you were given a choice: "Walk across the field the way it is and take your chances" or "Here's a button you can push to deactivate the land mines so you can walk across safely." Which option would you choose? Unless you enjoy Russian roulette, you'd choose the latter. Clarifying expectations with your partner up front, or as soon as a question arises, is the equivalent of deactivating the minefield. It doesn't mean you won't stumble every now and then, but it greatly reduces the chances that your partnership will be blown to smithereens when an expectation is not met.

Many of your expectations should be covered in your formal agreements with each other. Basic understandings, such as how much money each of you will invest, what your working hours will be, and how profits will be shared, should be clearly spelled out in your partnership agreement. Beyond the formal legal agreement, there are a host of expectations you and your partner need to discuss to avoid future conflict.

Let's examine some common areas of complaints of the partners I interviewed and how addressing expectations could help prevent trouble.

Working Hours

> Susan and Carol are equal partners in a floral business. Susan invested $20,000 dollars more than Carol, and Carol is supposed to work twice as many hours for a few years to compensate for that disparity.

✧

Issue:

For a period of two months during her divorce, Carol was unable to work more than an average of 30 hours per week, even though the partnership agreement spelled out that she would work 45 hours a week.

Clarifying Expectations:

Susan had an expectation of Carol that wasn't being met. They had several choices to consider, depending on how long this situation would probably continue, how Susan felt about the temporary inequity, whether Carol could make up the hours at a later date, and so forth. The key is to renegotiate expectations early in the process, not after weeks have gone by and Susan's resentment has built up to an explosive level.

Job Performance

> Gerry is in partnership with three other people in geographically separate areas of the country. All of his partners have full-time jobs and are compensating him for working on their project full-time by sending him a monthly check. He has little daily communication with his partners, and the four of them have gotten together only once. His partners rely on a weekly progress report to keep them informed about whether their money is being used wisely.

Issue:

Gerry acknowledges that his work style is creating a problem. "I start very slow in the beginning, and then shoot up in results after several weeks. My partners think I'm fooling around and not getting anything done."

Expectations:

Part of Gerry's job is to educate his partners about his workstyle. He needs to tell them up front, "You're going to think by about week four that I'm not performing, but the project is incubating. By week eight, I will be making some serious progress, and by week 16—our agreed-upon deadline—I'll deliver the final product to you."

Role of Partner

> Lisa found self-employment too isolating and lonely. She brought in a partner so that she would have someone to talk to and share responsibilities with. Her friend Bridget contributed enough cash to buy a 40 percent equity interest in the company and to be considered a junior partner.

Issue:

Lisa was bitter about her partner's regular absence from the business. She reported that Bridget seemed to find it difficult to be "tied down in the office" or to work any kind of regular schedule. She would often call Lisa from her car phone, or leave long, complicated memos she'd written after getting the urge to go to the office at midnight. The companionship Lisa had sought in a partnership was not there, and she regretted selling 40 percent of the business.

Clarifying Expectations:

Lisa had expectations of Bridget that she didn't check out ahead of time. She assumed that a partner would automatically become a companion, and yet, if she had looked at Bridget's previous work record and talked with anyone Bridget had worked with, she would have discovered that Bridget was more of a loner. Bridget was attracted to the prosperity that could be earned in partnership but had little interest in "wasting time with lots of chitchat and boring meetings." The first step for this team is to communicate honestly with each other about what each expects of the other's role as partner. Only then can they ask for what they want and determine whether this partnership can meet the needs of both parties.

Office Etiquette

Roger and three friends—two other men and a woman—aspire to reach the highest compensation level in an international network marketing company expanding overseas. They have pooled their resources as a team to grow their organization as fast as possible. They have been friends for years and work well together in most regards.

Issue:

Roger has a gripe. Whenever they hold their weekly staff meeting, his female partner, Madeline, takes the lead, organizes the agenda, and monopolizes the meeting. Who gave her the title of boss? He left his job to do network marketing full-time so he wouldn't have to deal with a boss. Lately, he's been feeling like Madeline's employee, not her partner.

Clarifying Expectations:

A partnership agreement is not designed to cover minutiae such as how staff meetings will be run and who will establish the agenda. Yet having this unresolved expectation can create friction. Roger and his partners need to discuss how meetings will be handled—how often they will meet, how the agenda will be set, who will facilitate the meetings, where they will be located, and so forth. Madeline came to the team with the most experience in the company, so she expected her partners to welcome her leadership. She failed to see that her dictatorial behavior was alienating her from the group.

Working Habits

Scott and Adam share an office and a computer in the spare bedroom of Adam's house.

Issue:

Scott is a neat freak, and he can barely handle spending every day in Adam's cluttered home. Lately, what's really been bugging him is that when he shows up at 9 a.m., Adam is still in bed.

Clarifying Expectations:

This is tricky, because Adam is contributing the rent-free place to work. Adam often sleeps late because he worked late into the night. He is more of a night owl than a morning person. He and Scott need to negotiate working hours that are ideal for each of them. As far as Adam's cleaning up his place, Scott's expectation is unlikely to be met, given Adam's lifestyle and aversion to order. To expect Adam to radically adjust his work habits or home environment is unrealistic. Scott and Adam will need to acknowledge their incompatibilities and find ways to work around them for the partnership to work.

Other Expectations

Here are just a few more of the long list of expectations that you might not address in a partnership agreement but that you would want to cover with your partners. Take a lunch hour to sit with your partners, and run down this list to be sure that you articulate your expectations and find agreement.

Working Hours:

- Number of hours per week you will work.
- Time of day when you will start and end work.
- Whether you will work nights or weekends.
- Whether you take a Sabbath break.
- How you will observe secular and religious holidays.
- How much vacation time each of you will take.

- How you will handle sick time.
- If you tend to work in long stretches or prefer to take frequent breaks.

Social Style

- How much contact during the workday you wish to have with your partner?
- How you will communicate with your partner—in person, voice mail, e-mail, phone, or fax?
- How often you will eat meals together?
- Whether you will eat meals out, together, or bring in leftovers and eat on your own.
- How much you will socialize with each other outside of work?
- How you handle punctuality and tardiness.
- Who you will talk to about confidential matters related to the company?
- How you will speak to each other—tone of voice, style for expressing anger?

Dress Code

- What you will wear at the office.
- What you will wear when meeting with clients.
- What you will wear when meeting with prospects.

Other Details

Write down some of the other details you feel need to be clarified in conversation or in your partnership agreement. No issue is too small for discussion if it's on your mind.

50 Questions to Answer in a Partnership Agreement

Written partnership agreements should answer the following 50 questions. You and your partner must decide whether to seek an attorney's assistance to draft the agreement, or an accountant to guide you toward the best tax structure for your needs. You can save a great deal of money by discussing ideas with your partner on your nickel instead of in your lawyer's or accountant's office. Many partners prepare a draft agreement and then consult with an attorney to have it formalized. (Refer to *The Partnership Book*, listed in Recommended Resources, for guidance on preparing your own partnership agreement.)

Company Name, Location, and Hours

1. What are the partners' names? Are the partners individuals, corporations, or limited liability companies? What is the designated name and purpose of the partnership?
2. Will we trademark and register the company name?
3. Where will the office be located—will we rent, lease, or own? Will any of us work out of a home office full-time or part-time?
4. What will be our working hours? What autonomy will each partner have to set his or her own hours? Do we need to service clients during any established period of time each day? How often will we meet to discuss the business?

Contribution

5. What is each partner contributing to the business in terms of
   - Money?
   - Skills?
   - Collateral property?
   - Tools and equipment?

- Intellectual property (patent or copyright)?
- Network and professional contacts?
- Reputation?
- Working hours?
- Insurance, benefits, company perks?

Accountability

6. How will we measure job performance and hold each partner accountable for meeting expectations?

Taxes

7. What partnership structure will we choose, and how will that determine our taxation?

Liability

8. What is the extent of financial liability we will have for our partners' behavior? Will the partners' contractual commitments and representations of the company bind me?
9. What is my liability if my partner does something illegal while representing the company? What business structure do we need in order to minimize my risk of such an event?
10. Who is responsible for what percent and kind of company debt?

Authority

11. How will authority and decision making be structured? Will we operate by consensus or based on share of ownership? What happens in the event of an impasse or stalemate? Will partners have the authority to control certain functional areas of the company without the approval or involvement of the other partners? What is the authority to act on behalf of the company without unanimous agreement? For example, can one person alone settle an account with a vendor or client?

Sheila is listed as president for incorporation purposes, but our business cards say co-president. We make major decisions for the company by consensus, but Sheila makes day-to-day decisions related to sales and marketing without asking me, and I manage the office.

12. What will be the procedure for borrowing money in the company name? When will borrowing require approval of the other partners?

    My partner and I weren't happy when our third partner told his uncle that he could lend us money to the tune of $100,000. My partner couldn't figure out why we weren't ecstatic and grateful for the available cash. He didn't consider that we think his uncle is an idiot and we didn't want his uncle's involvement in our company.

13. What is the scope of expense account authority before needing to consult with the other partners?

    Jeff and I started a communications company together because he had the sales experience and I had the technical knowledge. He would land the client and I would travel around installing the systems. He often took clients out to lunch and dinner on the company credit card, so after receiving astronomical credit card bills, I figured it was just a good sign of how many clients he was entertaining. I didn't find out until we were audited two years into the partnership that he took his family out to dinner a few times a week, also on the company credit card. Since I wasn't using our credit cards in the same manner for my family, we agreed that it wasn't fair. We set a limit to how much Jeff would charge for meals each month, and he settled with me for the non-business charges during the last two years.

Responsibilities

14. Who will handle what—how will your roles and responsibilities be divided? Who will have what management duties?

15. How will workload be assigned and monitored?

My partner, Al, and I got along great in the struggling years, but when we hit it big it was a different story. Once we reached a certain income level, Al became very comfortable and lazy. He started spending entire days out on the company boat instead of coming into the office, while the staff and I worked our tails off to grow the business to the next level. Al worked as hard as we did in the beginning, so it never occurred to us that we needed to get clear up-front about such basic expectations as how much effort each of us would continue to put into the business on a daily basis. I just assumed he'd keep working as hard as I did. You know what happens when you make assumptions!

Choosing Personnel

16. How will we choose an attorney, accountant, consultant, or any other professional service provider?

I was in an awkward situation because one of my partners was married to an attorney, and another one was married to an accountant. They each thought that their spouses should be brought in to do that professional work for our company. I wasn't sure that their spouses were the most capable or that they gave us the objectivity we needed. My vote on this issue was an unpopular one and I took a lot of heat for it. I was viewed as being disloyal and I think it harmed my relationship with my two partners because I took that stand. I eventually caved in and agreed to what they wanted.

17. What process will we use to expand and admit new partners?

18. How will we hire employees, contract workers, or any other professional who joins our organization?

When we started our company, it was easy to have a rule that no one was hired without meeting everyone in the company and full consensus that he or she was a good hire. Now we're 23 employees. Do we still have a prospect meet every employee? That's unrealistic! Yet we value the team environment and want to sustain it in the hiring process.

19. How will we select vendors?

Ever since we began, we've been buying office supplies from a good friend of my partner's. I met a guy who can sell us the same stuff at about 25 percent less. My partner doesn't want to switch vendors; it would be too difficult for him to cancel his friend's account. I understand his dilemma. Still, I've got to get my partner to see that business is business!

Insurance

20. What kind of business liability insurance will we purchase? How will we choose the carrier?
21. Will we purchase insurance to cover fire, lightning, earthquake, or flood?
22. Will we provide medical, life, or disability insurance or a pension plan for ourselves or our employees? How will we choose the carriers?
23. Will we purchase key man insurance—a policy that pays the company in the event of a partner's death or disability? (Banks often require this insurance to approve financing.)

Compensation and Ownership Percentage

24. What determines ownership percentage for partners?
25. If one of us had the idea for the business, should that partner receive compensation or additional ownership rights?

My partner and I have a 50/50 partnership in terms of responsibilities, but a 55/45 percent split on revenues and stock. It's only fair that my partner get some credit for coming up with the idea for the product, even if now, we share the workload equally.

26. How will profits be apportioned?
27. What percentage of profits will be withheld for reinvestment back into the company?
28. How will salaries be determined?
29. How will company perks—such as the company boat, company car, or box seats at the stadium—be assigned?

When my partner and I decided to bring in a third partner, we got into some heated debate about whether to give him or her the same perks as we have. I felt that we should get better perks (like a company car) to reward us for bootstrapping the company for the first couple of years. My partner saw perks as a recruitment tool. He wanted to attract the best candidate by giving him or her the same level of benefits as we, the two founding partners, enjoy.

30. What benefits will we provide, including insurance, sick and vacation time, paid leaves of absence or sabbaticals, and company perks?

Leaves of Absence

31. How will we plan for the possibility of disability, illness, or catastrophic event in the partner's family? (What will we do when some life event interrupts a partner's ability to work productively?)
32. What length of absence from productive work will constitute the need to renegotiate the partnership agreement?

When I entered into a partnership with Jerry, he was 68 and I was 42. I didn't give his age a second thought because he hardly acted it. After four years, though, he started to slow down. His family wasn't helping matters either. With his oldest unmarried daughter always bringing her rowdy children over for baby-sitting and his youngest in trouble with the law, Jerry barely paid any attention to matters in the office. Then his wife got sick and he took two different leaves of absence to take care of her. That was the last straw.

I confronted Jerry and got him to agree to change our ownership from 50/50 to 70/30.

Accounting

33. What financial statements are all partners entitled to? How regularly will they be prepared? (A bank loan will require quarterly statements.) Do partners have the right to see a financial statement whenever they ask for one? Who will take care of the books?

    I was an idiot for not ever learning how to read a financial statement, or never reviewing our books. That was my partner's turf and I left him to it. When he said we were out of cash, it never occurred to me that it was because he was buying his wife and family luxury items. It wasn't until he informed me that we'd have to file bankruptcy that I discovered what a mess of the books he had made, and how he'd been stealing from the company. Our financial problems were his fault, but I share some of the blame, too. I handed him too much responsibility. I should have kept closer tabs on where our, and my, money was going.

Outside Employment

34. Will there be any limits on who can engage in other outside business activity and what types of activity?
35. Will we forbid conflicts of interest and direct competition? What will be permitted or restricted?

Termination/Dissolution

36. What will happen to the business assets if one of us dies?
37. How will we determine the value of the business if one of us wants to buy out the other?
38. If a partner relocates and must leave an active role in the partnership, do we have to pay out his or her share? Can he or she remain an investor?

39. If a partner quits, will the reason he or she quits matter? Will we pay him or her the same amount whether he or she takes ill or joins another partnership?

George's wife got cancer and he decided to leave the company so he could concentrate on taking care of her and his family. We made arrangements for the remaining two partners to buy out his interest over a period of five years, resulting in a 50/50 partnership between the two remaining partners. We were generous with George because we felt compassion for his circumstances and we knew that he wasn't leaving to work for a competitor.

40. Can a partner sell or give his or her share of the business to anyone at all? If not, what are the restrictions and what will be the approval process?

41. If a partner quits or dies, will the other partners have the "right of first refusal" before the shares are sold or transferred to a third party?

42. If a partner quits to join another firm or to start another business, what kind of noncompete clause do we wish to have?

43. What will be the process for firing a partner for incompetence or malicious behavior? If a partner becomes alcohol or drug dependent and is no longer performing up to expectations, or if he or she should be arrested for a crime, how will we handle it?

My partner's behavior was erratic and moody. He was often late to the office and would skip out for two or three hours for lunches. I suspected he had a drinking or drug problem but I didn't know how to bring it up. Then a client approached me and complained that my partner had been drunk while giving a presentation. It was one of the most humiliating and horrifying moments of my career.

44. Who will we sell to, and how will we engage in the process if an outside buyer becomes interested in the company?
45. Upon dissolution of the partnership, how will shared assets be divided?
46. Who gets the rights to trademarks, copyrights, patents, customer lists, and files? Under what conditions and for how long?
47. Who can continue to use the company name and logo?

When my partner and I split up, we agreed that he would continue to operate the business on his own, still using the company name and logo. I went into business for myself and I was forbidden to service my old clients, use the company logo, or compete directly for business in my ex-partner's geographic area. In exchange for these agreements, he paid me what we agreed was a fair price.

48. Will we utilize mediation or arbitration to settle conflicts or dissolve the partnership? If so, how will we choose the mediator?

We were advised by our lawyer not to have a 50/50 partnership when we incorporated. He said we needed to identify someone who has the final authority to make decisions. We committed to mediation if we disagree, rather than abandoning our preference for a 50/50 partnership.

Amending the Agreement

49. How often will we revisit the partnership agreement and how do we amend it?
50. If a partner fails to make a financial or other anticipated contribution as specified in the partnership agreement, what are the consequences? Under what circumstances will the partnership agreement be revised?

My partner and I agreed to invest $10,000 each into our business and we wrote the partnership agreement accordingly.

> When it came time to write the check, my partner had a bunch of excuses for not having the money, so I put up the entire $20,000 and he was supposed to pay me back within 60 days. That was four months ago, and he still hasn't come forward with any money. Whenever I bring the subject up he gets real defensive and tells me that he'll have it for me shortly. I'm going to insist that the partnership agreement be revised from the 50/50 partnership we currently have to 80/20 until he invests the cash he committed to.

✧

Choosing a Partnership Tax Structure

If you are forming a joint venture, you may stop here, with just a written document of your agreements. If you are joining with others for a partnership you expect to continue beyond a particular project, you should formalize your agreements and create a legal structure that assists you with tax planning and protects you more completely than an informal letter of agreement. This step is usually done with an attorney, although there are many Internet-based incorporation service companies, which will give you the ability to complete all the necessary paperwork without the assistance of an attorney at a fraction of the cost. This alternative is appealing if you are well versed on your choices, have limited time and money, and you and your partners feel comfortable moving forward without legal assistance. There are books that address doing business in your state, provide sample operating agreements, and tell you what offices you have to contact and what the fees are.

Four Common Forms of Legal Partnership

Four common legal forms of partnership—partnership, limited partnership, incorporation, and limited liability companies—are explored briefly here. Let's look at the basics of each type:

Partnership

Partnerships convey personal liability in varying degrees to each of the partners, depending on the state in which they are filed. If you haven't carefully "looked before you leaped" and/or you are not comfortable with all aspects of your potential partner, you may consider this arrangement too risky. You could be held personally responsible for any action your partner takes, even if you are only a silent partner. Consider what happened to one individual I interviewed:

> I joined a good friend's existing business as her new partner. To my horror and surprise, one day the IRS showed up because my partner hadn't paid taxes in the early years of the business. She owed an astronomical amount to the IRS. As her new partner, I was suddenly liable for her previous debt. I took out a 25K loan on my charge cards to help repay the debt, and the IRS seized all of our business assets. I won't get paid back until the debts to the IRS are paid off. My partner's error was one of carelessness, not maliciousness or deceit. Still, I should have done a better job of looking at the books before I signed on as partner.

According to attorney Jan Caldwell, a legal partnership is formed when two or more individuals engage in business for profit. Each partner is personally liable for all debts incurred by the business. If a creditor has a claim against your partnership and partnership assets are insufficient to satisfy that claim, each business partner's personal assets can be seized to pay business debts. Profits and losses are reported on individual tax returns; the partnership pays no taxes. A legal partnership ends when one of you leaves the partnership unless you identify another alternative in your written agreement.

According to the Uniform Partnership Act, each partner can legally perform all acts that are necessary to running the business unless otherwise stated in the partnership agreement.

That means that partners can buy equipment and incur debt without the other partners' knowledge. Even if a written agreement limits a partner's authority, if an outside customer or vendor thinks that a partner is acting on behalf of the other partners in the normal course of doing business, all the other partners are still responsible for that partner's actions.

> Our written partnership agreement limited the spending authority of each partner to no more than $1,000 without the others' approval. We started the process of getting rid of one of our partners when we suspected he was embezzling from the company. We were furious when we discovered that he had charged $30,000 on company charge cards, without our knowledge or consent, to buy items for his own personal use. He bought his kids a new computer and his wife some expensive jewelry and a fur coat. He was the CFO, so he hid the expense without our catching it until it was too late. Because he was representing the company when he made those purchases, we became liable for the debt as well.

In the absence of a written agreement for how profits and losses are to be shared, it is deemed equal. In the event of a disagreement without a written agreement, all profits, assets, and debts will be split equally.

Limited Partnership

Limited partners are investors. They are liable for business debts and losses only to the extent of their investment. To be given the protection of a limited partnership, the investor can't be involved in management or day-to-day operation of the business. Typically, limited partners have cash they are looking to invest, hoping for a substantial return. They may not participate in management or decision making and maintain their liability protection. Limited partners are investors, and the company is run by a general partner. Although the limited partners do have liability protection, the general partner does not.

Incorporation

Unlike a partnership, in which partners have unlimited personal liability, an adequately capitalized corporation is considered a separate legal entity from its owners. This gives owners personal liability protection. A corporation will continue to exist even if one or more owners departs or dies. Taxes are treated differently, depending on whether you form a C or an S corporation.

With an S corporation, the most common form of incorporation for small business owners, the business does not pay federal income tax. Profits flow through to owners and are taxed only on the owners' personal income tax returns. Losses are deductible on personal returns to the extent you have invested and have personally guaranteed the corporation's debts. This ability to deduct losses makes an S corporation attractive to people who expect to lose money for a few years before making a profit. A C corporation pays income tax itself, and you, as an employee, pay tax on what you earned.

Corporations can be costly to set up and require following certain regulations, which is why many partners elect instead to take the risks of forming a less formal and long-term entity. One major warning must accompany any discussion about incorporation. A widely perceived myth is that incorporation protects you completely from losing your assets in the event of a business failure, a lawsuit, or other financial disaster. You must familiarize yourself with the concept of "piercing the corporation veil." That means: If anything done by you or your partner is construed as fraudulent or grossly negligent, incorporation status will not protect you. Do not look at incorporation as a foolproof method for protecting yourself against an unethical or grossly incompetent partner—and make sure to keep your required corporate paperwork up to date.

Limited Liability Company

Limited Liability Companies, or LLCs, have become very popular in the last few years. A relatively new form of business, approved by the IRS in 1988, LLCs merge the benefits of general partnerships and S corporations. LLCs are essentially partnerships that have liability protection. They are beginning to become the most common form of legal partnership. They are easier to set up and operate than a corporation, requiring only a simple operating agreement. Whereas a corporation requires a great deal of formality (such as taking minutes and designating a board of directors), LLCs are much more informal. LLCs do not pay income tax themselves. Like S corporations, the income flows through to the members, who then pay individual taxes.

As with anything else, LLCs also have their downside. The informality of the process can be more detrimental than advantageous to some kinds of partners, who would benefit from the structure that incorporation demands. However, you can build into your LLC agreement all of the structure you desire. If a company is going public, it will need to convert to a corporation before the public offering.

There are other kinds of partnership arrangements, beside the ones mentioned here, that may also be appropriate. If a company already has an official partnership, it might convert to an LLP—limited liability partnership—instead of a limited liability company. An LLP is often used for professional service firms because they have been run as partnerships before.

Some states are now recognizing one-person limited liability companies. This may be an option for you for individual liability protection when you want to partner with another company.

I encourage you to read one of the books in the Recommended Resources section at the back of this book or to seek the counsel of a lawyer or an accountant who is experienced in small business partnerships. Use this section of the chapter as a launching pad for an in-depth exploration of your alternatives.

The Importance of Checks and Balances

Some of the most heart-wrenching stories I heard in my interviews were those told by partners who neglected to put a system of checks and balances into their partnership structures. They assigned to one partner the responsibility for handling all of the financial details of the company, including completing all of the paperwork for incorporation, or whatever legal form they chose. And then that partner failed to follow through and the results were disastrous. This can easily happen when one partner's background is financial and the other partners have little understanding of or interest in such matters. I recommend that you hire an outside accountant either to do your bookkeeping or to regularly audit the books. Even if your strength isn't financial analysis, you should become well acquainted with the financial reports from your company and how to interpret them.

You may be thinking: "That isn't necessary. I can trust my partner." That's what the people in the following three stories thought as well:

Embezzlement

Our CFO embezzled $200,000 over a period of five years through company credit cards we didn't even know we had. He had the nerve to use my Social Security number to apply for the cards, so once he stopped making the payments, my credit was ruined. When we caught him, he was fired, but he got away with it, with no financial penalties or prosecution. The attorney general said corporate bylaws have to state specifically how much each of the partners can spend. We hadn't designated any limit on credit cards. (The CFO wrote the bylaws!) This guy took money out of the company to pay the bills, and then doctored the numbers on the financial reports to hide his transactions. We didn't suspect a thing for several years, until we were bringing in all kinds of new business but the CFO kept telling us we were broke.

IRS

I trusted my colleague to take care of paying all of the taxes. I didn't worry about it until I happened to be in the office on a Saturday and I saw a piece of mail addressed to him from the IRS. I opened it and discovered that we owed several thousands of dollars in penalties for not paying our payroll taxes.

Failure to Incorporate

My ex-partner told me she had filed the paperwork for an S corporation. I trusted her to complete the details and didn't concern myself with it until we were sued by a customer who fell on our front walk and broke her hip. Then I discovered that she had "never gotten around to filing the paperwork." Nor had she gotten around to purchasing liability insurance, as she had promised. I was unable to protect myself from a $20,000 hit that came straight out of my personal assets. I could kick myself now for not checking up myself on these essential matters. Needless to say, I'm no longer working with this partner.

Conclusion

It may take you and your partners some time to put together a partnership agreement that answers the questions I urged you to address in this chapter. In the meantime, write a letter of understanding that at least articulates your agreements, at this moment in time, about contribution, compensation, and workload. This letter is not a substitute for a full partnership agreement, but it will serve as a short-term step while you work out the details.

If you choose to work with an attorney to draft your agreement, attorneys Denis Clifford and Ralph Warner, founders of Nolo Press and authors of *The Partnership Book,* advise you to locate a lawyer who deals regularly with small business issues. Ideally you will find someone willing to minimize your up-front legal costs, since you are a prospective client who will bring additional business once your venture is launched and profitable.

Ask in advance of your meeting how much you will be billed for an initial consultation. If you haven't already chosen someone to work with, you may choose to interview more than one lawyer. That will depend on whether you are being charged for the initial consultation and how much time you wish to put into this process.

If you draft your own contract and partnership agreement, a lawyer might insist on translating it to legalese—for your protection.

Do your best to discuss disagreements as much as you can outside of your lawyer's office. An attorney is a very expensive mediator. (I recognize that you may need legal guidance to help you settle some disagreements.)

You will be tempted to procrastinate or shorten this process. If you do so, you will be joining 80 percent of all small business owners. That makes you normal; it doesn't make you well prepared or protected. Think of these steps as the foundation you are building for your new home—your partnership. If you build your partnership on bedrock, the wind and rain may blow but your partnership will stand solid. If you don't take the time to form a solid foundation, your partnership may be knocked over at the first strong wind.

CHAPTER 6

Appreciate Your Differences

"My partner has taught me that there is no one way."

—Ellen Parlapiano

Unless you partnered for the sole purpose of raising capital, your primary motivator for getting together was to combine your different strengths. This is the foundation of your success, as well as your most basic challenge. How many times have you muttered in exasperation, "Why can't my partner be more like me!"

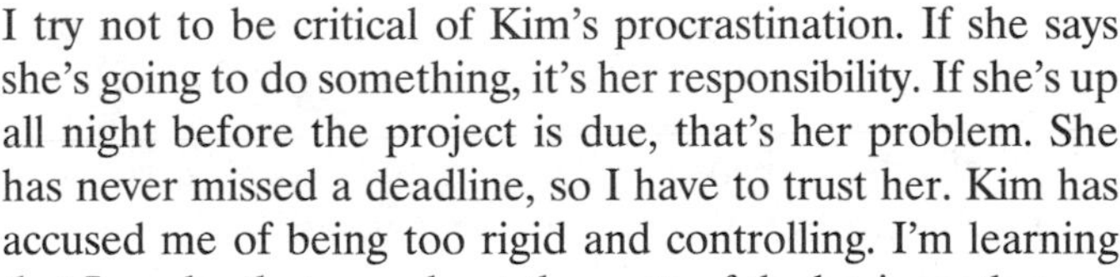

> I try not to be critical of Kim's procrastination. If she says she's going to do something, it's her responsibility. If she's up all night before the project is due, that's her problem. She has never missed a deadline, so I have to trust her. Kim has accused me of being too rigid and controlling. I'm learning that I can be that way about the parts of the business that are my responsibility, but I have to let her do her job her way.

John Gray, author of *Men Are From Mars, Women Are From Venus,* and Deborah Tannen, author of *You Just Don't Understand,* have helped millions of husbands and wives laugh and learn about how their gender differences influence marital and business communication. Popular four quadrant personality tests, such as the Meyers-Briggs and the Platinum Rule, have been educating audiences for years about how to handle the most difficult people in their office, why they can't get along with their bosses, and what happens to communication when "opposites attract."

Though you may be resistant to being placed in one of four personality quadrants, or being generalized as a "typical" man or woman, the fact is that many people have found insight and humor in this research. You will discover that you aren't as unique as you thought you were. Partner conflict is often rooted in gender- or personality-related communication styles.

In Chapter 6, we will examine how gender and personality styles impact communication with your partners and how you can use this knowledge to become more effective. Warning: This chapter is filled with generalizations. If a particular generalization doesn't apply to you, consider yourself the exception to the rule. Perhaps in your partnership the typical roles assigned to gender are reversed. Or maybe half of the pointers in the personality profile section make sense to you but the rest don't ring true. Take back to your partnership the insights that work for you and leave the rest.

Differences That Strengthen and Challenge Your Partnership

"In all intense relationships the paradox is, whatever you most value also gets you in the most trouble."

—Jeff Klunk

"Incompatibility is the norm—it's the chemistry for growth."

—Ed Shea

Let's consider for a moment the range of differences you and your partners may encounter in your partnerships. Here are some examples gathered from my interviews:

✧

My partner lives in suburban Connecticut, and I live in rural Ohio. Most of our partnership takes place on the phone and via e-mail because neither of us will ever move to the other's location.

✧

My partner keeps us moving forward, and I keep us grounded. He's the one who always has a great new idea, and I'm the one who says, "How are we going to pay for that?"

I have 25 years' experience as a corporate executive. My partners are clinical psychologists. They've never worked for a corporation in their lives. We're often talking in different languages.

I'm really great at sales—I even enjoy it. My partner goes into the bathroom and throws up before we give a presentation to a prospect because she is so frightened.

My partner is a quick decision maker, but I prefer to move more slowly. She's Miss Instinct, and I'm Mr. Due Diligence.

My partner procrastinates on everything and needs a deadline to keep her motivated. You can set your clock by me. I prefer plenty of time to work at a leisurely pace.

My partner and I will never be good friends. He's a conservative Republican and I'm a left-leaning Independent. We have little in common except for the business.

I'm 65, and my partner—my son—is 40. We steer the gray-haired clients over to me, and the younger ones gravitate to my son.

My partner is obese and timid about making public appearances because of being overweight. I've been slim all my life and I love the limelight. She's in charge of back-room operations, while I'm out doing speaking appearances, which suits us both.

✧

I've got five children I'm supporting as a single mother. My partner is single and plans to stay that way—especially after seeing what my life is like.

My daughters are infants, and my partner has teenage children. While I'm worried about paying for day care, she's concerned about saving for college expenses.

I follow the 3-foot rule—I'll tell anyone about our network marketing opportunity who is nearby. My partner prefers sending out cassette tapes to a mailing list of strangers and won't even discuss the business with friends, family, or co-workers.

I recently graduated from chiropractic school and joined an existing practice of 25 years. My partner is preparing for retirement, and I'm just beginning to grow my practice.

I am a Conservative Jew and my partners are all Evangelical Christians. I was worried at first that they would try to proselytize me, but they've been very respectful of our differences.

I am a black woman, partnering with a Hispanic man, a white man, and a Chinese woman. We're a mini-version of the United Nations.

Depending on what lens you are looking through, you will focus on the differences or the similarities among you and your partners. Finding differences isn't difficult—in fact, when you consider how dissimilar you and your partners are, you may wonder how you can work together at all!

The most successful partnerships I've seen delighted in these differences and made the most of them. Diversity is viewed as a blessing rather than a curse.

The Platinum Rule

"My greatest pleasure comes from making my partner happy. It's win/win for both of us."

—Tony Alessandra, Ph.D.

The Golden Rule—"Do unto others as you wish to be done unto"—is a useful creed for promoting kindness but a disastrous philosophy for communicating with your partners and employees.

Human nature is to speak to others the way we wish to be spoken to rather than the way others need to receive the communication. Tony Alessandra, author of this book's foreword, advocates following the Platinum Rule: "Do unto others the way they wish to be done unto." Learn how your partners think, feel, and wish to be spoken to, and communicate with them in their preferred style rather than your own natural style.

Helping your partners feel understood, listened to, appreciated, and respected is a powerful tool for creating a rewarding relationship and the secret to building rapport. The people I interviewed who have masterful alliances have mastered the Platinum Rule.

You can find plenty of detail about the Platinum Rule, including a questionnaire to determine which of four personality categories is your dominant style, in Dr. Alessandra's book, *The Platinum Rule.* Most people know what their style is—and their partner's—simply by reading the following descriptions (summarized here with the author's permission). These descriptions have been validated with thousands of people. You will probably see yourself as a blend of all four categories, with one style more predominant than the others. If after reading this section you don't find yourself aligned strongly with any of the categories, don't concern yourself. Some people are such a blend of all four that they find it difficult to pinpoint themselves into any one category. If you are one of those people, you probably have a slightly predominant style, but not one so noticeable to yourself or others that it blatantly stands out when you read the category descriptions. That's okay. Tune in to the parts of each description that ring true for you.

Let's look at each of the four categories and how aspects of each style can create trouble when communicating with your partners.

Director

You are a forceful, confident, competitive, and decisive risk taker. You dive in headfirst as if you, and you alone, have the answer. You are awesome at your best, and insensitive at your worst. You are a natural leader, propelled by your need to be in charge. You are more interested in meeting goals than pleasing people. You will initiate change, and you thrive on crisis. Juggling multiple tasks, you are apt to solve practical problems quickly.

You are only comfortable delegating if you are confident that it will produce results. You are impatient with abstract ideas and frustrated when others aren't as competent or motivated as you are. You may be accused of being an egomaniac. You often take yourself too seriously. You would benefit from taking more time to relax and smell the roses.

Caution: You will grow impatient with a partner who isn't moving at the pace you would like or who is not performing up to your "standards." You aren't apt to be subtle about your complaints, either! In fact, you can be downright demeaning, and your partner may feel pushed around. Lighten up, and remember that you, and the business, are not the center of the universe.

Socializer

You are an outgoing, optimistic, enthusiastic talker. You are always in search of a fun time and a good audience. A team player, you care about relationships. You find stability more attractive than risk, and you are slow to change. Fast-paced, energetic, playful, persuasive, you are long on ideas and short on follow-through. You will start projects and look to others to finish them. Highly intuitive, you'll make big decisions on scant data. You seek admiration and acceptance. More than anything, you crave the approval of your peers. Above all, you want to make work fun.

Caution: When work stops being fun, you'll look for more enjoyable pastures elsewhere. If you aren't partnered with someone you can laugh with, or if you aren't finding pleasure in your work, the partnership won't last long unless you find a way to get your laughs elsewhere. Your lack of attention to follow-through will anger your partner unless he or she readily agrees to handle the details or you have a staff to assist you. Since you crave approval, you are vulnerable in a partnership that doesn't recognize you or express appreciation of you. If you are paired with a director, you will struggle because the pace of change is faster than you are comfortable with.

Relater

Laid-back is your middle name. You are low-key, calm, discreet, friendly, and personable. People are attracted to your tranquility and stability. You yearn for a slow steady pace and prefer to walk solidly down the middle of the road. You prefer to make change slowly, and you'll want to see a plan before you get started. A cooperative team player, you will carefully consider the impact of change on others. You are a good listener, though you hate conflict and aggressive behavior, so you won't respond well to hostility or complaining. What people love about working with you is that you are dependable. You will quietly do what you are told without rocking the boat. Once committed to a project, you will persist like a bulldog. You shine on a project that requires a great deal of routine and detail work.

Caution: When you are working with assertive partners, you may bow to them and agree to do what they say just to avoid conflict. You will quietly build resentment if you don't speak your mind. Your loyalty and persistent nature will lead you to stick with a partnership through the good times and the bad. As honorable and advantageous to your business as that may be, watch out for hanging on too long in an unproductive partnership if it's better for you to say good-bye.

Thinker

You love clarity and order, and can be counted on for your thorough, meticulous attention to details and follow-through. You cherish efficiency and accuracy. Correct procedures are important to you. You'll use logic, rather than emotions, to make a decision. Self-controlled and cautious, you can appear to others as lacking spontaneity and being distant. You will share information on a need-to-know basis only when you are sure it won't come back to bite you. After studying problems intently, you are hard to budge when you believe you've mastered all the facts or thought something through to its logical conclusion.

Caution: Your perfectionist demands may drive your partner batty, especially if you hold him or her to your impossible standards. Your obsession with organization and frugal ways may earn you the label of uptight or overly rigid, especially if you are partnered with a socializer or a director. Since you prefer to work with people who are calm and thorough (another thinker or relater), you will have to stretch out of your comfort zone to tolerate the emotional intensity of working with a director or a socializer.

Communicating in Consideration of Your Differences

Director/relater, socializer/thinker, and director/thinker teams are the most likely business partnerships because they reflect the effort to strengthen a business by bringing together complementary skills. If you and your partner fall into one of these combinations, here are some ideas for turning incompatibility into a strong team:

Director/Relater

A director learns to be more patient and responsive from a relater. The relater learns how to quicken the pace. The relater absorbs from the director how to take charge and accept risk. The relater adapts to the director by giving information succinctly. Directors can develop sensitivity and empathy, and act less unilaterally and quickly. The relater can say no occasionally without being overly sensitive to the director's feelings. The director can help the relater feel more nurtured by offering a genuine compliment and showing interest in his or her personal life.

—✧—

> When we're having a staff meeting, and we're going into the second hour, I'll suddenly get up and say, "Okay, Gwen, you've maxed me out. I can't do this anymore. We've got to give this a break." Gwen has learned to let me walk away; she knows we'll pick it up again when my brain clears up.

—✧—

Socializer/Thinker

The socializer learns discretion from the thinker. The thinker becomes more relaxed and sociable around the socializer. The socializer will learn to talk less and listen more, focusing on the task at hand. The thinker can show concern and appreciation for the socializer, and the socializer can try to be more objective. The socializer can develop the ability and commitment to follow up on promises and tasks, while the thinker can become more spontaneous.

—✧—

> My partner isn't the kind of guy who usually shows any sentiment or emotion. So I was even more touched when he sent me some flowers following a really rough client meeting, with a card that said, "Thanks for hanging in there and putting up with so much grief." I saved that card—he gave it to me two years ago!

—✧—

Director/Thinker

Each member of this team gives up his or her need for personal control. The director needs to respect the thinker's needs for guidelines and policies. The thinker needs to be more direct and open with the director about his or her concerns. When the director initiates a new project, the thinker must respond in a shorter time frame than what is comfortable. The director will come to appreciate the well-organized and thoroughly reasoned analytical work of the thinker.

Jack is constantly bombarding me with new ideas while I'm trying to systemize what we already have. I used to think I had to respond immediately to every new proposal he dreamed up, but now I say: "I can't do that now—it'll go on the list." Instead of getting mad at Jack for being unreasonable, I take the time to educate him about what kind of time and resources it will take to produce what he's asking for. Usually he's good at backing off, unless he's really fired up. Then I've learned to drop what I'm doing and listen.

The Platinum Rule in Action—A Working Example

"We've become more than partners, more than father and son. We're friends. It wasn't easy at first, but it was the only way we were going to make this business work."

—Tom Wood

George and Tom Wood are a father-and-son team running a successful partnership for a network marketing company, the Peoples Network. TPN offers people the ability to cash in on the digital satellite industry and access TV programs, Internet and TV shopping, and thousands of other products. When I interviewed them, they shared how their business partnership had been transformed from unproductive and irritating to an outstanding relationship exceeding their dreams. Best friends and dynamic business partners, George and Tom recast their relationship from father and son to equal partners with the highest respect for each other's contributions and strengths.

George is a thinker. Early in the partnership, by his own admission, George overwhelmed Tom with a need for what Tom calls exhaustive detail. Coming from a lifetime corporate career in top management, George found that the transition to self-employment was a rough one and that working with his son was not an easy task. Tom recalls that the early years of partnering with his dad were characterized by throwing new ideas at his father (shooting from the hip most of the time like a classic socializer) and then feeling frustrated when his father didn't immediately show enthusiasm and support.

Tom laughs when he remembers the day he brought his dad into TPN. He handed George the contract and asked him to sign it. George told him he needed time to read it, and Tom replied, with genuine puzzlement, "Why?"

The light went on when they saw Tony Alessandra's eye-opening presentation of the Platinum Rule on TPN's success channel. Watching the lecture on TV about the challenges of working with an opposite personality, George and Tom realized they were fighting over their differences rather than leveraging them. George thought to himself, "Tom's doing this business so well. Why am I arguing with success?" Tom realized that it hadn't been fair to expect his father to venture into new territory without a road map. He began to see the benefit of his father's attention to detail and to appreciate the grounding his father provided to the business. I asked Tom and George what some of their greatest challenges have been as a socializer/thinker team and how they have used the Platinum Rule to convert their frustration into appreciation and effectiveness.

Tom said:

> When we run an event I let my father work out the details. He loves that part and I don't. I couldn't imagine anyone liking it and that's why I had never delegated it to him; that was before we learned the Platinum Rule.

> The promotion and marketing of the event are not my dad's strengths, so he delegates that to me. Now that we understand each other, we approach all of our prospects with the Platinum Rule. That alone helped triple our business in the last six months.

George recalls:

> Faxes almost became the final straw of our business partnership. I couldn't understand why Tom threw away faxes that I hadn't read yet. He said he'd tell me the summaries, but that drove me crazy; I wanted the detail. To solve it, we put the fax machine in my office, but that didn't work because Tom was doing most of the faxing. Finally we devised a system where Tom had the fax machine in his office and put every fax into a box after he had read it. That little discipline was hard for him as a socializer but it made the partnership work.

Because your learned response is to relate to others according to the Golden Rule, you will need to unlearn that tendency and replace it with strategies like those outlined here and in the Platinum Rule. It takes time to perfect this skill, so be patient with yourself as you learn. George and Tom report that it was a full six months before they reaped the benefits of a dramatic improvement in their relationship.

It takes skill and practice to convert criticism to tolerance and then to gratitude. If you succeed, you will enjoy your partnership more and your clients will have the advantage of tapping into the full range of your talents.

Bringing the Platinum Rule Teachings into Your Relationship

A Partnership Communication-Building Exercise

Here's an opportunity for you to contemplate, and then communicate to your partner, how both of your personalities positively affect your partnership relationship and the productivity of the company—and how they may be limiting it. As we've reviewed, every personality strength brings with it a weakness as well. Partnerships always celebrate and struggle with the differences among their team members.

—✧—

Take a moment to complete the following sentences. Put your partner's name in the blank, and ask your partner to do the same. Then, in a scheduled partner meeting, discuss the results.

I appreciate the following strengths you, bring to our partnership and our company.

Strengths: ______________________________

____

____

The strengths that you bring to our partnership and our company also challenge me in the following ways:

Challenges: ______________________________

____

____

I appreciate your putting up with the following characteristics of my personality that I know drive you a bit nuts!

____

____

____

____

Here's what I'd like to suggest we do differently, so that we communicate more effectively and irritate each other a little less:

____

____

____

____

—✧—

Gender Issues

"Recognizing gender differences frees individuals from the burden of individual pathology."

—Deborah Tannen, Ph.D.

I warned you earlier about generalizations—here they come! If you aren't the "typical" man or woman, some of these insights may not apply. If you are, you will find this section enlightening, as it will explain why certain dynamics exist in your partnership, whether you are partnered with a man, a woman, or both. Drawing primarily from *Men Are From Mars, Women Are From Venus* and *You Just Don't Understand,* we will explore how gender-related needs and behaviors may affect your partnership. We'll examine the patterns that can occur in three different scenarios: a male/male partnership, a male/female partnership, and a female/female partnership. If you have more than one partner, all of these categories may apply. We'll take a look at the potential strengths and pitfalls of each arrangement.

When Two or More Men Partner

Men engage the world as individuals in a hierarchical social order in which everyone is either one-up or one-down. Life is a contest, a struggle to preserve independence and avoid failure. Conversations are negotiations to achieve and maintain the upper hand and to protect oneself from others' attempts to push one around.

Men make decisions without consulting their partners. They feel aggravated if they can't act without talking first. If a man makes a decision, he may be resistant to explaining his reasons, as he interprets being asked as not being trusted. Men feel oppressed by lengthy discussions about what they see as minor issues.

A man is more concerned with being respected than liked.

A man's competitive nature makes it difficult for him to talk to another man about how he feels, or to admit problems in business or at home. He is more likely to talk about politics or sports than anything personal. If there is a woman in a partnership with two or more men, the men will more likely talk to her about personal issues or conflicts they have with their male partners.

Men are more comfortable dealing with conflict if there are roles and a clear set of expectations, as in sports. Men are more likely to express conflict intellectually than emotionally. Their approach is solution oriented. If you set up rules and procedures ahead of time, you'll increase the likelihood that a male partner will deal with tension without avoidance or withdrawal.

Men are hindered by their insistence that they must act independently and solve their problems without help. They need to learn that it's okay to make mistakes or ask for assistance.

—◆—

> Patrick and Bob own PB&J's Sandwich Shop. Patrick is in charge of ordering the food and Bob takes care of customers. When they first opened the business a year ago, they had an unspoken agreement that they would divide the work evenly, each one helping the other whenever it was needed. Recently, however, Patrick has been drowning in paperwork and staying late into the night after Bob has already gone home. Patrick refuses to ask Bob to stay longer hours so he can get home at an earlier hour. The paperwork has always been his responsibility and he doesn't want Bob to think that he can't handle the workload.

—◆—

Because the primary concern of most men is creating and sustaining their freedom and control, partnering with another man can be tricky. Here are six strategies for successful male/male interaction in a partnership:

1. Give each partner his own areas of responsibility. Allow him to make decisions autonomously.

2. Establish agreed-upon weekly routines for discussing and resolving conflict. Two conflict-avoidant men will start seething with resentment if issues aren't dealt with above-board. Regular partner meetings will help keep concerns from being buried. Discuss issues in a logical, calm, problem-solving manner. To the extent that you can formalize your process for resolving tension, you will be more likely to bring conflict to the surface, and resolution will be more likely.
3. Recognize the tendency to focus more on business operations than relationship building. To give the partner relationship the attention it needs, participate in skill-building exercises like the ones in this book, or get together at the gym or over dinner outside of work. Consider hiring a coach or consultant who is experienced in working with business partners.
4. Two men in partnership can use their natural competitiveness to their advantage, motivating each other to increase sales and perform at a higher level. Go out of your way to express appreciation or regard for your partner's performance, despite the temptation to downplay your partner's achievements so that you feel superior.
5. A partnership of two or more men needs to be a safe place to make mistakes. Don't pull away your respect when your partner screws up; affirm your partner's abilities and skills in the face of difficult times—when he least expects your support. Your ego may judge your partner for not being perfect, but you don't need to always verbalize it.
6. Men in partnership do not need to rid themselves of competitive aggression. They can channel the competitive energy they feel toward their partners into combating the competition instead.

When a Man and a Woman Partner Together

Male and female partners can get into a pursuit/withdrawal pattern that becomes a vicious cycle until one of the partners steps out of his or her role. Here is how it may manifest:

Men often pull away and silently think about what's bothering them, rather than discussing their fears and concerns. When a man is worried about a problem he goes into his "cave" (a place of solitude John Gray describes in *Men Are From Mars, Women Are From Venus*), or tries to forget about the problem by distracting himself. He becomes distant, forgetful, unresponsive, and preoccupied until he solves the problem.

While a man fights for his independence, a woman struggles to preserve intimacy and avoid isolation. A woman will misinterpret her partner's silence and distance. When he's silent he is focusing on solving his problems. He's saying, "Leave me alone until I figure this out." She decodes: "I'm ignoring you. You aren't important to me. I'm even thinking about ending this partnership." Silence triggers a woman's worst fear—abandonment. He may not even be thinking about the partnership at all, but she will start feeling paranoid, in the absence of communication and rapport. Even if his problems aren't work-related, she may assume that they are about the business and her.

A woman has a very different approach to solving problems: she wants to talk about it, preferably with her partner. Talking helps her explore the issue and to feel closer to her partner. While a man needs silence to solve a problem, a woman needs to talk about it.

Women crash like waves, and sometimes they need to hit bottom in order to feel better. If a man assumes that her change in mood is due to his behavior, he'll try to snap her out of it before she is ready, which will spark an angry response from her. When a male partner reassures his female partner by telling her that their situation isn't so bleak, she hears her feelings being belittled or discounted.

She says: "I'm worried about cash flow this month. We've barely got enough to meet payroll." He says: "Don't worry yourself about it. We'll pull through—we always do. Be optimistic." (He has the positive intention of making her feel better. What she feels instead, is invalidated.)

Since a man is so solution oriented, he has to be careful about not invalidating his female partner's feelings. In his effort to fix her problem, or to assure her that everything is taken care of, he will tell her that what she is worrying about is no big deal, or that her concerns are unfounded. His well-intentioned approach to fixing everything will cause her to feel disrespected and discredited. At times, his unconscious desire to be in a one-up position to his partner will lead him to share information and knowledge in a way that makes her feel inferior or stupid. Men can use a tone of voice that sends the message "you are incompetent," or "I am smarter than you."

On the other hand, men complain about women setting up "improvement committees" as soon as they partner. A man appreciates advice only if it's solicited. When a man feels that his female partner is trying to improve him, he will resist any suggestions she makes. Ironically, only when she makes him feel respected and accepted for who he is, will he be more likely to ask for feedback and advice, and receive what she has to say.

When a man is spending too much time with his female partner he'll need to pull away and she'll notice increased moodiness, irritability, passiveness, and defensiveness. The more a woman tries to get her male partner out of his cave, the longer it takes, accelerating the pursuit/withdrawal cycle. He'll spring back like a rubber band if she gives him the space he needs, rather than chasing him into his cave and complaining about his distance.

Conversation between a male and female partner can be frustrating to both. A woman uses dramatic phrases and exaggerations to express her feelings more fully. A man might take her literally. A woman will tell a story with lots of detail, keeping him in suspense about the bottom line. Building suspense adds more feeling to the story. A man gets impatient with a woman's detail because he assumes that all the details are necessary for him to find a solution. When he doesn't see their relevance, he starts to think: "Get to the point already!"

This dynamic is illustrated in the following dialogue between Alex and Tara, equal partners in a firm that supplies medical equipment to hospitals around the country. Alex has been out of town for several days on a sales trip. While he was gone, a lawyer called and told Tara his client was suing their firm for selling faulty equipment five years ago. Tara cannot find the invoices that will show them what equipment they sold the client. She has been anxiously awaiting Alex's return. She wants to give Alex lots of details he's not all that interested in hearing. Alex just wants Tara to get to the point:

Tara: Alex, welcome back. The worst thing happened while you were gone.

Alex: What could be that bad?

Tara: Sorry to jump right in with bad news. How was the sales trip?

Alex: Fine—I'll tell you later. What's the problem?

Tara: It happened after lunch on Monday. The air conditioner broke; it was like a sauna in here and I had just decided I was going to leave when the phone rang.

Alex: Is that what's wrong? The air conditioner broke? Why is that so bad?

Tara: No, that's not the problem.

Alex: It would save time if you would get to the point.

Tara (*hurt at his tone of voice*):

A lawyer called and said County Hospital is suing us for selling faulty equipment. I haven't been able to find the invoices to see what equipment we sold them—it was over five years ago.

Alex: Relax, I know just where they are.

Alex would have preferred if Tara got straight to the point. It only took her five sentences to get there, but after starting with her alarming sentence, "The worst thing happened...," Alex was unable to hear the rest until he knew what problem he would have to solve.

Here are nine strategies for successful interaction between a male and female partner:

1. Men: If you want to please your female partner, listen attentively to what she has to say, without rushing to solve the problem. Work on using body language and expressions like nodding your head, or repeating key points in your own words, to indicate that you are listening. If you are hearing her, but not listening, she'll know the difference.
2. Women: To suit your male partner, get to the point. In staff meetings, you'll need to follow an agenda and not allow the discussion to get too far off track. At times you've got to keep the emotions out of the discussion and just talk business.
3. Women: The phrase "Could you please..." is a turnoff for most men. Instead of saying, "Could you take care of payroll this week?" (of course he can—are you questioning his competence?) say, "Would you take care of payroll this week?" That way he feels like he is making the choice, and his capability isn't being questioned.
4. Men: Don't take a woman's words literally. If she uses lots of exaggerated expressions like "always" and "never" and "we're going to go out of business," recognize that she is expressing her deepest fears, and she is looking for reassurance—it doesn't mean that it's all true.
5. Women: You will trigger a man's defenses if you speak to him in a disapproving tone, implying that you don't trust or respect him. A man will misinterpret some of your actions as a sign of lack of trust, even if you never intended it that way. Every time you tell a man how to do something, or

correct the way he's already completed a task, your metamessage to him is that you don't trust him to act competently without your help. Don't start your sentences with "Why didn't you...?" A subtle switch to "How come...?" instead of the loaded word "Why...?" seems to lessen a man's defensiveness.

6. Women: Give your male partner plenty of time alone when he needs it, without holding it against him or complaining about it. If you try to force him to interact with you when he's not in the mood, it will only backfire. Get out of the office and away from your partner if you find it difficult to get out of his way. He'll come back to you in a short time.
7. Men: Don't lecture your female partners.
8. Women: If you've got an issue with your male partner, take it up with him in private. Don't embarrass him by raising the matter in front of someone else.
9. Men: Pick and choose when to play the role of Mr. Fix-It. A woman appreciates Mr. Fix-It, unless he comes out when she is upset. After she's been heard, then you can offer solutions. If she comes to you and asks you to fix the broken computer, and that's right up your alley, go for it. If she comes to you and wants to vent about how incompetent the customer service department is at the computer store, don't try to solve that problem until she's done complaining. She may just want you to listen to her, and affirm her feelings.

When Two or More Women Partner Together

Now that my partner and I aren't getting along, I wake up in the morning and I don't even want to go to work. It doesn't matter that we are making a ton of money, or that our clients love us. I still get a stomach ache being in the office when she and I aren't talking to each other. I wish I could stop caring what she thinks of me, or whether we're friends—but I can't. Lately, I've been thinking about selling the business to her, just so I don't have to feel this way every day.

When two or more women are in partnership, if the relationship isn't working, the partnership won't work in the long run. Tension in the relationship is very distracting and painful—which is why women spend so much time trying to work things out. Female partnerships are just as vulnerable as male partnerships, but for completely different reasons. Female/female partners will frequently confront and process conflict, sometimes at the expense of getting anything done. They must be careful to not overly process or analyze their relationship, or they will spend an inordinate amount of time working out partnership issues.

Women feel comfortable seeking help, so they are more likely to recommend bringing in a consultant to help solve business or relationship problems. (Men are more likely to pay for an accounting or legal professional than a relationship coach.)

Hopefully, in a female/female partnership, each partner is emotionally down at different times, relying on the other to keep the momentum and optimism going while she rebounds. When a woman doesn't feel safe going into despair, rage, frustration, or any other negative emotion, she pretends that everything is fine and turns to addictions, like overeating, to hide and repress her feelings. Two female partners have an opportunity to create a working environment that encourages and allows the natural pattern of a woman's feelings to unfold. PMS is real, and women also need to be sensitive to hormonal cycles.

Two women may spend a great deal of time talking about personal/family life issues. Sometimes, a woman will vent to her business partner about frustrations with her husband, children, neighbors, or anyone who is bothering her. This kind of sharing may not be welcome, and could become a drain on her partner's energy. On the other hand, some partners use personal sharing to bond together.

Women appreciate frequent gestures of affection and appreciation, even something as simple as a scribbled note of thanks, a compliment, or offering to pick up lunch. You can never give a woman enough praise.

Women feel it is natural to consult their partners at every turn. They expect decisions to be discussed first and made by consensus. Interdependence between two female partners doesn't scare them, it appeals to them. It reinforces their connection and intimacy.

Here are seven strategies for successful interaction between two or more female partners:

1. Compliment your partner on a presentation done well, how she handled an employee relations problem, or how she is dressed. Frequent daily gestures go further than an effusive remark made every once in a while.
2. Over time, you will be able to predict when one or both of you are likely to head into a down cycle. It may be timed with your menstrual calendar, Monday mornings after you leave the babies in day care, or after you've been a single parent for two weeks while your husband has been traveling. Listen to your partner's anxiety and frustration, and affirm her ability to pull through. Above all, don't let yourself get pulled down with her.
3. Don't hesitate to bring in outside help when one or both of you suggest it. If you choose your assistance wisely, an outside perspective can be enlightening and helpful. Make sure you both choose the professional, or at least have a vote, so that neither of you feels pushed into receiving help from someone she doesn't feel good about.
4. Check in with your partner about how much personal sharing each of you is comfortable with, and when. You may find that your partner welcomes chatting over lunch but not while she's focusing on work. If so, you may need to curb your desire to share spontaneously until it's a better

time for your partner. Or, you might tell your partner that you care about what is happening in her life but you would prefer talking about it after work.

5. Don't spend too much time confronting relationship issues. Set up weekly partner meetings rather than processing every day. Agree to postpone some discussions until the partner meeting, if it can wait. Develop a tolerance for living with grumpy days rather than calling into question your partnership every time one of you isn't feeling super about the other.
6. Though your natural tendency may be toward consensus management on every decision, such an approach will slow down your business. Define areas of responsibility where you each have autonomy to make decisions without checking with your partners first, and establish which decisions will be made jointly.
7. Hold regular partner meetings, every day or at least once a week, to satisfy your need for relationship building and to reinforce your connection as partners. If you start drifting apart from your partner because you both get too busy, the partnership may start falling apart.

Partner Commitments to Address Gender Challenges

You and your partners might have scanned the previous suggestions for enhancing your interaction, nodded your heads, and said to yourselves, "Yes, that makes sense." You might even already be doing some or most of these suggestions. I also know how busy you are and how good intentions can quickly be replaced by your "to-do" lists.

Write down two commitments from the strategies suggested here, or any others you may come up with on your own, to enhance your communication between male/male partners, male/female partners, or female/female partners. Agree to give these a try for at least a few months. Be bold—try one or two you haven't done before and see what happens to your relationship!

—⟡—

To enhance our gender communication skills and improve our partnership, we commit to the following two positive actions:

1. ____

____

____

2. ____

____

____

—⟡—

Conclusion: Look for Common Ground, Accept Unmet Needs

When it comes to honoring the differences in your relationship, remembering the serenity prayer might help:

> *God grant me the serenity to accept the things I cannot change, the courage to change the things I can, and the wisdom to know the difference.*

I interviewed a woman in a professional partnership with three men. Though she is nationally respected as an expert in her field, her male colleagues tend to either ignore her contribution or to appear jealous when she succeeds in a manner that doesn't include them. This was a source of great pain and aggravation to her for many years. She is committed to staying in the partnership, which is financially lucrative and rewarding in many other ways. Though she accepted that she was unlikely to change her partners, she still had needs for recognition and praise. To fill those needs outside her partnership, she started a nonprofit organization for women outside of the company. This organization provides her with a place where she is nurtured and revered by an audience that showers her with appreciation and praise.

As your partnership progresses, you will begin to see more differences than commonalities, especially if your partner starts to irritate you. Search for common ground in your shared commitment to the company, in your personal history together, and in your private lives.

⟡

> I brought in a partner to my business who was a devil of a guy to get along with. In fact, everyone hated him. But he invested a ton of money and saved the company from going under, so we tolerated his hostility. I didn't think the guy had a soft spot, or that we had anything in common, until one day I came into work shaken up because my baby daughter was about to have a serious operation to repair a heart defect. Roger noticed I was strung out. He called me into his office, closed the door, and said, "I haven't told many people about this, but we lost a child right after birth." That moment broke the ice between us.

⟡

Successful partners come to peace with their differences and relish them. View your partners with compassion and respect for their orientation and points of view. If you learn to tolerate and respect your differences, you may even come to appreciate them.

Once you stop trying to make your partners into clones of yourself, you will see how valuable their unique approaches can be to you and the business. They will help open your eyes to new possibilities, do the kind of work you'd rather not do, balance and anchor you when you are going off half-cocked, and give you something to laugh about.

CHAPTER 7

Conflict Resolution

"It's not how similar or different you are; it's how you handle differences when they arise that counts."

—Clifford Notarius and Howard Markman,
We Can Work It Out

No human relationship is immune to struggle. This is true for business partnerships as well. Managed conflict will lead to a stronger and more successful business. Unresolved conflict will weaken your business and deplete the energy of all partners involved.

While interviewing 120 individuals who are currently, or have been, in a business partnership, I frequently heard stories that revolved around dissension and conflict resolution. Though each situation was unique, certain themes repeatedly surfaced. This chapter portrays common scenarios that trigger partner conflict, safeguards to prevent similar occurrences, and solutions for repairing such conflict if it does occur.

In a healthy and productive relationship, the vast majority of conflicts can be avoided or mended through slight or significant changes in partner communication and behavior. If you determine that your differences cannot be resolved, see Chapter 9 for an exploration of the issues to consider when dissolving your partnership.

Common Triggers for Conflict—and Their Safeguarding Measures

Trigger One: Criticism Is Delivered Poorly

Criticism that begins with "you" (as in "you should have done a better job on this report"), attacks your partner's character ("you're lazy"), or slips into generalizations ("you're always late") won't solve the problem. All it does is launch a futile cycle of attack and defense. Criticism that is poorly timed, especially if it embarrasses your partner in public, also fuels anger and resentment that leads to dysfunctional communication.

Safeguards and Solutions:

Avoid dumping—bringing up a long list of complaints all at once—which leaves your partner feeling overwhelmed, hopeless, and defensive.

Communicate your criticisms as requests for action rather than attacks of character. Don't express complaints globally ("You never do any work around here") but, rather, specifically ("I don't like running the opportunity meetings by myself while you're playing golf. I'd like you to help me with the meetings on Saturday morning for about three hours").

Begin your sentences with "I" ("I wanted the sales report done before the investor meeting, and it's not. You said you would take care of it, and I'm angry that it's not ready.") Then shift your complaint to a request ("It's essential for us to have the sales report finished before we meet with the investors. Is there a reason why this would be an impossible deadline for you to meet?").

The use of "I" statements as a method of creating more effective communication is illustrated by these confrontations between two dentists arguing over perceptions of workload.

The first scenario presents an example of hostile and ineffective communication:

⟡

Susan: Jackie, when are you going to work your fair share around here? You see half the number of patients I do, but you take home the same paycheck I do. You don't seem to care any more about the patients, and this song and dance you have about your alcoholic husband is really starting to wear thin with me. You said this wouldn't go on for longer than a few months, but it's been six months and you've gotten away with this long enough!

⟡

The second scenario involves negotiating a new working relationship:

⟡

Susan: Jackie, I asked for this meeting because we need to discuss how we're going to allocate the patient load in the office. When you see half the number of patients I do, and bring home the same paycheck, I feel resentful and burned out. I realize that you are under enormous pressure at home, and it must be very hard to manage it all. I agreed to help out for a period of time, but it's gone on too long for me and I'm starting to reach my limit. We need to negotiate a new understanding of how patient care and profits will be shared between us as long as you are only able to work 20 hours a week.

⟡

Don't plunge ahead with critical feedback without preparing your partners. Ask their permission to proceed. Give them an idea of what it's about so they can decide if they are ready and willing to hear what you've got to say. (For this technique to work, the person who is receiving the feedback must be willing to address the issue within a few days. If the discussion is postponed for weeks at a time, with one excuse or another, resentment will build.)

Trigger Two: Criticism Becomes Contempt

"One zinger will erase 20 acts of kindness."

—Clifford Notarius and Howard Markman

Once you make a verbally abusive comment, it's hard to retract it. Damage can be undone, but it takes a lot of work and time. Unresolved criticism escalates into contempt when you insult and psychologically abuse your partner. When disdain overwhelms your relationship, you entirely forget your partner's positive qualities. Your communication is peppered with insults and mockery. Your body language and tone of voice demonstrate a lack of respect for your partner, and your head rings with an inner script of righteous indignation ("How could you be so stupid and incompetent? I would never do something so idiotic!"). When contempt escalates, you may even be thinking about revenge.

Safeguards and Solutions:

Marital research shows that you must have at least five times as many positive as negative moments with your spouse if your marriage is to be stable. The same could be said of a business partnership. For every argument that implies "I don't like who you are" you will need at least five situations when you convey appreciation to your partner to counterbalance the negative impact of being criticized.

Ironically, your chances of changing partners are greatly improved if you accept them for who they are. Dr. John Gottman, a marriage counselor, warns: "It is difficult for change to occur except in a climate of acceptance." You may be so fed up with your partners' idiosyncrasies that you can no longer discuss the issues civilly or with a generous spirit. The problem is, the more contempt you express for your partners' behavior, the stronger will be their resistance to change. They'll hang on to their dysfunctional behavior for dear life, insisting, "I am *not* a bad person, and you do *not* have the right to criticize me so harshly!"

If you communicate contempt, your partner will respond defensively. If you offer love and acceptance, your partner will want to please you in return. This basic psychology applies to parent/child relationships, marriages, supervisor/employee relationships, and of course, business partner relationships.

Make the shift to communicating tolerance rather than indignation (you don't have to endorse behavior to accept that it's a reality). Work at keeping the good will alive in your relationship. Good will encourages self-motivated change, which is much more effective than change imposed by others. Point out when your partner does something right rather than focusing on what he or she is doing wrong, and you will see your partner do something right more often!

I can hear you objecting: "But you haven't met my partner. There is no way I'll accept what he's doing!" Unless what he or she is doing is bad enough for you to leave the partnership, your chances of changing the behavior become greatly improved by tempering your judgments and making your partner feel respected.

Trigger Three: A Partner Is Unhappy Being Self-Employed

You've heard about the "kick the dog" syndrome, when a disgruntled employee comes home and takes out his or her workplace frustrations on the family dog. Some partner-related conflict is triggered by circumstances that have nothing to do with the partner relationship itself; it is symptomatic of an unhappy partner's displacing resentment onto the partner relationship.

I joined Erin's small computer software company after I was forced into early retirement from my position as vice president of a large bank. It was a rough adjustment from driving the company car and being responsible for hundreds of employees to sharing one tiny office with Erin and making my own cup of coffee. I took out most of my resentment on Erin. I yelled at her when the Internet service went down and I couldn't reach anyone useful in customer service. I expected her to answer the phone like she was my secretary. It wasn't her fault; I just needed some time to get off my high horse. I don't know why she put up with me, but thank God she did, because now we are an effective team.

Safeguards and Solutions:

The first safeguard to this conflict—understanding your motivations for partnership and being clear about what you want the partnership to offer you—is found in Chapter 2. If you partner for the wrong reasons (perhaps early retirement leaves your ego wrecked and your bank account empty, so you rush into partnership), the chances become higher of running into this kind of conflict. In the scenario above, the gentleman just needed some time to make the transition, and then the partnership worked fine. In this case, you might need to give your partners grace while they make a difficult adjustment or cope with personal trouble in their lives. The fact is, you are partnered with a person who must handle a host of personal and family issues that will affect his or her working life. It is unrealistic to think that your partner can erect a solid wall around work that will keep out such distractions. To the best of your ability, choose compassion over anger, and know that someday the shoe may be on the other foot. When your partners are *truly* out of line, gently suggest that they are taking out on you a frustration that belongs elsewhere and request that they find another way to deal with it.

Trigger Four: Arguing About Past Versions of Reality

Partners can spend a great deal of time and energy going into the past, describing their version of what happened, what was said, or what was promised, and then arguing about whose version of reality is correct. Both partners are absolutely convinced of their points of view and are bent on convincing the other that his or her memory of that same conversation or event is inaccurate.

Lauren and Holly own a jewelry store. Custom jewelry must be ordered at least one month ahead of delivery. Lauren and Holly just discovered that neither of them placed an order for a pear-shaped emerald necessary for a customer order. The customer has just called and said he will be in the next day to pick it up.

Lauren: We don't have the emerald. You forgot to call and order it.

Holly: I didn't forget; you said you would call because I had to leave early the day that customer was in.

Lauren: I don't remember ever telling you that I would call. That's your job.

Holly: What are you talking about? I remember, as if it were yesterday, you telling me you would take care of it.

"Memory matching is a game that produces no winners," warn marriage counselors Howard Markman and Scott Stanley. Lauren and Holly will never settle this argument if they continue along these lines. Most people have a difficult time letting go of their convictions.

Safeguards and Solutions:

Here's another way that dialogue between Lauren and Holly could have gone:

Lauren: We don't have the emerald. You forgot to call and order it!

Holly: I didn't forget; you said you would call because I had to leave early the day that customer was in.

Lauren: I think I would remember if I said I would call. Maybe you are right; I could have forgotten. Look, regardless of who forgot to call, we don't have the emerald and the customer is going to be here tomorrow. What are we going to do now?

Holly: I will call our supplier right now and see if I can have an emerald rushed to us today. From now on, why don't we meet for a few minutes every morning before the store opens, and make sure we called in all the orders from the day before?

Lauren: Sounds good. You and I don't need this kind of stress.

—✧—

With this approach, the partners team up to solve the problem rather than fight each other. Lauren shifted the direction of the dialogue by acknowledging that Holly's point of view *could* be accurate, even if it's not what she believes. Such an admission doesn't mean that Lauren's perceptions are wrong—she is only admitting that it is possible. By doing so, Holly doesn't get angry, and they are able to brainstorm a solution to this current problem and how to prevent future occurrences.

Don't persist in arguments about what one of you said in the past—it will get you nowhere. If you find yourself arguing about whose memory of the past is accurate, stop yourself; concede that both of you see the same event differently and that you will get nowhere arguing about it. (This hazard is minimized when there are more than two people involved in the discussion, although several people can still have different perceptions of the same reality.)

When you are stuck in an argument about the past, shift the focus into the future—what will you do going forward, regardless of what happened in the past, and how can you avoid this kind of misunderstanding again?

Write down your agreements; don't rely on subjective memory. When you are making verbal agreements, repeat for the other what your understanding is so there is no confusion.

Trigger Five: Rushing Into Problem Solving

Most partners try to prematurely solve problems before they have developed a thorough, mutual understanding of the issues at hand. Therefore, they don't produce lasting solutions or specifics about how such plans will be implemented. If they don't deal with underlying issues in a constructive way, they will constantly be dealing with crises related to the problem.

Partners often try to solve problems at inopportune times, such as when some event triggers the discussion or argument, or when something is on your mind at a time that isn't good for your partner. Witness the following example:

> It was an awful day. I got a flat tire on the way to work and had to climb under my car, in 80-degree weather, in my best suit. The first thing I hear when I get to the office is a message on the machine from a vendor telling me that one of our parts is back-ordered for two weeks. That was followed by a phone call from one of my biggest clients threatening to move his account if we don't move up our delivery schedule. Just when I'm worrying how to keep this client happy, my partner comes out of his office and tells me he wants me to sign off on a new piece of capital equipment, to the tune of $10,000. And of course, he needed my approval right that minute. I couldn't even think straight. I told my partner I needed to take a walk, and it would have to wait a few hours.

Safeguards and Solutions:

Schedule regular partner meetings to air concerns and give problem-solving the time it requires. If possible, postpone emotional issues until the partner meeting. Establish daily or weekly meetings, and stick to them no matter how busy you become. Don't rush decisions that need ample discussion or consideration. Partners who thrive don't make resolutions on the fly, whenever the business drives them. They drive the business. They are mindful of the need to communicate when each partner can be present for the discussion.

Before you register a complaint with your partner, check in to see what kind of mood he or she is in, how receptive he or she might be to hearing what you have to say, and if this is a good time to discuss a concern. If your partner says "Not now!"

don't push the issue. Ask your partner to commit to a time to discuss your concern that would be better for him or her.

Trigger Six: Varying Opinions of Work Output

We tend to value our own contributions, skills, and efforts more than our partners'. When the business is in startup mode, money is scarce, or the company is in trouble, we may blame our partners for not working hard enough. When the company is thriving and cash is flowing in, partners will frequently start grumbling about who worked harder to bring the company to success. One of the most frequent fights between partners relates to the perception that one partner is working less than the other but is still receiving the same salary or equity. Disgruntled partners will start watching each other, putting each other on a time clock of sorts, and comparing their work schedules. This was a common complaint I heard:

Andy worked as hard as me when we first joined up to launch our network marketing business. Three years later the residual income topped $10,000 a month for each of us. Now Andy seems to think he is always on vacation. He rarely comes to the office anymore. He's missed the last three partner meetings; he's usually golfing or out on the boat. If he is satisfied with his income, and doesn't want to work any harder to grow the business, I wish he would just tell me and stop pretending that he is still committed to this partnership.

The partner this gentleman is complaining about has a very different perception of the problem:

I don't know what's wrong with Richard these days. He accuses me of not working just because I don't come into the office. Of course I'm working—look at how many people I've brought into our business in the past year. I prefer to build our business by getting out and meeting lots of prospects. Richard would rather sit in an office and talk about our plans. Frankly,

I find meeting with Richard mostly a waste of time. All he does is get on my case for not working hard enough—no wonder I don't ever want to meet with him.

—✧—

Safeguards and Solutions:

Partners need to differentiate between work style clashes and genuine issues of nonperformance. The tendency is to assume nonperformance when in fact it may be, as it was in the previous example, that one of the partners works best late at night, at home, or on the golf course. The key is: Is the partner fulfilling his or her responsibilities to the best of his or her ability? Or is his or her commitment to the company beginning to wane, as evidenced by working less?

If it is a case of nonperformance, the unhappy and overworked partner needs to calmly express his or her concerns without falling into the trap of attack and condemnation. Instead of "Where the hell have you been? What do you think this is, a country club?" try something like "Hey, I need you here. We're depending on you to manage the office while I'm on the road. What's keeping you from being able to do that?"

In the cycle of the business, partners will shine at different times. For example, some visionaries do much better in the beginning than when the product has been created and work has become more routine. Don't expect partners to work at exactly the same speed and with the same passion in all phases of the business. Depending on their personalities, what's going on in their families, their skills and goals, their health, and any number of other variables, they will approach work with varying commitments, hours, and abilities at different periods of the business's development.

No one has a true 50/50 partnership on every given day. The partners who thrive over the years give each other space around work hours and trust each other implicitly. They take a long-term perspective and express this kind of attitude:

> You can't be in business for 10 years and not have personal problems that affect the business. Life isn't that good! Luckily, we both went through family turmoil at different times. There have been periods when I've leaned on Leona, because I wasn't operating at full capacity, and vice versa. We're 50/50 partners; one of us pulls more weight than the other at certain times, but over time it's balanced.

Refer back to Chapter 4. Establish your performance standards, and rather than worrying about number of hours worked, focus on whether each partner is meeting the goals he or she committed to. The real issue is what the partner is contributing to the business, not how many hours he or she is working. Remember, most people gravitate toward entrepreneurship because they want freedom and control. The last thing your partner wants to feel is that he or she is on a time clock that you installed.

Trigger Seven: Invalidating Your Partner

Here are some statements that are sure to cause resentment every time:

- "That's ridiculous."
- "You don't know what you're talking about."
- "I don't care what you say, I'm not changing my mind."
- "That will never work."
- "That's a silly thing to be upset about."

Though you may have a valid objection to your partner's suggestion, communicating it in this manner will only trigger an angry or hurt response.

Safeguards and Solutions:

When you disagree with a suggestion or statement made by your partner, take a moment to catch your breath, remember your appreciation of your complementary differences, and ask questions, rather than reflexively invalidating your partner. Try to understand where your partner is coming from and how he or she reached a conclusion or idea. Give enough time to the discussion to fully explore your concerns about your partner's suggestion. Allow your partner to educate you and to try to sell you his or her idea. If you still disagree, articulate why you feel concerned without attacking your partner for being a loser.

Keep an open mind; you never know when your partner's "ridiculous" idea could lead to something sensational. Remember that because the power of your partnership lies in your complementary differences, occasionally one of you is going to make a suggestion for the business that the other finds absurd. If you thought alike all of the time, you wouldn't need each other.

Louie and Beth owned an independent bookstore. They were losing business to a chain store that opened in a nearby mall and needed to find some creative ways to boost sales. Louie suggested arranging chairs and couches around the store and encouraging customers to relax and read any book they wanted. They would even supply free coffee. Beth thought this was risky and that profits might actually drop even further—she was afraid they would turn into the local library. But she agreed to give it a try. To her surprise, the new setup worked wonders. Beth and Louie boosted sales, and their profits grew by 30 percent over the next six months.

Trigger Eight: Threatening or Belittling Your Partner

During my interviews, I was saddened to discover what I call the "battered partner syndrome." It happens when a nasty, controlling partner gets together with a timid, insecure individual who worships the other partner as a mentor (rather than as an equal partner) and doesn't feel ready to stand on his or her own. The tyrannical partner dominates the relationship by demeaning the other partner and repeatedly threatening to leave the partnership if he or she doesn't get his or her way. Such people know that their partners feel dependent on them, and they take advantage of this vulnerability. The longer this goes on, the lower the self-esteem of the abused partner drops. Ironically, when weak partners finally extricate themselves from these poisonous relationships, they realize after a few years of recovery that they were, in fact, much better businesspersons than their abusive partners ever were.

Safeguards and Solutions:

Refer to Chapter 3 and watch for the warning signs of a dysfunctional partner before you even get together. Get counseling if you feel that your partner is abusive to you in any manner.

Trigger Nine: Unwelcome Advisers

As we will cover in greater detail in Chapter 8, when you partner with an individual, you are often partnering with his or her family as well. One of the most common complaints I heard was from individuals who felt subjected to unwanted and unsolicited advice from their partners' family members. Most frequently, it was a father or a spouse who was intruding:

> Cindy and I started a beauty shop together. Cindy was the perfect partner until she got married! All of a sudden, she couldn't make a single decision without asking her husband. It wasn't long before she started to bring Richie's ideas back to the shop with her. "Richie says we should cut our prices," or "Richie says we should stop giving free introductory manicures to our customers." Richie barely knows anything about the hair-cutting business, and I don't see his name anywhere on the checks we write. We ran this business for six years without him and did just fine. Now I feel like I'm married to Richie too.

Conflict erupts because the partner who is being bombarded with advice feels ganged up on. This partner also resents that problems cannot be effectively handled at the office, when and where they need to be handled, because one of the partners keeps needing to check with his or her spouse. This tendency increases when relatives and spouses are tapped for investor money or provide personal funds that allow the partner to keep afloat while the business is getting off the ground. Then the partner feels even more obliged to include these outsiders in the company decision-making process, and critiques more closely the performance of his or her partners.

Safeguards and Solutions:

If a partner's parent or spouse will be involved in the business in an active way, or as an investor, the extent of that person's involvement in day-to-day operations should be agreed to by all partners and systematized in some manner. If the way you make major decisions is to converse with your family, keep that to yourself. When you express your opinion, although it might have been influenced by your advisers, express it as your point of view. See Chapter 8 for further detail.

Trigger 10: The Partnership Connection Is Threatened by Alliances

When more than two people partner, alliances might be formed between partners that set up a cliquish, grade school atmosphere. If two partners are in conflict, sides are drawn and each partner tries to find allies in and support from the other partners. Partners express feeling left out, being jealous of a closer relationship between other partners, or feeling resentful of being coerced to make decisions they don't agree with because "majority rules."

In the beginning it was fine with me that Anne and Heather did most of the traveling while I stayed behind and watched the store. Then Anne and Heather became close friends, sharing inside jokes and family secrets, and socializing together after work. They started acting like I wasn't even part of the business. They would neglect to consult me on business decisions, and when I disagreed with one of them, the other always came to the defense of the partner I disagreed with. When I saw them giggling together in the store, it just made me sick. It reminded me of grade school. I felt left out, but I didn't know how to complain without sounding like a baby.

Safeguards and Solutions:

This partner needs to express her feelings to her partners, even though she is concerned that it will make her appear overly sensitive. If she doesn't, she will likely leave the partnership or explode in an unproductive way on some day that puts her over the edge. Her partners may be entirely unaware of the impact their friendship is having on their third partner. She needs to be careful to communicate her complaint in "I" terms. If she expresses her feelings about being left out of the loop and asks for a way to have a closer relationship with her partners, her partners might respond compassionately—if she doesn't attack them for having their valued friendship. She might suggest that they include her in more meetings, or it might help to alter their roles slightly so that they all have more access to each other and the customers.

Beware if you find yourself grumbling about one partner to another. Such gossiping is extremely divisive and destructive to a partnership. Take your concern directly to the person you are upset with, either privately or at a business meeting, instead of spreading your unhappiness around the firm. If you and your partners are dissatisfied with the performance of one of your partners, seek professional help for exploring how to remove that partner from the business—if that's the direction you and your partners need to take (see Chapter 9).

Trigger 11: Making Significant Decisions Without Considering Your Partner

Chapter 4 discussed the importance of clarifying your authority and how decisions will be made. You and your partner may agree to certain unilateral responsibility, but some major decisions should be made as a team. When one or more partners don't follow expectations and make major decisions without checking with their partners first, it can incite a near riot.

Randy and Mike own a limousine service. Mike discovered when he returned from vacation that Randy had signed an agreement to lease four additional limos that weren't planned or budgeted for.

Mike: You leased these limos without asking me. We're partners, or did you forget?

Randy: You were gone for a week and this deal couldn't wait. We got a great price.

Mike: But we don't need four new limos right now. That's a heck of a lot of money to spend for something we don't really need.

Randy: We both agreed that we were going to retire the four oldest limos by the end of the year. I just accelerated the time a bit. I thought you would have agreed or I wouldn't have gone forward. Why don't you trust me?

Mike: I do trust you, but I don't feel good about such a major expenditure without being involved in the process. Next time, check in with me first, okay?

Safeguards and Solutions:

The first step is to ensure that each partner is aware of, and committed to, the expectations established around decision making. When partners go outside those boundaries, it is either because they didn't understand what the rules were, they are blatantly rebelling against the restriction, or, as in the previous example, they honestly believe that making an exception to the rule is in the best interests of the company.

Recognize the difference between positive and malicious intent. If your partners meant well but did something that makes you uncomfortable, calmly let them know your concern and talk through how to handle something like this in the future. Your partners will feel angry, hurt, and unappreciated if they did something they thought was fabulous for the company and you only spotlight the fact that you weren't included. However, your partners need to understand the impact of leaving you out of such decisions.

If you notice your partners regularly ignoring the boundaries you've established for decision making and purchasing, it's either time to renegotiate your understandings or to find new partners. Such actions indicate a lack of respect and regard for your partnership. Some entrepreneurs won't stand for anything that restricts their sense of freedom and control, and they are poor candidates for partnership.

Give each partner the authority to act as independently as possible. The more autonomy you give each partner, the less likely he or she will be to rebel against constraint or to make vital decisions without you.

Trigger 12: Personal Habits That Interfere With Work Performance

Like your spouse, your partners will have personal habits that irritate you. Perhaps you don't like the way they snap their gum, or smoke cigars, or arrive 15 minutes late for every meeting. Minor irritations can escalate into major roadblocks when they begin to interfere with company performance. When a partner's personal habits are destructive to the partnership, they must be addressed:

> When Eric and I first started our CPA practice, I never suspected he had a drinking problem. I didn't get my first hint until our clients started to mention his excessive drinking while lunching with them. I didn't want to believe it, so when I finally questioned him about it and he denied it, I gave him the benefit of the doubt. I had to break my denial when he didn't show up at an important client meeting. I called to ask him why and he admitted he had been out all night and he wasn't up to attending. I told him that he needed to get help

with his drinking problem if he wanted to stay in our partnership. When I gave him the ultimatum, it was the incentive he needed to get to AA. Five years later, my partner is still sober and we've built a well-respected practice together. He thanks me now for forcing him to quit drinking.

✧

Safeguards and Solutions:

Distinguish between irritating and intolerable behavior. You can address irritations in partnership meetings or discussions by making small requests for change:

✧

When you show up late for our meetings, I feel irritated since I'm always on time and I'm wasting time waiting for you. What do we need to do to make it easier for you to get to our meetings on time?

✧

My partner and I have a no-smoking policy in our office, even though he's a smoker. He understands that I won't work around secondhand smoke.

✧

Sometimes you will have to learn to live with the behavior that irritates you, or adjust your conduct or attitude to make it more tolerable. You and your partners could waste many precious hours trying to change nuisance behaviors in the other instead of focusing on the business at hand.

✧

My partner has this habit of cracking gum all day that used to drive me batty. He's trying not to smoke at the office, so I didn't want to ask him not to chew gum. I turned on the radio in the office so I wouldn't hear it, and it wasn't such a big deal anymore.

✧

These kinds of occurrences are different from the alcoholism scenario, when a partner's personal habits severely impact his or her ability to function. Sometimes, however, behavior crosses the line from an annoying personal habit to insupportable behavior in the eyes of the other partner.

This partner made a difficult decision:

—⟡—

My partner started cheating on her husband with one of our customers. At first she tried to hide it from me, although I suspected. Then one night I caught them together in the office when I returned after dinner to get some work done. I was repulsed, not only by seeing my partner naked with a customer, but by the idea of partnering with someone so lacking in personal ethics. I talked with my husband about it. Although she and I had a successful business, my husband and I decided that as long as she continued this affair, we didn't want to be associated with her. I gave her a choice; she chose him over me, and we ended our partnership.

He dumped her four months after our partnership ended—but I wouldn't consider taking her back.

—⟡—

When an irritating personal habit crosses the line to destructive behavior, professional counseling may be necessary to remedy the problem. It can be very awkward to approach your partner with your concerns on such personal matters. But if it's seriously affecting your business, you have to. Approach your partner with compassion, rather than blame or judgment. If your partner denies the problem and refuses to seek help or correct the situation, you may have no choice but to end the partnership.

Trigger 13: Failing to Publicly Acknowledge Your Partner's Contribution

When meeting prospects, customers, and trade associates, partners should take great care to present their business as a partnership. I interviewed two men who came close to ending their partnership over this issue. Paul joined Greg's company a year after Greg had started it, but they agreed to be equal partners. The problem was, Greg regularly said "my business" when meeting with clients, which really got under Paul's skin:

> My partner, Paul, complained to me that I always referred to our business as "my" business and he didn't like it. He got so mad at me once following a client meeting, he threatened to leave the partnership over it. I never even realized I was doing it. It's an old habit left over from the days when I ran the business myself. Once I paid attention to his complaint, I learned to bring him into the conversation and it became second nature.

Partnerships are particularly vulnerable to this conflict if one of the partners is the "inside person" and the others are out on the road representing the company. The most strain is caused if the partner who is the media representative for the company, when receiving acclaim on radio or television, doesn't acknowledge the contribution of other partners to the product receiving recognition.

Safeguards and Solutions:

Watch your language when speaking about the business, and include your partners in the discussion, even if they aren't there, whenever possible. Although your ego may resist, your clients and colleagues will likely view your enterprise as stronger when you can provide your partners' skills and knowledge as well as your own. (Why else do so many entrepreneurs call themselves "Smith and Associates" when it's really only Smith doing all the work?)

Sometimes, as with the situation between Paul and Greg, the habit of speaking in "I" terms instead of "we" terms is not intentional. If it is, you'll need to confront your partners and request that they work on making the change. If they don't, it's indicative of the way they feel about your partnership, and you'll need to decide how big a deal that is to you. For Paul, it was a big enough deal to get out of the partnership. Others might feel this way about it:

⟡

My partner's goal is to be president of a large corporation. His ego is the size of Texas, and he seldom acknowledges my contribution to the company. You'd think he ran this business by himself, but there are 10 of us working together. It used to really bug me, but now I feel kind of sorry for the fellow. He'll never be satisfied with what we're doing, or feel important enough. Recognition for my contribution would be nice, but I don't need it to be happy.

⟡

Trigger 14: Geographic Distance Forces Artificial Intensity

Modern technology has spawned partnerships between individuals who rarely see each other in person. Their business is conducted via fax, e-mail, voice mail, and phone. When the partners do get together, they often schedule marathon meetings—over several days, a weekend, or even a week at a time.

This kind of meeting structure can be extremely draining. The partners work nonstop with little sleep, trying to cram in as much as possible in the short time they have together. The tensions build and they start getting on each other's nerves. As one partner said to me, "We accomplished a lot but we destroyed our relationships."

Safeguards and Solutions:

⟡

My partners and I get together for one three-day weekend a month for business planning, because we live in different parts of the country. We used to spend the entire weekend doing more work than is humanly possible and hating each other by Sunday night. We got a lot accomplished but we all dreaded these weekends. Once we decided to bring our wives to the meeting and have a little fun. We spent the first night relaxing and talking. I've partnered with these guys for two years and I realized I hardly knew anything about their lives. We spent Saturday catching up on business while the wives went shopping. Saturday night we went out on the town. On

> Sunday we only worked until the middle of the afternoon and left early to get back home at a reasonable time. We got less work done, but we had more fun and now we're all looking forward to the next business weekend.

These partners discovered the secret for safeguarding their relationship against the pressure of marathon meetings. Plan to spend at least a portion of your time together just relaxing and getting to know each other, as you don't have that opportunity to do so during your regular workweek. If appropriate, include your significant others. You can structure demanding work sessions, but don't look at the entire time you reserve to meet as dedicated to accomplishing business tasks. Or, look at it another way: One of your business tasks as a partnership is to strengthen your relationship with your partners. Give your relationship as much priority as the tasks at hand. Although you may get "less" done, your partnership is more likely to endure.

Trigger 15: Avoiding Problems Until You're Ready to Explode

Just as some people do in marriage, business partners will often avoid dealing with a problem for as long as they can. Worried about rejection, frightened of a hostile reaction, unskilled at confronting others, they stick their heads in the sand and hope the problem will go away. Some resentments will pass if you just wait long enough and work on developing greater acceptance. But often a buried resentment becomes a crisis when it is ignored too long. Then, when the partner raises the concern, he or she does so with rage and pent-up hurt and frustration.

> My mother and I joined up to sell a network marketing product—a skin-care line—that we both had great results with. I didn't think Mom and I would be able to work together in a business but it's actually been really cool. The only problem was, we were always late for opportunity meetings because we rode together; there was always one last thing Mom

had to do before we left the house. She's my mother and I didn't know how to tell her to hurry up.

One day, I got so fed up with waiting for her, I drove off to the meeting without her. Mom was so hurt and angry, she didn't even talk to me at the gathering. I felt really bad about offending her, but I was sick of being late. We talked after the meeting and agreed to drive in separate cars. That way, she could take her time and I could be punctual.

Safeguards and Solutions:

The obvious safeguard to this problem is to bring up complaints before they build to an intolerable level. For this to work, all partners must commit to open communication and dedicate themselves to keeping the partner relationship healthy and free of buried resentments. Essentially, you have to be more committed to the health of your partnership than to protecting your own comfort zone when handling conflict. Equally important to the success of this commitment, each partner must learn to handle *receiving* criticism without reacting in a hostile manner that discourages others from registering a future complaint.

If you deliver a complaint to your partner in the middle of an angry outburst, you are unlikely to encourage a receptive response. If you and your partner reach an explosive level, at least one of you needs to have the maturity and self-control to stop for a moment and become centered and calm before reacting hysterically. Even when you are enraged, you can force yourself to take a deep breath, tell your partner you need to leave the room, and say that you will be back to discuss the problem when you are calmer. (If you do leave, make sure you agree with your partner to discuss the issue within a few days, so the problem doesn't get buried.) When you resume the discussion, let your partner know that the reason you are so angry is because this resentment has been building for a long time but you've been hesitant to bring it up.

Take a look at your conflict resolution style. If you are the avoidant type, you will need to watch for your tendency to avert conflict at the price of effective communication with your partner. Schedule regular partner meetings where at least a part of the agenda is devoted to discussing relationship concerns, or hire a coach or mediator to help you and your partner keep communication lines open.

Trigger 16: Bossing Around Your Partner

An egotistical director, with an intense need for control and strong opinions about the way things should be done, partnered with a more timid, laid-back thinker type is a team ripe for conflict. The aggressive partner might treat the timid partner like an employee—or worse, a slave—caught up in the need to have things done "right" and according to his or her schedule. The quieter partner may swallow feelings of resentment and then either explode with hostility, which will catch the director by surprise, or leave the partnership.

Safeguards and Solutions:

Chapter 6 discusses in detail the Platinum Rule, which illustrates how your predominant personality style impacts communication. If you are opposites, you'll both need to adjust your natural styles to reduce conflict. For example, director types must learn to lighten up and be less controlling, while thinker types must learn to assert themselves. It will help a great deal to understand where your partners are coming from and to look for positive intentions behind their sometimes ineffective approaches.

Directors need to watch their language. They should use "Please," "Could you," "Would you like to," and "I'd like your opinion on" instead of "Why didn't you," "I need this by," "You have to," and "I've decided."

The key is to become conscious of your own behavior, rather than running on automatic. When you want to boss your partner around, you can learn not to act on that impulse.

Trigger 17: Disagreeing About How to Handle a Client or Customer

My partner wanted to travel with her husband whenever he went away on business trips. She would be out of the office for a few weeks at a time, several times a year. We were in a service business where superior customer service was critical. I believed in staying in close contact with our customers. My partner was never around to fulfill that commitment. If a problem came up with one of her customers, I'd have to handle it when she wasn't there. Her attitude was: I'm bringing in some big business to this company (and she was), so you and the customers will have to learn to live with this minor inconvenience. She and I had a fundamental difference in the way we viewed the customer. She saw the customer as a sale, and I saw the customer as an ongoing relationship.

Safeguards and Solutions:

You can reduce the likelihood of this kind of conflict by dedicating some time to evaluating your partners before joining with them in your enterprise. Refer to Chapter 3 for ways to ensure that you select a partner who feels the same way about a customer, for example, as you do. When I spoke with partners who reported an excellent working relationship, they invariably stated, "We have the same values and commitment to the customer."

Let's say that you and your partner share fundamental values but still differ at a particular moment over how to handle a customer or client matter. If you are locked in your positions, search for your mutual interests, as recommended by Fisher and Ury in *Getting to Yes.* Behind your differing positions, if you examine them closely enough, is an interest you share. If you can articulate what that is, then you can negotiate a compromise solution that will please both of you.

For example, Jerry and Frances own a chain of Midwest floral shops. Jerry is the controller and operations manager. Frances is the chief floral designer and is in charge of customer service. Their partnership is disintegrating under the strain of an ongoing argument that is rarely resolved to their satisfaction:

Jerry: We've got to watch the bottom line. We can't keep giving our customers such extravagant arrangements. When the designer in you takes over, you strip away our margin.

Frances: What differentiates us from our competitors is that we go the extra mile. If we do it your way, we'll lose our competitive edge and the profits will disappear completely.

What are the mutual interests behind these two opposing positions? (Remember to consider their *partnership* interests, as well as the business.)

The following is a list of some of their possible mutual interests:

- Increase profits.
- Please customers.
- Have a satisfying partner relationship.
- Grow the business.
- Distinguish themselves as unique in the flower business.

When Jerry and Frances recognize their mutual interests, they can search for a solution that would meet these interests, rather than arguing about whose position is right. Perhaps they can:

- Raise prices.
- Buy materials at a deeper discount.
- Develop a wider range of floral selections, allowing Frances to offer her elaborate arrangements for a higher price.

- Create additional products, other than flowers, to bring in additional revenue.

This kind of brainstorming will only occur if the partners let go of fighting over their positions and look for what they share in common. It takes practice to solve business problems in this way, but after achieving positive outcomes you'll tend to use this approach more often.

Trigger 18: Threatening to Leave the Partnership Whenever There Is a Disagreement

My husband, Stephen, and I wrote our marriage vows. One of our vows was, "We will work to resolve any conflicts arising between us without threatening the foundation of our marriage." What we meant by that was: We expected that conflict would arise between us. We declared a dedication to working out our differences and to not calling into question our relationship every time we were angry with each other. We understood that we needed this commitment in place to encourage ourselves to stick it out when we were having rough times. Sometimes in partnerships, one or more partners develop a habit of running away from resolving emotionally charged conflict by simply threatening to leave if they don't get their way, or by expressing hopelessness about the relationship whenever conflict arises. For example:

> I don't know how we ever thought we could work together. We're as different as night and day. I didn't realize that working with you was going to be so much hard work. It seems like we'd each be better off breaking off this partnership and finding someone more suitable.

If that kind of statement arises after weeks and months of trying to resolve your differences, it might be entirely appropriate. But if a partner talks like this every time an argument erupts, the partnership won't progress very far.

Safeguards and Solutions:

Threatening to end your working relationship every time you and your partner argue creates an unsafe atmosphere for working out conflict. Issues get buried underground and then explode in a damaging manner. Partners become hopeless and pessimistic about resolving their problems. Taking a bully approach to your partner ("Do it this way or I'm leaving") or the self-centered approach ("If I get you to change and do it my way, I don't have to make any changes myself"), might give you what you want in the short term, but it will eventually destroy your partnership. Save your threats for those moments when you feel so strongly about what you are insisting on that you *are* willing to dissolve the partnership if your concern isn't resolved to your satisfaction. Even if you are overcome with frustration at times, try to avoid using the threat of exiting as a weapon for manipulating your partner. You may win the battle, but you'll lose the war.

Trigger 19: Losing Your Temper and Saying Something You Regret Later

I interviewed two partners who admitted to being hot-headed Italians with fast tempers and a shared inclination to fly off the handle when one did something that the other didn't like. Over time, they developed a communication system that circumvented their natural tendencies to say something they would regret later:

> My partner and I came up with an agreement. If he did something that really ticked me off, I would say, "I have a concern." And vice versa. When one of us said that phrase, the other would immediately respond, "What are you concerned about?" We would listen, without getting defensive, and repeat back what we heard. Then we'd talk it out until it was resolved. The "I have a concern" phrase alerted us that we had a problem that needed immediate attention—it was a red flag that one of us was really upset and the issue needed immediate

resolution. Sometimes it took enormous self-control to say "I have a concern" instead of "You stupid idiot, why didn't you...?!" But using that phrase started out our discussion calmly, on the right foot.

—⟡—

Safeguards and Solutions:

Any partner who has a tendency to flare up in anger needs to master strategies for keeping his or her temper under control and for channeling his or her concerns to other partners in a productive way. The tendency can be to put the responsibility on the "at-fault" partner ("If only he wouldn't do X, then I wouldn't have a reason to lose my temper"). You will have disagreements with any partner during the course of your partnership—that is a given. How you respond to those disagreements is entirely within your control.

Often, partners with hot tempers have to develop the self-discipline to put a pause into their response, whether by walking out of the room until they calm down or by asking for the conversation to be postponed until they have their reactions in check. Watch your language with your partner. If you wouldn't talk that way to your spouse or your mother, it's a good sign that your temper isn't under control.

Trigger 20: Failure to Take Responsibility for Your Own Actions

Once you make up your mind that your partners are at fault, you will gather evidence that supports your position, making it difficult to see any evidence to the contrary. You may take the focus off how you are contributing to the problem and blame your partners for all that ails you or the company. It's called scapegoating, and every partner does it from time to time. It's painful to look at a mirror and see your own faults. It's much easier to blame someone else; our business partners are natural prey.

Let's say that your perceptions are accurate and your partner *is* seriously skill-deficient or culpable in a particular circumstance. You are entitled to your angry feelings, and you might be right. However, Susan Page, author of the inspiring book *How One of You Can Bring the Two of You Together,* notes that "The booby prize of life is being right."

According to Page, the problem with being right is that's all you get. You get to be right. You don't get to solve the problem. You don't get to be closer to your partner. You don't get to reduce the conflict in your relationship. You don't get to stop feeling angry. Being right is a dead end. Being right makes you helpless because the "right" view is that the problem is your partner's fault. If the only solution to a problem is that your partner has to change, you are in a weak position, because there's nothing you can do to remedy the situation except convince your partner to change.

Safeguards and Solutions:

Shifting the focus back on yourself, and looking for your responsibility in any partner conflict, will be difficult, but you can learn to do it. Your role is *always* there for you to examine, whatever the issue. Remember the serenity prayer—you can't always control your partners' actions, but you can control your own. The quickest way to resolve an argument is to make a sincere apology for your own wrongdoing, even if you think your partner has also done wrong. The fastest way to get your partner to admit to problems is to be willing to acknowledge your own.

Practice an interior monologue to bring you back on track when arguing with your partner. Here are some useful statements that can help:

- "I value my partner too much to be having this kind of fight. It's just not worth getting this upset."
- "I know my partner has positive intentions."
- "I'm sure we can figure this one out together."

- "If I calm down, I can look at my part of the problem and do something about it."
- "I trust my partner to work this out with me."

The best solution to this conflict trigger is to drop the need to be right. The more you realize what an empty victory being right is, the easier it will be to let go of a stubborn position.

The common sources of conflict we've just explored apply to any business partnership, close friendship, or marriage. But some unique conflict issues arise between friends in business together and families in partnership together.

Resolving Conflict With Friends

> We are both stubborn, volatile, hot-tempered, New York City personalities. We are great friends, but working together was like mixing fire and gasoline.

Friends who go into business together fall into some common traps if they aren't careful. They often avoid confronting issues and working out conflict with their partners because they are uncomfortable bringing their concerns out in the open and they fear jeopardizing their friendship. (The opposite can also be true; friends with a long history of a close friendship may be so secure about their relationship that they can talk to each other about anything.) Money issues in particular are the most awkward for friends to discuss with each other.

A partner in business with a friend may agree to do something out of friendship that isn't really something he or she feels comfortable doing. Such people hesitate to disagree with their friends, electing to withhold their feelings rather than create conflict.

A partnership between friends that isn't working may continue longer than other nonfunctional partnerships do because the parties involved are reluctant to admit that it isn't working and fear the end of the friendship when the partnership dissolves. (I interviewed many partners who most regretted the loss of a friendship when their partnerships went sour.)

Partners who start out as friends often have unrealistic expectations of how their friendships will translate into working together. Just because they have been drinking buddies, or raised their kids together, does not automatically mean they will have a viable business relationship. They will be working together in an entirely different setting, solving problems together, sharing power and control, and negotiating such sensitive issues as money and workload. Even the closest friends may clash in a business environment.

Jamie and Lisa were neighbors and best friends for years. When they discovered a new vitamin product that had great results for both of them, Lisa suggested to Jamie that they start selling the product to their friends and neighbors. Jamie readily agreed, and soon they had a successful business going. It was not long before trouble arose between them.

During their years of friendship, Lisa had noticed that Jamie didn't like to spend money. This had never been a problem for Lisa until Jamie balked at buying cassette tapes to promote the business and questioned every dollar spent on promoting the business. Jamie kept insisting they could sell plenty of products just through word of mouth, at no cost to them. That was the beauty of a network marketing business, she argued. Lisa maintained that friends and neighbors could buy only so much product and they would have to find a new market before they ran out of friends to sell to. She wanted to grow the business more aggressively than Jamie did and was willing to spend money to accomplish that goal.

Jamie and Lisa couldn't reach an agreement. In the end, they decided to split up and each work with her own downline, rather than let the joint venture ruin their friendship.

Friends in partnership together who have the easiest time handling conflict share the following characteristics:

- They are equal partners in their contributions, skills, abilities, and investments.
- They are each comfortable telling the other their true feelings.
- They agree to put the friendship first and to not allow the business to jeopardize their relationship.
- They know how to wear two different hats: friend and business partner.
- They have compatible work styles and personal values.
- They each genuinely want the best for their friend and partner.

Unique Challenges of Family Partnerships

> Being in partnership with my son is the greatest thing in the world. When you flip the switch and appreciate your son for his goodness and talents, and stop telling him where to go and how to be, you get a friend.
>
> —George Wood

> When you grow up as a kid admiring your dad and hoping you can become like him, and then you become his peer, you've reached a mountaintop.
>
> —Tom Wood

In my research, I discovered many examples of family partnerships that work. (For plenty of examples of husband/wife partnerships that work, see *Honey, I Want to Start My Own Business: A Planning Guide for Couples.*) Some of these family partnerships are not merely working but are exceptional. The love and respect between father and son, mother and daughter, or brothers and sisters is evident to a greater degree than is common with a family of origin. This achievement didn't come easily for some of these partnerships, but as they worked out their conflicts and climbed out of the limiting roles of "son" or "father," they developed close, productive partnerships and friendships. Below are direct quotes from some of my interviews, as individuals shared with me their secrets to preventing or handling conflict in a family partnership:

> I'm in partnership with my dad. The way my dad treats me as his business partner is amazing. He knows that I idealize his intelligence, wisdom, and experience. He knows that if he says, "That's a dumb idea," I respect him so much for his business acumen, it would hit me hard. So he lets me figure things out for myself, and just directs me. I've made mistakes that have cost him money, but my dad has created a work environment where I have permission to learn.

> We use a technique in all of our staff meetings—the debrief. At the beginning of every meeting, each person in the meeting has to do a mental and physical check and report in: "I'm preoccupied," "I didn't sleep well," "I'm concerned about my daughter's graduation," and so on. It gets rid of stuff you don't know about but keeps bubbling up. The person who speaks has the floor as long as he or she wants, and there are no judgments or conversations about whatever is shared.

> I see my role as parent to help my kids grow and gain more freedom. I focus more on mentoring, and encouraging my daughters to make decisions, than holding on to control. My job is to be their safety net and sounding board.

> When I call my adult son and business partner, but I just want to talk to my grandchildren, I'll say, "This is Grandma. Let me talk to the kids." If I'm calling with my business partner hat on, I'll say, "This is Evelyn. I'm calling about business."

I swapped roles with my son. I've always been the promoter—the "you can make it happen" kind of person. We entered a contest for our network marketing company and I was exhausted toward the final deadline. One day I told my son: "That's it, I'm giving up." He said: "You can't give up." Here's my son, my partner, telling me not to let him down. So with my tail between my legs, I found a way to do it. I used to be the guy who pushed him to be the best he could be. Now I wasn't being Dad, I was being a partner.

When my wife says to me, "Is someone going to take out the garbage?" I can hear, "Hey, schmuck—you're the one who is supposed to take out the garbage; why didn't you?" Similarly I learned that my father and business partner wasn't saying "Schmuck—you didn't take out the garbage" when he asked me to do something. He was saying "Maybe you should consider...." I learned not to hear everything coming from him as a criticism.

I'm in partnership with my 22-year-old son, who lives with me. He'll get enthused about his social life and stay out until 2 a.m. I would get onto him for staying out so late, because the next day he'd be unproductive. He thought I was being a nagging mother. Finally I told him, "This isn't your mom talking, this is your business partner. You aren't functioning the way I need you to be." Then he'd listen.

When my mom critiques my work, I welcome it as feedback and I always appreciate it. If she criticized the way I raise my kids, it would be a different story. So she's careful to keep her criticisms to work only.

At one point I called my father and told him not to call every day and ask about orders. It made me feel like I was answering to him. He thought he was being a nice guy and caring, but I felt like I was being harassed by an investor.

My mom and I have business meetings in a restaurant, so we are in a public environment. We put on the partnership mask, and then when the meeting is over, we put the family mask back on. When it comes to business, my mom treats me like an adult and an equal partner. But when some guy has broken my heart and I need a shoulder to cry on, she's right there as my mom.

I worked in business with my dad and two brothers. We had the "kitchen table" agreement. If we were screaming at each other in the business, Friday night when our families would go out to dinner together, the fight ended at the restaurant door.

When we're working together, I call my dad by his name, Jim, and he calls me by my name, John. We never call each other "Dad" or "Son" at the office.

There are hundreds of consulting firms in the country that offer excellent resources and assistance to members of family businesses. If you are struggling in your relationship, I encourage you to seek such counsel. See the Recommended Resources section in the back of this book.

Honoring Personal Boundaries

Given the intimacy of a partner relationship, expectations around personal boundaries need to be spelled out, especially in opposite sex partnerships, or conflict will erupt. There are no established rules here, as I discovered in my interviews. I met male and female partners who were married to other people and yet shared a hotel room when traveling to save money (with the blessing of incredibly trusting spouses). I spoke with partners who had evolved from a romantic sexual relationship to "just friends and business partners." I also got to know some business partners who fell in love with each other after working together for a period of time. I even met a business partner who fell in love with, and married, his business partner's spouse (after their business partnership split up and both partners divorced).

The secret to success is making expectations related to personal space and boundaries explicit and mutual. Perhaps you are a touchy-feely kind of person. Touching your business partner on the shoulder is not intended as a sexual expression, but one of affection. You will need to find out if your affectionate touch toward your business partner is welcome or offensive.

Maybe you call everyone "Hon" or "Sweetie," but your business partner—or your partner's spouse—doesn't appreciate it when you refer to him or her that way. Are you a private person who prefers to keep all details about your personal life under close guard, or are you apt to confide regularly in your partner about the fights in your marriage, your last date from hell, or the troubles you are having with your sister? Just because you regard your business partner as a friend or confidant doesn't mean your partner desires the same relationship with you.

I interviewed two individuals who were secretly in love with their business partners. In both cases, they shared this information with me privately, not in the presence of their partners. The affection was not mutual, and their unrequited love proved so painful and awkward that one gentleman admitted to me he had begun refusing to travel with his female partner because it was too difficult for him to control his sexual feelings for her while staying in the same hotel with her. Both of these partnerships are in jeopardy.

The issue of personal boundaries applies to same-sex partnerships as well, though it may not focus on sexual issues. You still need to get comfortable with how much personal sharing you will do, what secrets you will hold within the partnership and withhold from friends or colleagues, whether hugs and affection are appropriate—even how much attention you pay to birthdays and other personal life events. Essentially, no matter what sex your partner is, you are negotiating how much distance you want between your personal life and your working relationship with your partner.

> My partner shocked me by throwing a surprise birthday party for me when I turned 50. She invited all of our clients, and I have to say, for me, it was one of the most humiliating experiences of my working life. My partner, a much younger woman than I, didn't comprehend that I had no desire for everyone I work with to know that I turned 50! I keep my age to myself, especially in my working relationships. I felt really exposed. I never told my partner how I really felt because I didn't want her to think I was ungrateful.

Stepping across the line of your partner's personal boundaries can destroy your partnership. If you don't establish ahead of time what your expectations are, one wrong step can critically injure your partnership. In some partnerships, these issues are never discussed because they quite simply never come up. My caution to you is this: If any questions about personal boundaries do arise, address them in the early stages, before misunderstandings occur. Though these can be the most sensitive and embarrassing conversations you have with your partner, ignoring these issues will only endanger your partnership.

Conclusion: Practice Makes Perfect

If you feel overwhelmed by all the occasions for conflict we've explored, remember this: A minor change in just one partner approach can make a major difference in your relationship.

The tendency of most entrepreneurs is to attribute their partnership problems to some deeply ingrained personality characteristics of their partners', which they insist are fixed and unchangeable. Robert Schwebel, Ph.D., author of *Who's on Top,*

Who's on Bottom, asserts: "Many individuals see themselves as fair, cooperative people trying to deal with unreasonable or mistaken partners."

The single most important step you can take to reduce the conflict in your partnership is to take responsibility for your own actions and to view every problem as an experience you participate in creating. The next most important thing you can do is to acquire patience and a long-term perspective.

> *"With successful discussion of disagreements, partners grow confident of their abilities to tackle whatever is required of them to find mutual happiness. When disagreements lead to chronic fights and discord, partners become pessimistic about their relationship and lose confidence in their ability to make the relationship work for them."*
>
> —Clifford Notarius and Howard Markman,
> *We Can Work It Out*

The term "conflict resolution" suggests that any conflict between partners can be resolved. But one of the fair and prudent approaches to conflict resolution might be the dissolution of your partnership. As I mentioned before, "till death do us part" is not an expectation of any business partnership. Some partnerships deteriorate to the point that ending the partnership is the right thing to do. If you are considering such action, refer to Chapter 9 for an exploration of the issues involved in ending a partnership.

Conflict resolution is not some course you take so that you'll never argue with your partners again. The nature of human relationships is to engage in conflict. The question isn't how you and your partners can develop a conflict-free relationship but rather how you and your partners can build a strong and healthy relationship, managing whatever conflict arises in your work together. If you can shift from resenting your incompatibility to appreciating the ways your differences complement each other, conflict will become your friend, not your enemy.

CHAPTER 8

Defining Spouse Involvement

"My partners understand that a woman is also the CEO of her household."

—Martha Rogers, Ph.D.

When you partner with someone who is married or in a significant relationship, and who is also a parent, you are partnering with your partner's family as well. No matter how separate from the business you choose to keep your own family, their presence will influence your work together. This book devotes an entire chapter to this subject because one secret to successful partnering is to understand and accept this reality. This chapter will highlight the choices you have regarding boundaries between work and home, as well as how to handle emotionally charged issues such as jealous spouses and partner affairs.

The Good News

In many successful partnerships, long-standing business partners become as close as family. Husbands and wives of partners come to know each other well, they watch each other's family grow up, and their kids relate to business partners as they might to an uncle or aunt. This comment from a computer executive conveys the deep satisfaction a close partnership can bring:

I refer to my former partner's daughter, Elisa, as my godchild. I've watched her grow up since she was just a tot, tearing apart our offices whenever she had the chance. When she started dating, I felt as protective as a father would. When she graduated high school I was there cheering her on. When her father suddenly died during her first year in college, she turned to me whenever she needed some "fatherly" advice—even though I was no longer in partnership with her dad. I was honored when she asked me to give her away in marriage a few years ago. I don't think I could love Elisa more if she were my own child.

⟡

I repeatedly heard in my partner interviews expressions of gratitude for a spouse's contribution to the business. Whether the spouse is there as a cheerleader, as a direct contributor with needed skills, or as the one who brings in a steady paycheck while the business is launched, his or her support is integral to the success of the venture.

⟡

My partner and I meet every Sunday morning. She has two small children and so do I. My husband watches all the babies on Sunday mornings while we have our meetings. I write a schedule on Sunday nights for the week, including day-care runs, meals, and evenings when I'll be tied up in meetings. Some nights he puts the kids to bed. Thank God I have a supportive husband; I could never do my business without him taking such great care of the family.

⟡

My partner and I try to avoid confrontation at all cost. We react poorly, getting defensive and not listening well. We asked our wives, who have much better communication skills than we do, to help us facilitate our partner meetings. Since they are motivated to help us grow our practice, they were delighted to be involved.

⟡

My partners and I get together on occasional weekends, because we live a few hundred miles from each other. Our spouses hang out together, take care of the kids, do all the cooking, and give us the space we need to get our work done. Sometimes we feel like one big extended family.

⟡

Involvement of Your Spouse in Choosing a Partner

My wife, Sue, is my Geiger counter and lie detector test. I've been in several partnerships and joint ventures over the years, and I have her meet anyone I am considering going into business with. A couple of times I ignored what she said, like when she warned me away from two partners. Both times, it backfired on me. She sees things I don't see, and she's not as naive and trusting as I can be. I've learned to trust her judgment.

Partners vary widely on how much they involve their spouses in the partner selection process. Here are four possibilities:

1. In some marriages, such a decision would never be made solo. The wife or husband is integrally involved in the process from day one. He or she might help the entrepreneur find a partner, be a partner himself or herself in the business along with the spouse, and/or be actively involved in the interview and evaluation process. The partnership is considered a joint endeavor.
2. In some marriages, spouses are involved in the evaluation process, although they will have nothing to do with the business going forward. They are consulted for their opinions, and they have veto power if they feel strongly that a potential partner is bad news.
3. In some marriages, spouses give their "stamp of approval" after the partners are well on their way toward signing an agreement. Essentially, by the time spouses and partners meet, the entrepreneurs have made up their minds to go forward. The spouse can influence the decision at this point, but it's a bit like stopping a train already moving down the tracks.
4. In some marriages, spouses have no involvement at all in the partner selection process. They aren't consulted, nor are they particularly interested. They trust their spouses' judgment entirely and leave the decision up to them.

Which one of these sounds most like your marriage, or your partner's? If you aren't sure, discuss it with your spouse. No choice is better or worse than the other. The key is to be sure to involve spouses to the extent that they wish to be, if they can be helpful to you. Avoid excluding a spouse who wishes to be involved. When, and if, your partnership creates any tension or difficulty for your marriage, your spouse will be less supportive if he or she wasn't consulted at the beginning.

Ask Your Spouse These Questions at the Outset

1. To what extent do you want to be involved in selecting and evaluating my prospective partner(s)?
2. Do you want veto power if you feel strongly that my prospective partner(s) won't work out?
3. What concerns are important to you that I should address when selecting my partner?
4. How much input do you want in our business on an ongoing basis?
5. Do you want to meet my partner's spouse and family?

Boundaries Between Work and Family

Partners vary widely on their preferences for merging work and family. Most of the people I spoke with insisted that their way was the correct one for creating a successful partnership. I heard "Never socialize with your partners!" And some insisted, "Get to know your partners and their families really well before considering a partnership with them!"

What's clear is that most individuals have strong feelings about how much to socialize and share of a personal nature with a partner. It's important to honor your spouse's preference, your own, and your partner's.

Here are some variations on the theme of blending work and family:

My partner and I never socialize outside of work. We keep the fence between work and home really high. The last thing I want to deal with is what happens if my partner and I split up and our social life is intertwined with theirs. It would be like a bad divorce.

Our wives are best friends and both stay-at-home moms. They hang out together all the time, and our families get together a lot on weekends. We went into partnership after being friends for years.

We don't mix socially with my partners because by the time I'm home, the last thing my husband and I want to do is hang out with my partners. I barely see enough of my family as it is. We do, however, get together with my partners and their spouses for certain holidays and company events.

My partner married my wife's sister, so we're together all the time. My partner and I would come home from work arguing about one thing or another, and our wives would say, "Stop it. We're going out tonight. Lighten up."

My husband was annoyed with the intrusion of my partners into our after-hours private time. I stopped taking calls from my partners on Sunday mornings and after 9 p.m. to give us some uninterrupted time together. The rest of the time the business has my attention, and he's okay with that.

Our venture was located in my business partner's home, so there was no way to avoid interacting with her family. My husband didn't interact too often with us, though, since he was always working in his job.

I'm keeping at arm's length socially from my partner because we're going through hard times in the business. If we go out, I don't want him looking at what my wife is wearing, or what kind of jewelry she's got around her neck, and making assumptions about how much money we have.

My partner and I got an apartment together to save money so we could put more cash into the business. Our boyfriends hang out with us as a foursome, but we both need space, too. We schedule time in the apartment so each of us gets time alone with her lover. We didn't want our boyfriends to start resenting the business or feeling crowded by our business partners always being around.

I'm in partnership with my sister and brother. We had to get clear about how much our families would socialize together outside of work and how we'd keep work conflicts separate from the family. Sometimes we all get sick of each other and we need a break.

I was furious with my wife for telling her business partner something about me that I considered very personal and private. Imagine my shock when I heard about it from the husband of my wife's business partner. After that, my wife and I talked specifically about what I considered appropriate to share with her business partner and what kinds of personal details I preferred to keep between the two of us.

Solicit Your Spouse's Input on These Questions

1. How much would you like to socialize with my partners' spouses and families?
2. What concerns do you have about socializing with my partners' spouses and families?
3. What boundaries do you want me to set to keep our family life separate and private? Is there anything you prefer for me not to share? Are there times in our days or nights together when you don't want me to have contact with my partners?

4. Do you ever feel that my business or partnership intrudes too much into our marriage or home life? If so, what would you like me to stop or do less of?
5. If I travel with my partners, what expectations do you have about what I do or don't do?

Tensions Between Partnership and Family

When you are married and in a business partnership, you are simultaneously involved in two intimate relationships with potentially conflicting needs. Friction originates when you feel torn between doing what is best for your business and your partnership, and what is right for your spouse and family. Tensions can arise in a marriage when the boundaries between work and home are not clear or are disrespected. You may have to cope with an insecure or jealous spouse who is threatened by your business relationships. When business partners and family don't integrate well, it creates great hardship in the partnership and the marriage. Your business partnership can become a lightning rod for any deep and unresolved conflicts in your marriage.

⟡

> My partner, Ken, and I are in an upscale fashion business. My partner's wife weighs about 300 pounds and buys her clothing on sale at K-mart. It's particularly embarrassing when she joins us on business travel, because she definitely doesn't fit the image of the company. She's intensely jealous of me (I'm about 120 pounds and a former model) and of my close relationship with Ken. Ken has confided in me that he would like to leave her, but they have a special needs child and he feels responsible. Our business is stuck; we can't do what it takes to expand, because the more successful we become, the more Ken starts resenting his wife's attitude and appearance. Eventually, he may have to choose between the business or his marriage.

⟡

On the following pages I've listed 13 conflicts shared with me during my partner interviews. Each conflict is followed by advice on how to handle it, should a similar situation arise in your marriage or partnership. Note that recommendations in this section are intended to be brief, to just get you pointed in the right direction. These issues are complex and are not easily addressed in a sentence or two; each of these conflicts could generate an entire chapter's worth of advice by itself! I strongly recommend seeking the professional help of a marriage counselor or business and relationship coach if you and your spouse struggle with any of these conflicts.

From the Point of View of the Partner

Conflict 1: My husband was also self-employed when my partner and I began our business. We started doing better in our business than he was doing in his. He was so jealous of our success that he tried to tear us down and put roadblocks in front of us.

Recommendation: Do what you can to support spouses in finding employment that will satisfy them and help boost their egos. Involve them in your business as much as possible, so they feel partially responsible for your success.

Conflict 2: My husband is a career employee. He's flipping out about the risk involved in my business. He condemns my partner for everything that goes wrong because he can't handle the ups and downs of the business, and he has to have someone to blame. He won't relax until we start bringing in some steady income.

Recommendation: Distinguish between uncomfortable and intolerable risk. Commit to your spouse that you won't let the business create any financial circumstances that he or she would find intolerable, even though they may be uncomfortable. (For example, you'll go $10,000 into credit card debt, but not $20,000.)

Keep spouses out of their panic zone by respecting their limits, and you may find them more tolerant of the risks you need to take.

Conflict 3: My partner has gotten involved with a controlling man who is trying to tell us how to run the business. He's totally taken over her life. Frankly, I think the guy is a psychopath. Our business has come to a standstill because I don't want to be involved with this guy in any way, but she won't give him up.

Recommendation: At times you may need to make tough choices between honoring your need for safety and integrity and continuing in your partnership. If an unreasonable, unethical, or dangerous spouse is interfering with your business, and your partner will not respect any limits to the spouse's involvement, dissolving the partnership may be a necessary alternative to putting yourself and your business in jeopardy.

Conflict 4: The most exciting moments of my life have occurred during my partnership. My partner is the only one who can really understand what I am feeling at moments of highs and lows in the business. My husband is jealous of the kind of intimacy I share with my partner, even though it's not sexual.

Recommendation: Even though you might believe that your spouse can't understand what you are going through in the same way as your business partner would, share with your spouse your emotional experiences related to the business if he or she is willing to listen. Be careful of too many late-night private conversations with your partner that make your spouse feel shut out and suspicious. If you are sensitive to your spouse's feelings, rather than annoyed by them, you'll more naturally offer the compassion and reassurance your spouse is looking for.

Conflict 5: My wife and my partner's wife used to be best friends. Then they had a falling out, and now they aren't talking to each other. It's made it very difficult for me to keep working with my partner. My wife badmouths him and his wife all the time and keeps pressuring me to leave the partnership.

Recommendation: One of the downsides of socializing with a business partner, or a business partner's family, is that you risk your working relationship if your friendship, or your spouse's friendship, falls apart. You might not be able to continue both the partnership and your marriage if your spouse is too hurt or angry to forgive and move on. On the other hand, I interviewed business partners who were once lovers, broke up, and still remained business partners. In time, people are remarkably resilient and able to work through emotional upheaval, allowing the partnership to continue.

Conflict 6: My partner asked her husband's advice all the time—he was like a third partner. "Harry said we should..." and "Harry said we shouldn't...." I started feeling like Harry was really running the business.

Recommendation: You and your partner must be clear about the level of input a spouse will have in business operations. Agree to officially solicit outside expert advice and opinions only if everyone agrees. If a spouse will be actively involved in advising the business, get that out on the table and legitimize the spouse's contribution. If the spouse will remain behind the scenes, only offering advice to his or her own spouse in off-hours, encourage the partners to consult their spouses when they desire, but to speak their own minds in partner discussions. Even though your opinion may be shaped by your spouse's input, communication with your partner will be more direct and straightforward if you begin sentences with "I think" instead of "Harry thinks."

Conflict 7: My wife and I have been drifting apart for years. Now I find myself confiding about personal problems more to my business partner than my wife. I must admit, my relationship with my partner has become more intimate and meaningful than the one I have with my wife.

Recommendation: Decide how committed you are to sustaining an intimate relationship with your spouse. A close marriage takes work and dedication—it won't happen just because you are married for a number of years. If you are drifting apart, you'll need to put effort back into reviving your original connection with your spouse—if it's important to you. Beware of channeling your needs for intimacy into your business partnership, asking your partner to fill a role that really belongs to your spouse.

From the Point of View of the Partner's Spouse

Conflict 8: I don't like the way my wife and her partner are spending money to grow their business, but they don't listen to my advice. I think I should have a say, since the business impacts my lifestyle. My wife tells me to butt out where I don't belong.

Recommendation: Clarify with your spousc what authority you each have over business expenses that affect joint accounts or your lifestyle. For example, you may agree that monthly expenses of more than $250, or one-time expenses of more than $500, require your spouse's input and approval. Where you agree that approval isn't necessary, unsolicited advice can be ignored. Where you agree it's a joint decision, respect that commitment or you may enrage your spouse.

Conflict 9: My husband sees far more of his female business partner than he does of me. I trust that he's not sexually involved with her, but sometimes when he comes home late at night after telling me they were working late at the office, I do worry. When I bring it up, he gets really angry and defensive and accuses me of not trusting him enough.

Recommendation: Invalidating a jealous spouse's concerns never works to reassure him or her; it only worries the spouse even more. Rather than arguing about your spouse's feelings, do the opposite of what your defensive reaction might lead you to do. Show compassion and tenderness, and give even more physical and verbal affection than you are accustomed to giving. Over time, if your spouse is getting what he or she needs from you and feels secure in your marriage, the jealousy should diminish.

Conflict 10: My spouse travels a lot with her business partner, a handsome guy a few years younger than me. Of course, they get separate hotel rooms, but sometimes, when she calls me late at night from the hotel after having dinner and a few drinks, I start thinking: "My wife is an attractive woman. I wouldn't blame him if he wanted to go to bed with her." He's married, but how do I know what kind of guy he is?

Recommendation: The jealous spouse may wish to spend some time with his or her spouse's business partner, to get comfortable with the partner's character and feel more trusting. If feasible, the spouse could travel every now and then with the partners on business. Some of the resentment might be coming from the spouse's feeling stuck at home in a thankless role while the partner spouse is out in the limelight. In that case, make sure that your spouse is receiving lots of praise and recognition for his or her contribution.

Conflict 11: My wife's business partner isn't carrying her load. Meanwhile, she's still taking home half the revenue of the company. I've tried to convince my wife to get rid of her deadweight partner, but she is being loyal to her for some stupid reason. I want to see my wife succeed, but my resentment toward her partner makes it very hard for me to be supportive.

Recommendation: Agree to address the issue your spouse raises rather than just ignoring it and hoping it will go away—which will inflame your spouse even further. Perhaps you might agree to confront your partner if she doesn't start performing by a certain time, or you might request that the equity ratio be reapportioned according to actual work produced. Reassure your spouse that you won't allow this situation to continue forever. If you ignore your spouse's concerns, he or she will start resenting your business and will pull away his or her support.

Conflict 12: I'm working alone in my home-office. My husband is out at his business with his partners and customers. When he comes home from work; I want to talk, but he's been with people all day, and he wants space to himself.

Recommendation: Give spouses a transition time, after they arrive home, to be by themselves and to do what they need or want to do. If you don't pounce on them as soon as they walk in the door, they may be more open to conversation later on, after they have recharged.

Conflict 13: My husband has no problem strategizing and planning for the future in his business—he and his partners know exactly where they want to be in one year, two, even five years into the future. But I can't get him to talk about our future at all—he's too busy or tired from working all day in the business. I miss the dreaming we did when we were dating.

Recommendation: Make talking about your marriage and future together fun! Get creative with a Saturday night date; shift the mood by talking over a glass of wine or a gourmet dinner. Conversation about the future may take place in "every now and then" moments rather than in a marathon meeting. If you make it seem like something else to add to your spouse's to-do list, he or she will naturally rebel, so invite your spouse to dream with you in a fun and unusual way.

The Key To Merging Partnership and Family

The secret to managing the challenge of engaging in a business partnership and a marriage at the same time comes from a statement in the first chapter in this book: "Approach a business partnership with the same significance as a marriage." Respect the intimacy and power of your business partner relationship. We often think of a marital affair as sexual in nature; realize that your partner relationship is the focal point of a large portion of your passion, time, and commitment. You are creating something with you partner—conceiving and raising a business—and often spend more time working together than you will spend at home. It's only natural that your spouse will at times resent the competition for your time and attention. Go out of your way to reinforce the sacred, special nature of your marriage. Every spouse wants to feel that he or she is number one.

When your partnership blends well with your family, it is also natural for your partner to become a member of your family. In the best of all worlds, you won't feel split in conflicting directions. Rather, you will fell blessed with the more intimate, rewarding, adult partnerships in your life. Your spouse will fully encourage your partnership and will develop a positive relationship with your partner in his or her own way.

Ideally, your partner relationship will enhance your marriage by improving your communication skills and your tolerance for difference. When you bring these skills back into your marriage, you will improve your marriage as well. If your partnership and business make you happy, you'll be a better spouse and parent. And let's hope that your business success, achieved in partnership, rewards your family with prosperity and financial security.

Hold the dream of a perfect merger between family and business. But don't leave it up to luck, simply hoping to find the right partner or an accommodating spouse. There is plenty you can do to select the right partner and create a partnership and a marriage that support each other. It will take commitment and dedication to make it work. Put your partner and your spouse on the same team, and you will have far more power and energy available for building your business and a satisfying family life.

CHAPTER 9

Terminating a Partnership

"The decision to separate may be the result of discussion and planning, or it may occur spontaneously. It may be mutually agreed on, but more often it is not. Whether the decision is made in an angry shouting match under a streetlight, in a cool and controlled exchange from opposite sides of a living room, or silently by one who lets absence inform the other, the scene is so important to the participants that even years later they can recall the details. Other scenes from a relationship may grow hazy and confused, but not this one, for this moment carries with it the potential for finality."

—Diane Vaughan, *Uncoupling*

I met Ari as a fellow guest on a midday television program dedicated to helping people pull through midlife crises. We chatted companionably on the way to our cars and decided to continue our conversation over lunch. When I asked Ari how he had come to start his consulting firm, his brow and jaw muscles tightened perceptibly, and without even knowing I was writing a book on business partnering, he shared the following:

I went through the worst kind of divorce you can imagine 10 years ago. And it wasn't from my wife. My business partner sold out on me, pulled the rug right out from underneath me. My partner, Jeff, and I built our company from nothing to sales of $60 million a year. We worked together night and day for eight years. There was nothing I wouldn't have done for the guy. I thought I knew him better than my wife—we certainly spent more time together. But Jeff got greedy, and behind my back, because he owned 60 percent of the firm, he found a buyer. He forced me to sell out; I couldn't afford to buy him out. Everyone thought I was so lucky—getting this big pot of money. But I didn't care about the money. I lost my best friend and my favorite job in the whole world. The betrayal was so shocking, it took me years to get over it. I started my consulting practice—solo, I might add—a few years after I was bought out. It took me that long before I could function in another business.

Countless times, when I interviewed people like Ari who had "partnership disaster" stories, I discovered that they had enjoyed a successful partnership—made money, created a worthwhile product, got along well for the most part—but had endured an unfortunate ending. These individuals would then paint the entire canvas of their partnerships as disastrous. But I came to view these circumstances as successful partnerships with devastating endings.

How is it that ending a partnership is considered one of the secrets for creating a successful partnership? Should a discussion about termination even be included in a book aimed to assist entrepreneurs with developing satisfying partnerships? A relationship guide for partners would not be complete without some useful discussion about termination issues. Every partnership will end eventually. It is my hope that after creating a superb partnership, you won't end on a sour note. But in case you do, this chapter will walk you through some of the challenges you'll need to negotiate.

Mutual Consent—The "Friendly" Divorce

Partnerships may split up by mutual consent, in an entirely agreeable fashion. Such circumstances often revolve around the sale of a company and consensus among all partners that it is time to move on to other ventures. Partners may retire or start new companies. Great celebration and prosperity can accompany this kind of dissolution. The partners "marry" to accomplish a specific mission. When that goal is achieved, the partnership comes to a halt—much to the glee of all involved. They came together to conceive and bear a child. Once the child is born and operating independently in the world, the marriage dissolves, for everyone agrees that the marriage's only purpose was the birth of that one child (or company).

Don is a dotcom multi-millionaire with this story to tell:

When my partner Chuck and I got together to launch our Internet company, we barely knew each other. We met through mutual friends and were immediately trusting of each other because we both respected the people who recommended us to each other. I had a great idea. He had money and a network behind him to make it happen quick. We put the deal together in less than a week. We were launched in 30 days, profitable in 90. A year later we went IPO. We never pretended we were in this for the long haul. We wanted to make a mint, and then sell our shares and get out. That's what we've done. I don't ever have to work again, and I don't plan on it. Life's too short! I'm perfecting my golf game!

Sometimes partners conclude that they would rather be doing something else with their lives and mutually agree to dissolve the partnership in order to pursue their individual life dreams. In this case, there can be regret because the partnership is ending, but there is little animosity in the process. The partners may have great love and respect for each other and genuinely want the others to be happy in their lives.

Gary, a novelist, reflects:

My best friend, Steve, and I were in business together for many years, managing apartment properties. It got old and boring for both of us. The excitement of starting a new business was long gone. We'd both answered too many crisis calls in the middle of the night because someone's toilet wasn't working. We talked for a year or so about ending the business so that he and I could semi-retire and do other things. I wanted to write a novel that had been stirring inside of me for years, but I never got to it. Steve was a fisherman and he wanted time to fish, and to compete in fly-fishing competitions. Finally, we decided to go for it. We sold the business to a friend of ours. He still hires us from time to time to consult with him, but for the most part, he's doing fine without us, and Steve and I are enjoying our freedom. Who knows, maybe I'll get this novel published someday.

At times, the ending of a partnership coincides with the failure of the enterprise. In the best of circumstances, the partners don't blame each other for the company's poor performance but rather humbly accept the fact that they gave an idea their best shot and it didn't work.

Jenny and Jason were twins who elected to go into business together right out of college. They had always been very close, had similar interests, and both wanted to be independent. They shared a love for dogs so they opened a dog grooming shop together, right in the hometown where they were raised. At first, the media gave them a big boost. "Local twins come home to open a business." Old friends and neighbors brought their dogs to them for grooming. They were optimistic that all would work out well.

Then they were given a rude awakening. Competition moved in. Another dog grooming shop opened up at the other end of down, charging less than they were. Their margins didn't allow them to reduce their prices without losing profitability. To add to this, the veterinarian who regularly referred customers to them retired, diminishing their source of referrals.

Jenny and Jason gave it the old college try for about a year and a half, but then Jason was recruited by a friend of his to work elsewhere. Jenny decided she was tired of trying to scratch out a living. They sold their dog grooming equipment on eBay and moved on.

Like soldiers in battle together, partners can get extremely close. The winding down process, though mutual, can be a painful one as the partners face the end of their company and their partnership as they know it. This anguish is different, however, than in the cases we'll discuss later, when blame for poor performance is part of the mix. This pain stems from the loss of a dream and a partnership that worked well—even if it didn't translate into business success. If the partners have worked well together, there is a high likelihood they will regroup and move on to a new venture together.

A Tip for a Mutual and Friendly Dissolution

Even if you are ending on the best of terms, and the decision is entirely mutual, don't be surprised if there are still tense moments during the dissolution process and if your relationship shows the strain. Even if you are excited about the new directions you are headed in, you may still grieve the loss of your current partnership. Negotiating any kind of financial settlement will challenge even the best relationships. Change of any kind is hard on the psyche; you may need to give your partners grace when they say things that are a bit out of character or act in ways that mean they aren't their usual, friendly selves. In time, if your relationship is strong and cherished, you may reconnect again as good friends once the awkward termination process is behind you.

Unexpected Dissolution of the Partnership

Life circumstances, often unplanned, have a way of influencing the termination process. Partners die, get sick, become disabled, move away, marry, have babies, encounter natural disasters, and redesign their lives in all kinds of ways that make the partnership no longer fit their life maps. Family difficulties might demand attention and require letting go of an all-consuming business, a divorce might create the need for a steady salary, a jealous spouse might insist that the partnership be dissolved, or a midlife crisis might spur a partner into reevaluating how he or she spends his or her waking hours.

Carol reflects on a previous business partnership that regrettably ended:

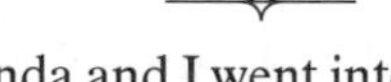

> My good friend Linda and I went into business together, selling arts and crafts supplies, since she and I were into arts and crafts as a hobby. We had a storefront and we also sold through the Internet. We were doing great, but then Linda's oldest son was in a tragic car accident. He survived, but was left paraplegic. Understandably, Linda needed to devote herself to his care. She had little time for the business. It was too much for me to handle on my own. Although I could have searched for another partner, I didn't want to. I didn't think I could find another partner as good as Linda was, so I thought it would be best if I just got out of it too. We sold the business to a nice young couple who were looking for exactly what we offered. I'm now working for them as an employee! Although at first it was hard to get used to, now, it suits me just fine. I'm still doing what I love, without some of the headaches of running a business.

This kind of dissolution is sometimes mutual (as in the case of a natural disaster that destroys the business), but not always. Often, one partner encounters a circumstance in his or her life that prompts him or her to sell out to the other partners. The business might stay, minus the contribution of one of the partners. Or the business might dissolve because the partners can't reach a satisfying buyout agreement, or because the enterprise is too dependent on the skills and contribution of the exiting partner to survive without him or her.

If you are lucky, all members of the partnership are accepting of a radical change at the same time. If not, the termination process can be quite hostile, as the partner being "left" goes through a grieving process that usually includes a great deal of anger. Even though the partnership isn't ending because it was a dysfunctional relationship or because the company wasn't successful, the hostile termination is a reflection of the deep wounding some partners experience when losing a relationship they highly valued.

Kevin, an entrepreneur, was still fuming when I interviewed him about the partnership he had lost a few months earlier. Their painting company had been doing well; the relationship he shared with his partner, Jim, was the most rewarding he had ever encountered. He thought they would be partnered for years. But Jim shocked him at a breakfast meeting one morning by announcing that he had decided he "wanted to do something else with his time."

Jim was moving on to a different kind of work and wished to dissolve the company. As typically happens in a lot of partnership dissolutions, Jim sprung his decision on Kevin "out of the blue" even though he had been preparing for his exit over the past several months. By the time Jim made the announcement, he had one foot out the door, leaving Kevin feeling shell-shocked, betrayed, and extremely angry.

For the first time in my career, I enjoyed getting up in the morning and going to work. In a split second, my partner took that away from me. Friendship to me is really sacred. I considered my partner a close friend. I thought we were friends first, partners second. But to him, we were only friendly partners. Once our work together didn't suit him anymore, the friendship was gone, too. The loss is so enormous, it's like a death. I lost a friend, our company, my dreams, my income, even my trust in human beings. I've been divorced before, and this is much worse.

Dissolving a relationship often begins with a secret. One of the partners starts to feel uncomfortable in the relationship, or begins to reevaluate the partnership and the business in light of new life circumstances. The partnership no longer fits. The dissolution process begins in solitary reflection. By the time a partner goes public with the desire to exit, he or she has often been emotionally preparing for such an action for months. Such people have already moved through the anger, denial, blaming, bargaining, and sadness stages of ending an intimate relationship, reaching a level of acceptance by the time they drop the bombshell on their unsuspecting partners. It can take several months, if not years, for the partners to both reach the same level of acceptance about the dissolution, since the "surprised" partner needs time to recover and to move through the same grieving stages.

One of the most painful kinds of non-mutual dissolution is where the initiator starts cultivating another partnership before ending the current one. It feels no different to the involved parties than an extramarital affair.

One gentleman shared the following story with me:

> Things didn't go sour in our partnership until the last year. In fact, the three of us got along really well, and we built a multi-million-dollar company over a 10-year period. We had minor squabbles, like what kind of car we each should be driving, but that's about it. Then my partner, Wade, tried to sell the company without my other partner and I even knowing anything about it. It was really that dramatic. We thought he was home sick with the flu, but he was in Europe, putting together a deal with a French company in the hopes that he would be able to convince us to sell our shares and allow him to run the company for the French. They didn't want my other partner and me involved as part of the new plan. He negotiated the whole deal behind our backs, and then just sprung it on us for our approval. He thought that if he danced a few million dollars in front of our noses, we'd leap at the chance

to sell out and be happy about it. It took several months to reach agreement, since my partner and I were caught entirely off guard, and we felt really betrayed.

In the case where a partnership has been working well, the partner initiating the change will often start recasting the other partners in a negative light, reconstructing the history of the relationship and noting only trouble, in order to justify ending the partnership. Good times are forgotten or explained away. The exiting partner announces that the partnership was a mistake from the beginning, an error that he or she now intends to remedy. The partner hearing the unexpected news argues for a chance at keeping the partnership intact, but the plea falls on deaf ears because the initiator has already decided to leave.

This recasting process might protect the exiting partner against feeling regret or sadness, but it will infuriate the partners being left behind. Now they are not only coping with the unexpected ending of their partnership, but also with the loss of their belief that the partnership was a positive, rewarding experience. Such a blow often shatters their trust in intimate relationships in general. When all partners have fully dissolved their partnership and reestablished independent identities, or moved on to form another successful partnership, they may once again be able to see the positive qualities of their former partner and the relationship they shared. Though negative recasting can be essential to the letting-go process, it is often temporary, and within a few years it can be replaced with a more balanced and appreciative point of view.

A Tip for the Leaving Partner

Be gentle with your unsuspecting partners, who have not had months to process the decision you have made. Allow them to work through the process, and give them as much time as you can. Try to not make your partners the bad guys in order to make your exiting easier. Listen to them, and allow their efforts to remedy the relationship be heard even if you have already made up your mind. Be prepared for the anger and depression that your shocking news may generate.

Betty regrets the way she handled terminating her partnership with her ex-best friend, Judy:

> Oh goodness, what a fool I was. I wish I could take it all back and do it differently. I was young then—25 years old—and impetuous. I was working with my best friend at the time, but then I fell in love with George. George wanted me to come work for him instead. I couldn't do both. I had stars in my eyes and would have done anything for George. So I left my best friend high and dry. Just gave her a couple of weeks notice. She and I haven't talked since. The worst thing is, George is now history too. I should have given her more respect than that. She deserved better. I've been feeling guilty about it for 30 years!

Tip for the Partner Being Left

Losing an intimate relationship, and your company as you now know it, is a major upheaval in your life. You will pass through very predictable grieving stages, and the process often cannot be rushed. If you can, trust that when one door closes, another one opens. Remember the Hebrew expression Gam Zu Letovah, which means "This too is for the best." Shift your focus from devastation to curiosity about what the future holds. Once you have created new circumstances for yourself, this ending won't seem nearly as horrific. Seek counseling and the support of God, your spiritual community, family, and friends to see you through this difficult time.

Frank recovered from his loss and shares this happy ending:

> Busting up my partnership with Rick is the best thing that ever happened to me, although I didn't believe it at the time.

I was a drinking alcoholic. Rick enabled me to continue my drinking on the job. Finally, Rick had enough of my B.S. He walked out on me. Just packed up his things and had his lawyer contact me to work out the dirty details. He told me that it was because of my drinking and that I better get my act together. I was furious at the time. I felt really betrayed and I certainly didn't want to hear about my drinking.

This was hitting bottom for me. My drinking got worse for about six months. Without Rick to keep the business together and to make excuses for me to our clients, I quickly destroyed everything he and I built together.

The good news is, I landed in AA and I've been sober for three years, two months, and 14 days. I've got a good job now and I'm newly married. I owe it all to Rick and my buddies at AA. If he hadn't pushed me over the edge and made me accountable for my actions, I might still be drinking.

Ending a Troubled Partnership

In my former marriage, it got so bad, I didn't want to come home from work. Then, when my business partnership went sour, I'd get up in the morning and I didn't want to go to work. For a while, I had no place to go where I was at peace. Now, I'm remarried and I love being home again. My business partner left and I'm enjoying my work anew. What a difference a few years can make!

So far, we've been discussing partnerships that end for reasons unrelated to difficulties in the partnership relationship. The truth is, many partnerships will end primarily because the partners can't get along, or because in the eyes of one individual another partner is incompetent, unethical, or worse. Partnerships may crumble gradually over time, like a long-term marriage drifting apart, or may end abruptly in dramatic fashion. Endings can be relatively polite or reminiscent of the nastiest divorces.

Partners in business fight for custody (who owns what part of the company) and alimony (who is entitled to what financial share of the company) as viciously as couples in divorce court. When blame and money are involved, and respect no longer exists between partners, it is difficult to communicate civilly, which is why lawyers and mediators are often called in to assist with dissolving the partnership.

Here are eight red flags that signal the deterioration of the partner relationship, helping to identify when it's time to consider ending a partnership, or, at the very least, seek professional help.

1. You are starting to keep secrets from your partner or partners, or you suspect your partners are keeping secrets from you.
2. You wake up most days dreading going to work. You've been thinking a lot about finding another alternative.
3. You are consumed with anger toward your partner. You can barely have a civil conversation with each other anymore.
4. No matter how hard you try to resolve the conflicts that keep erupting between you, no solution ever seems to satisfy either of you for long.
5. You've lost respect for your partner or partners. Their approaches to business and to their personal lives make you feel ashamed or ambivalent about being associated with them.
6. You still like your partner a great deal, but you believe you would make better friends and colleagues than business partners.
7. Your partner seems to have entirely different values than you. You regularly clash over the direction you wish to take the company or how clients should be approached or handled.

8. The quality of your service or product is deteriorating. Rather than creating a prosperous, productive environment, your partnership is destroying the company.

The problem with this kind of partnership ending is that it usually follows a long period when partners have been struggling to resolve their conflicts but instead build animosity toward each other. In some cases, that hostility is well founded. Partners steal from each other, misrepresent themselves, renege on their agreements, and engage in unlawful or unethical behavior. Partners can be incompetent and worthy of the denigration they receive. Whether you are justified in your anger or not, most likely you'll still have to go through the ugly process of proving your point and settling the financial details of the company. Your partner may not share your point of view, no matter how convinced you are of its merits!

A Tip for Partners Ending a Hostile Relationship

Seek professional help. Some partners try to negotiate termination on their own without any outside assistance. It's possible, but extremely difficult if your relationship has fallen apart. The process will drag out when you get locked into a position. Other partners begin the dissolution process by calling their respective lawyers—and the billable hours start accumulating from that first phone call. Any money you and your partners are fighting over retaining might go toward paying the lawyers for terminating the relationship.

Mediation services are a valuable alternative, especially where partners will have some form of continuing relationship—as when they live in the same geographical or professional community. Hiring a mediator to help you work out the ending process can be significantly less expensive and faster than having your lawyers fight it out. Once a mediator helps the partners arrive at their own solution, it can be put in writing and considered legally binding. The mediation process encourages antagonists to arrive at a compromise solution.

Ideally, your written partnership agreement commits to trying mediation first, before seeking a solution through arbitration or attorneys. Your legal agreement might even designate who that mediator would be. You might wish to give mediation a try and, if it falls apart, then seek the more expensive legal counsel.

If you are a member of your local Better Business Bureau, you may be entitled to mediation services offered through its organization at no, or low, cost. Also, you can usually find mediation services in your phone book's yellow pages, or you can elect to use a professional consultant or business coach whom both of you trust and consider to be neutral.

Business Issues to Resolve When Ending a Partnership

Following are some of the primary issues you'll need to discuss and resolve when terminating a partnership. Scanning this list is a good reminder of why it is so important to choose a partner wisely! Partnership dissolution can be incredibly complex.

Distribution of Property—Who Will Get What, When, and How

Tangible Property

- Buy/sell agreement—how the company will be valued.
- Accounts payable and company debt.
- Accounts receivable.
- Office furniture and equipment, and other physical assets.
- Residual income from product sales, royalties, service contracts.
- Workbooks and other written materials used in the course of business.

Intangible Property

- Copyright or patent ownership of the product.
- The business name, phone number, and address.
- Product names and branded or trademarked names.
- The client list.
- Employees.

Issues to Resolve

- Damage control, if a partner's performance was harmful to current business.
- How current projects already committed will be completed. If a partner is leaving, how those skills will be replaced.
- How the winding down period will be handled.
- How clients will be informed of the dissolution.
- Renaming the company if necessary.
- Written literature—brochures and promotional pieces will need to be rewritten.
- Healing destructive emotions (anger, hurt, depression) that interfere with your ability to do the business.
- Handling any family repercussions of the termination (for example, wives of the partners are friends, the sister of one of the partners works there, and so on).
- What you will and will not say in public about your partnership.
- How the buy/sell agreement will be executed, if applicable.

You can begin a partnership in a moment—one conversation and you're off and running. Ending a partnership takes a lot more time. Count on a minimum of three to six months of negotiation and winding down; some partnerships require longer than that. Many of the partners I spoke to who experienced difficult terminations told me that it took a few years for them to regain their sense of equilibrium—and even longer for them to forgive partners who betrayed their trust.

Some people have never forgiven their former partners; they still carry an enormous grudge that embitters their business dealings to this day. These "walking wounded" have a tendency to romanticize how great everything was before their miserable partnerships occurred. They are stuck, unable to move on and create new, more satisfying alternatives for themselves now that their former partnerships have ceased to exist. It's easier for some people to see themselves as victims than to be in charge of their lives.

Whether your partnership ends poorly or well, it is a chapter in your life that will provide enormous learning and growth. As new opportunities arise, perhaps only in hindsight will you see how any particular partnership led you to your next steps. Usually, hindsight allows for a rewriting of history—re-framing your partnership experience, no matter how unproductive or dissatisfying it was, as an important experience leading to other positive outcomes.

My greatest hope for you is that your partnerships will end as superbly as they functioned when you were together. If you develop strong communication skills, solid respect for each other, and a commitment to a win/win conflict resolution process, the ending of your partnership can leave your relationship intact, even if the company dissolves. The lawyers might end your partnership as it is defined in a partnership agreement, but relationships continue on—in memories, in daily interactions with each other, and perhaps even in the new and separate directions you head in.

Ending your partnership agreement legally will never erase its effect. Once you journey down the entrepreneurial road in partnership, whether it be a happy or a horrendous experience, you are changed forever.

CHAPTER 10

The Secrets To Successful Partnership in a Nutshell

Unless you are one of those people who like to skip to the end of a book and read the last chapter first, you have now read more details about partnership than you probably even knew could be written. I hope this book has prompted you to ask the questions you need to ask and to settle in advance the issues necessary to begin your partnership on solid footing. If you are currently in a partnership, I hope this book has given you some additional ammunition to forestall the possibility that your partnership will deteriorate into a hostile relationship.

This book will still be a reference when new issues arise in your partnership that weren't on your mind during your first reading. Building a successful partnership, like building a marriage, is an evolving process; passages that don't resonate with you now may hit home at a different stage in your partnership. As you change partners over the lifetime of your career, each partnership can raise entirely different concerns and questions.

I believe that some elements of positive partnering come down to plain old good luck and serendipity. You happen to be in the right place at the right time, and you meet the right person. You have the good fortune of crossing paths with a quality individual, someone with integrity and a strong work ethic and passion for what he or she does. You and your partner develop a product and bring it to market at the ideal time to make a fortune, or to really make a difference in the world. Clearly, some aspects of positive partnering are left to the randomness of the universe. Nonetheless, as I wrote in my book *Create Your Own Luck,* there is far more in your control when reaching for a positive partnering experience than not. If you are willing to take the time and devote the energy, there is plenty you can do to create a superlative relationship.

If someone asked me, "What are the secrets to success when building a business partnership?" I would respond by taking this complex subject and breaking it down to eight steps—reflected by the first eight chapters of this book. Granted, no relationship challenge can be entirely resolved by following the eight steps of anything. Yet it is helpful when standing at the base of a mountain to understand what basic training, gear, and mountaineering skills we will need, given the experience of thousands of climbers before us, to get to the top with the least likelihood of injury or calamity.

Some climbers buy all the right gear, dedicate themselves to intense training, and still never leave the base because they lose their courage, or because outside events intervene. Others will beat the odds and make it to the summit without any of the theoretically required basics, making others of us wonder why we spent so much time and money taking the more careful approach. And then there are those who will do everything right and for whom misfortune, like bad weather, will sabotage their dreams anyway.

The eight secrets for success spelled out in this book are designed to synthesize two years of research into four to eight hours of reading. They oversimplify at times, but they also point partners to the cornerstones of any successful partnership. To review, here are the eight secrets for positive business partnering:

1. Approach your business partnership with the same respect you would give to a marriage.
2. Understand who you are and what your business needs are.
3. Look before you leap—evaluate your partner beyond the superficial.
4. Create a joint vision, and clarify your expectations and roles.
5. Formalize your agreements—begin with the end in mind.
6. Communicate with an appreciation for your differences.
7. Resolve disagreements before they disintegrate the partnership.
8. Define your spouse's involvement and address his or her concerns.

When it comes to developing a successful relationship, the tools and techniques you can use could fill your office library. When all is said and done, any successful partner relationship depends on these basic factors:

1. The ability to resolve conflict with a win/win approach.
2. Maintaining good will toward each other and wanting the best for your partner as well as for yourself.
3. Building a trusting relationship that is safe, accepting, generous of spirit, and tolerant of differences.
4. Focusing on gratitude for the gifts of your partner and your relationship rather than grumbling about what isn't perfect.
5. Sharing goals and working as a team to achieve them.

6. Taking responsibility for your contribution and acting with accountability and integrity.
7. Listening well and making your partner feel appreciated, heard, and understood.
8. Responding appropriately to feedback and requests for change.
9. Demonstrating a willingness to share control as well as credit for achievements.
10. Embracing the opportunity to learn and grow from whatever challenges your partnership brings your way.
11. Having the fortitude and resiliency to stay committed through adversity.
12. Keeping a long-term perspective and your sense of humor.

Partnership Vows—Creating Your Own Statement

When we marry, part of the ritual all of us engage in is to speak aloud our marriage vows. Some choose to adopt standard vows that originate in a particular religious or spiritual community. Others write their own vows. The purpose is the same, regardless of the words chosen: to proclaim to each other and to the community our positive intentions at the beginning of our journey together. For some couples, marriage vows become an anchor to return to when one or both find themselves straying from the unity they felt on their wedding day. Marriage vows serve as a reminder of what we dreamed of for ourselves and our partnership. We accept that the words are aspirations and are not always achieved on any given day.

Given the close parallels between business partnership and marriage, why not proclaim to one another your best intentions, desires, and commitments for your partnership, in your own set of unique partnership vows?

I invite you to spend some time with your partner creating a statement that expresses your vows to one another in your partnership. I leave you with a version of partnership vows I've created that you are welcome to adopt. I encourage you to find your own unique voice and to create vows that are especially meaningful to you. I trust that if you dedicate yourself to this activity, the words will come.

Partnership Vows

- I will respond to you with honesty and integrity, and do my part to create a safe and trustworthy relationship.
- I will take full responsibility for my own behavior and give you responsibility for yours.
- I will, whenever possible, choose
patience over impatience,
compassion over judgment,
openness over rigidity,
letting go over control,
gratitude over complaining, and
optimism over doubt.
- I will summon the courage and strength I need to manage whatever challenges our partnership, and the rest of my life, bring our way.
- I will take care of myself physically, emotionally, and spiritually, so that I have the resources to contribute to our enterprise as I have pledged.
- I will lighten up when I need to, so that we have an enjoyable and fun experience.
- I will communicate to you directly when I am troubled or angered by anything you have said or done, unless doing so would not be productive.

- I will work to resolve any conflicts arising between us in a manner that brings a satisfying resolution to both of us.
- I will strive toward tolerance and acceptance of our differences, with the hope of coming to celebrate them.
- I will respect you as my mentor and teacher, and be willing to learn from you at all times.
- I will join with you to create a prosperous enterprise that honors our deepest values and makes a positive difference in the world.
- I will, when the time is right, end this partnership gracefully, with respect for your contribution and appreciation for what we have been able to achieve together.

Recommended Resources

Books

Alessandra, Tony, and Michael J. O'Connor. *The Platinum Rule: Do Unto Others As They'd Like Done Unto Them.* New York: Warner Books, 1996.

Bugen, Larry. *Love and Renewal: A Couple's Guide to Commitment.* Oakland, Calif.: New Harbinger Publications, 1990.

Clifford, Denis, and Ralph E. Warner. *The Partnership Book: How to Write a Partnership Agreement,* 4th ed. Berkeley, Calif.: Nolo Press, 1996. For information, call 800-992-6656.

Edwards, Paul and Sarah, and Rick Benzel. *Teaming Up.* New York: Tarcher/Putnam, 1997.

Fisher, Roger, and Scott Brown. *Getting Together: Building Relationships as We Negotiate*. New York: Penguin, 1988.

Fisher, Roger, and William Ury. *Getting to Yes: Negotiating Agreement Without Giving In*. New York: Penguin, 1991.

Forward, Susan, and Craig Buck. *Money Demons: Keep Them From Sabotaging Your Relationships—and Your Life*. New York: Bantam Books, 1994.

Gerber, Michael. *The E-Myth Revisited.* New York: HarperBusiness, 1995.

Gottman, John. *Why Marriages Succeed or Fail.* New York: Simon and Schuster, 1994.

Gray, John. *Men Are From Mars, Women Are From Venus.* New York: HarperCollins, 1992.

Jaffe, Azriela. *Honey, I Want to Start My Own Business: A Planning Guide for Couples.* New York: HarperBusiness, 1996.

Jaffe, Azriela. *Starting From No: Ten Strategies to Overcome Your Fear of Rejection and Succeed in Business.* Chicago: Dearborn Publishers, 1999.

Jaffe, Azriela. *Create Your Own Luck: Eight Principles for Attracting Good Fortune Into Your Life and Work.* Boston: Adams Media Corporation, 2000.

Jones, Laurie Beth. *The Path: Creating Your Mission Statement for Work and for Life*. New York: Hyperion, 1996.

Maddox, Rebecca. *Inc. Your Dreams: For Any Woman Who Is Thinking About Her Own Business*. New York: Viking, 1995.

Mancuso, Joseph. *Running a Family Business*. Englewood Cliffs, N.J.: Prentice-Hall, 1991.

Markman, Howard, Scott Stanley, and Susan Blumberg. *Fighting for Your Marriage: Positive Steps for Preventing Divorce and Preserving a Lasting Love.* San Francisco: Jossey-Bass Publishers, 1994.

McGinnis, Alan Loy. *The Power of Optimism.* New York: HarperCollins, 1990.

McGowan, Judith H. *Inc. Yourself.* New York: HarperCollins, 1992.

Mellan, Olivia. *Money Harmony: Resolving Money Conflict in Your Life and Relationships.* New York: Walker and Co., 1994.

Olesen, Erik. *Mastering the Winds of Change: Peak Performers Reveal How to Stay on Top in Times of Turmoil.* New York: HarperBusiness, 1993.

Page, Susan. *How One of You Can Bring the Two of You Together.* New York: Broadway Books, 1997.

Parlapiano, Ellen, and Patricia Cobe. *MomPreneurs: A Mother's Practical Step-by-Step Guide to Work-at-Home Success.* New York: Perigee, 1996.

Poe, Richard. *Wave 3: The New Era in Network Marketing.* Roseville, Calif.: Prima Publishing. 1995.

Rigsbee, Edwin Richard. *The Art of Partnering: How to Increase Your Profits and Enjoyment in Business Through Alliance Relationships.* Dubuque, Iowa: Kendall/Hunt, 1994.

Roberts, Lisa. *How to Raise a Family and a Career Under One Roof: A Parent's Guide to Home Business.* Moon Township, Pa.: Bookhaven Press, 1997.

Schloff, Laurie, and Marcia Yudkin. *He and She Talk: How to Communicate With the Opposite Sex.* New York: Plume, 1993.

Seligman, Martin. *Learned Optimism: How to Change Your Mind and Your Life.* New York: Pocket Books, 1990.

Siebert, Al. *The Survivor Personality.* New York: Practical Psychology Press, 1994.

Snowden, Richard. *The Complete Guide to Buying a Business.* New York: Amacom, 1993.

Tannen, Deborah. *You Just Don't Understand: Women and Men in Conversation.* New York: Ballantine Books, 1990.

Tomzack, Mary. *Tips and Traps When Buying a Franchise.* New York: McGraw-Hill, 1994.

Ury, William. *Getting Past No: Negotiating Your Way From Confrontation to Cooperation.* New York: Bantam, 1993.

Vaughan, Diane. *Uncoupling: Turning Points in Intimate Relationships.* New York: Oxford University Press, 1986.

Weiner-Davis, Michele. *Divorce Busting.* New York: Simon and Schuster, 1992.

Wylie, Peter, and Mardy Grothe. *Can This Partnership Be Saved? Improving (or Salvaging) Your Key Business Relationships.* Dover, N.H.: Upstart Publishing, 1993. (This book is now out of print; to find a copy contact Dr. Wylie at 202-332-7571.)

Magazines

Business Start-Ups. 2392 Morse Avenue, Irvine, CA 92614; 800-274-8333.

Entrepreneur: The Small Business Authority. 2445 McCabe Way, Irvine, CA 92614; 800-274-6229.

Home Office Computing: Solutions for Today's Small Business. 411 Lafayette Street, 4th floor, New York, NY 10003; 800-288-7812.

Inc.: The Magazine for Growing Companies. P.O. Box 54129, Boulder, CO 80322; 800-234-0999.

Web Sites

Entrepreneur.com. This frequently visited, award-winning small business site delivers focused content, community, tools, and services to small and emerging businesses. I write a monthly column for Entrepreneur.com on topics related to the psychological concerns of home-based professionals.

infoUSA.com. This site is a leading provider of sales and marketing information to small businesses and Internet companies across the country. Visit the site to read my weekly column on sales and customer service tips for business owners and salespersons.

The Small Business Advisor. This award-winning Web site provides a variety of online information to help the entrepreneur and small business owner be successful. It includes book reviews, special reports, articles, tax information, and useful related links. Highly recommended!

Heartwarmers4u. A free e-mail service that sends you a daily message (6 days a week) designed to inspire you and give you insights on how people around the world are overcoming the everyday challenges they face. Most of the e-mail messages you receive are composed of stories written by your fellow Heartwarmers4u members. They cover every conceivable topic. Some can be sad, others happy—or even sappy. They may bring a tear to your eye, or a chuckle to your cheek. They can be fact or fiction, prose or poetry. Regardless, they will make you think and help you balance your life in ways that will make it more enriching and rewarding. To join the heartwarmers' list, send an e-mail to *join@heartwarmers.com*

The Small Business Advocate. Featuring hundreds of searchable audio archives, The Small Business Advocate is a leading-edge online resource and a weekday radio/internet talk show.

Founder and host Jim Blasingame has created a community where small business experts share valuable information, real world perspectives, and tips on how to be more successful in your small business. You can ask a question, find articles and links, read the newsletter, and much more. It's all free, interactive, and dedicated to small business.

Business Filings Incorporated. Business Filings (*www.bizfilings.com*; 800-981-7183) is the Internet leader in providing online incorporation services. It easily and affordably incorporates businesses and forms Limited Liability Companies in all 50 states.

NameProtect.com. This site has helped thousands of entrepreneurs, attorneys, and intellectual property professionals search and register their trademarks online. NameProtect.com offers full-service trademark protection with an easy three-step online process. Call 800-689-6223.

The Entrepreneurial Parent. EP is a community and career resource for parents on the home career track. Need some camaraderie or advice? Sign up for their free monthly e-zine—send a subscribe message to EPnews or visit their site for topics ranging from telecommuting to business startups to responsible parenthood. If you're an EP, you're not alone any longer!

Web Cards. This company creates full color printed postcards of your Web site. Announce your site, promote your specials, or keep in touch with your clients. Order online or call 800-352-2333 for samples. A proof will be posted on the Internet for your approval. Prices start at just $95 for 500 4" x 6" color postcards.

FSB Online. This is the online Web site of FSB (Fortune Small Business) magazine. It is updated daily with stories on small business news, management, marketing, e-commerce, finance, business travel, and the entrepreneurial lifestyle. Visit every Thursday to read an original column I write for FSB called "Balancing Act."

Legal Docs. This business provides legal forms online at *www.law.net/usalaw/ index.htm*. You can also use Electronic Legal Source at *www.e-legal.com.* Another possibility is *Partnership Maker* software from Nolo Press, 950 Parker Street, Berkeley, CA 94710; 800-992-6656.

Consultants and Advisers

Dr. Tony Alessandra is the author of several books and audiotape series, including *The Platinum Rule*, *Charisma*, *The Sales Professional's Idea-A-Day Guide*, and *The Sales Manager's Idea-A-Day Guide*. Call 619-459-0197, fax 619-459-0435, or find him on the Web at *DrTonyA@alessandra.com*, *www.alessandra.com*, or *www.platinumrule.com*. You can order products through *www.amazon.com*, or *www.alessandra.com*.

Associated Credit Bureaus, Inc. This international trade association represents more than 800 credit reporting agencies in the United States, Canada, and a dozen other countries. 1090 Vermont Avenue, NW, Suite 200, Washington, DC 20005-4905; 202-371-0910; fax 202-371-0134; *www.acb-credit.com*.

Azriela Jaffe, MBA., BSW., business/relationship coach and partner mediator. Web site for Anchored Dreams: *www.isquare.com/crlink.htm*. Works nationally, all coaching via telephone and online. 215-321-5269. For free online newsletters for entrepreneurial couples, or *Creating Your Own Luck*, send e-mail to *Az@azriela.com* or *azriela@mindspring.com*.

Better Business Bureaus. Contact the BBB in your local area or call 900-CALL-BBB to request up to three company reports per call. As a BBB member, you are entitled to free or low-cost arbitration assistance for your business and your partner relationship. Contact the Council of Better Business Bureaus, Inc., 4200 Wilson Boulevard, Arlington, VA 22203.

Diana Edwards, Ph.D. is a psychologist and trained mediator and can be reached at 1614 East Rancho Drive, Phoenix, AZ 85016; 602-248-9038 (business) or 602-248-9030 (home).

Ed Shea, MSW, LCSW has a telephone coaching practice specializing in imago therapy, marriage counseling, and partner mediation. He can be reached at 239 East Wilson, Elmhurst, IL 60126; 630-530-1060 or 630-530-1865; *coachimago@aol.com.*

Edwin Richard Rigsbee is a consultant and author of *The Art of Partnering.* He can be rcached at P.O. Box 6425-ESIG, Westlake Village, CA 91359; 805-371-4636; fax 805-371-4631; *EdRigsbee@aol.com*. Visit his Web site, *speakers.com/rigsbee/ articles.html,* for additional free partnering information; there are more than 30 articles there.

Fred Racey practices partner mediation in the North Carolina area.105 Briarpatch Lane, Boone, NC 28607; 704-264-7819.

Georgann and John V. Crosby, Family Business Roundtable, Inc. These family business consultants consult nationally on issues of change in the family and change in the business. 727 East Bethany Home Road, Suite 118, Phoenix, AZ 85014; 602-285-1207; *fbr@ix.netcom.com.*

EntrepreneurPR, specializes in small businesses and publishes *Entrepreneur Illustrated.* Cofounders John Nixon and Scott Smith can be reached at 3050 Fite Circle, Suite 209, Sacramento, CA 95827; 916-368-7000; fax 916-368-7008; *scott@entrepreneurpr.com.*

Jane Hilburt-Davis, co-founder of Key Resources, offers seminars, workshops, and private consultation for family businesses, "copreneurs," and closely held businesses. Lexington, MA; 617-861-0586.

Jan Caldwell, Esq. has a legal practice focusing on small business development and is a certified mediator. He is director of the American Association of Home-Based Businesses and works with mid-Atlantic clients. 9613 Page Avenue, Bethesda, MD 21814; 301-493-7890; fax 301-493-789; *jan@worldnet.att.net.*

Kathi Elster conducts business strategy seminars and partner mediation. 120 East 34th Street, #15L, New York, NY 10016; 212-481-7075.

Life Management Associates, a professional services firm located in Lancaster, PA, offers a full range of psychological services, including marriage, family, and individual counseling, organizational consulting, training, personnel services, and mediation services for business partners: 800-327-7770. Jeff Klunk, psychologist, partner.

Linda Locke is the editor of *MLM Woman,* a training and motivational publication for women in network marketing. She can be reached at *Regent@west.net* and *www.west.net/-regent/mlmwoman.*

Mary Tomzack, Franchise Consulting. 50 Law Road, Briarcliff, NY 10510; 914-347-3530.

Michael Mastros provides family and business mediation services from Washington, D.C., to Reading, PA. 320 North Duke Street, Lancaster, PA 17602; 717-393-4440; fax 717-393-5506;.

Performance Improvement Associates provides organizational marriage counseling, helping people who run organizations iron out differences. The business is run by Dr. Peter Wylie (202-332-7571) and Dr. Mardy Grothe (617-275-1254). You can e-mail Peter Wylie at *pbradwylie@aol.com* or send regular mail to 1666 B Euclid Street, NW, Washington D.C. 20009.

Richard Snowden, author of *The Complete Guide to Buying a Business.* Box 5491, Portsmouth, NH 03802; 603-436-2240.

Robert Sullivan, Information International, small-business consulting. Box 579, Great Falls, VA 22066; 703-450-7049; *bobs@isquare.com.* You can find his *The Small Business Start-up Guide* at *isquare.com* or by calling 800-375-8439.

Index

T

U

V

W

Azriela Jaffe is the nation's leading expert on entrepreneurial couples, and highly sought after by the media for her expertise on the emotional, interpersonal, marital and family concerns of self-employed professionals, entrepreneurial couples, and business partners. She is one of the country's foremost spokespeople on work/family concerns.

Azriela is the nationally acclaimed author/editor of eight books, including:

Honey, I Want To Start My Own Business, A Planning Guide For Couples (HarperBusiness, 1996).

Starting from No: Ten Strategies to Overcome Your Fear of Rejection and Succeed in Business (Dearborn, 1999).

The Complete Idiot's Guide to Beating Debt (Macmillan, 1999).

Two Jews Can Still be a Mixed Marriage: Reconciling the Differences Regarding Judaism in Your Marriage (Career Press, 2000).

Heartwarmers: Award-winning Stories of Love, Courage, and Inspiration (Adams Media, 2000).

The Complete Idiot's Guide to Flying and Gliding (Macmillan, 2000).

Create Your Own Luck: Eight Principles of Attracting Good Fortune in Life, Love, and Work (Adams Media, 2000).

Her books have been translated into German, Portuguese, Chinese, Japanese, and Korean.

Azriela writes a nationally syndicated column, "Advice from A-Z." Her column appears in some two dozen newspapers, magazines, and Web sites. She also writes a column for *Fortune Magazine Small Business Online* and *infoUSA.com*. She freelances for entrepreneurial magazines, including *Entrepreneur* and *Success*.

Azriela has appeared on well over 200 television and radio networks and programs, including CNN, CNBC, NBC, ABC, CBS, Fox, Bloomberg TV, Money Magazine TV, Wall Street Journal

Radio, NPR, USA Radio Network, Voice of America, *The Dolans*, *The Jim Bohannon Show*, *Sound Money*, and *Let's Talk Business*.

The Wall Street Journal named her first book, *Honey, I Want to Start my Own Business*, one of the best work/family books of 1996. Her work and expertise has been featured and/or recommended in virtually every major newspaper, entrepreneurial magazine, and women's magazine, including: *The Wall Street Journal*, *The New York Times*, *USA Today*, the *Los Angeles Times*, the *Chicago Tribune*, *The Philadelphia Inquirer*, *The Boston Globe*, *Business Week*, *Inc.*, *Money*, *Forbes*, *Fast Company, Success, Business Start-Up, Home-Office Computing, Woman's Day, Parenting,* and *Marriage*.

Azriela is the founder of Anchored Dreams, (*www.isquare.com/crlink.htm*), a coaching and consulting firm that provides practical assistance and emotional support to individuals, couples, and partners in business. Azriela also publishes three online newsletters for self-employed professionals, including the Entrepreneurial Couples Success Letter, the world's only newsletter dedicated to the needs and concerns of entrepreneurial couples and families.

Azriela is a member of the National Speakers Association and is a sought-after keynoter and workshop leader for entrepreneurial and women's conferences all over the country.

Before her current career as author, columnist, and speaker, Azriela worked in human resource management for three large firms in the Boston area, covering a 15-year span. She holds an MBA from Northeastern University and a BSW from Michigan State University.

Azriela lives in Pennsylvania with her husband, three small children, and a foreign exchange student.

She can be reached at:

793 Sumter Drive
Yardley, PA 19067
215-321-5269
azriela@mindspring.com, or *az@azriela.com*.